Translating in Town

BLOOMSBURY ADVANCES IN TRANSLATION SERIES

Series Editor:

Jeremy Munday, Centre for Translation Studies, University of Leeds, UK

Bloomsbury Advances in Translation publishes cutting-edge research in the fields of translation studies. This field has grown in importance in the modern, globalized world, with international translation between languages a daily occurrence. Research into the practices, processes and theory of translation is essential and this series aims to showcase the best in international academic and professional output.

A full list of titles in the series can be found at:
www.bloomsbury.com/series/bloomsbury-advances-in-translation

Related titles in the series include:

Collaborative Translation
Edited by Anthony Cordingley and Céline Frigau Manning

Community Translation
Mustapha Taibi and Uldis Ozolins

Global Trends in Translator and Interpreter Training
Edited by Séverine Hubscher-Davidson and Michał Borodo

Institutional Translation for International Governance
Fernando Prieto Ramos

Intercultural Crisis Communication
Edited by Federico M. Federici and Christophe Declercq

Retranslation
Sharon Deane-Cox

Telling the Story of Translation
Judith Woodsworth

Translating Holocaust Lives
Edited by Jean Boase-Beier, Peter Davies, Andrea Hammel and Marion Winters

Translating the Poetry of the Holocaust
Jean Boase-Beier

What Is Cultural Translation?
Sarah Maitland

Translating in Town

Local Translation Policies During the European 19th Century

Edited by
Lieven D'hulst and Kaisa Koskinen

BLOOMSBURY ACADEMIC
LONDON • NEW YORK • OXFORD • NEW DELHI • SYDNEY

BLOOMSBURY ACADEMIC
Bloomsbury Publishing Plc
50 Bedford Square, London, WC1B 3DP, UK
1385 Broadway, New York, NY 10018, USA
29 Earlsfort Terrace, Dublin 2, Ireland

BLOOMSBURY, BLOOMSBURY ACADEMIC and the Diana logo are trademarks of
Bloomsbury Publishing Plc

First published in Great Britain 2020
Paperback edition published 2021

Copyright © Lieven D'hulst, Kaisa Koskinen and Contributors, 2020

Lieven D'hulst and Kaisa Koskinen have asserted their right under the Copyright,
Designs and Patents Act, 1988, to be identified as Editors of this work.

Cover design: Ben Anslow

All rights reserved. No part of this publication may be reproduced or transmitted
in any form or by any means, electronic or mechanical, including photocopying,
recording, or any information storage or retrieval system, without prior
permission in writing from the publishers.

Bloomsbury Publishing Plc does not have any control over, or responsibility for,
any third-party websites referred to or in this book. All internet addresses given in
this book were correct at the time of going to press. The author and publisher
regret any inconvenience caused if addresses have changed or sites have
ceased to exist, but can accept no responsibility for any such changes.

A catalogue record for this book is available from the British Library.

A catalog record for this book is available from the Library of Congress.

ISBN: HB: 978-1-3500-9100-9
PB: 978-1-3502-7607-9
ePDF: 978-1-3500-9101-6
eBook: 978-1-3500-9102-3

Series: Bloomsbury Advances in Translation

Typeset by Deanta Global Publishing Services, Chennai, India

To find out more about our authors and books visit www.bloomsbury.com and
sign up for our newsletters.

Contents

List of contributors   vi

1 Translating in towns: An introduction   *Lieven D'hulst and Kaisa Koskinen*   1

Part 1   Translating in hegemonic regimes

2 Translation policies in Northern Italian cities during the Napoleonic era: The case of Milan, Genoa and Turin   *Michael Schreiber*   21

3 Habsburg Vienna: The institutionalization of translation in a hybrid city, 1848–1914   *Michaela Wolf*   41

Part 2   Upcoming local nationalisms

4 Bern in the nineteenth century: Emerging institutional translation in a multilingual state   *Valérie Dullion*   67

5 Mediating Flemish: Local language and translation policies on the French–Belgian border   *Lieven D'hulst*   91

6 Translating in an emerging language policy: Tampere city council 1875–1887   *Kaisa Koskinen*   115

Part 3   Interpreting in harbour towns

7 Consuls and other interpreters in Cork Harbour, Ireland   *Mary Phelan*   141

8 Maritime interpreters in nineteenth-century Barcelona: A failure story in translation policy   *Albert Branchadell*   161

Part 4   Translating for the public space

9 Translations in *Ljubljanski zvon*: The window into the cultural life of the late-nineteenth-century Ljubljana   *Nike K. Pokorn*   185

10 Translating in the 'expanded' town: Translation practices in nineteenth-century Nicosia and Cyprus   *Georgios Floros*   210

Name index   231

Contributors

Albert Branchadell
Professor in Catalan Linguistics and Translation Studies
Autonomous University of Barcelona
Spain

Lieven D'hulst
Professor in Translation Studies and Francophone Literature
KU Leuven
Belgium

Valérie Dullion
Associate Professor in Translation Studies
University of Geneva
Switzerland

Georgios Floros
Associate Professor in Translation Studies
University of Cyprus
Cyprus

Kaisa Koskinen
Professor in Translation Studies
Tampere University
Finland

Mary Phelan
Lecturer in Translation Studies
Dublin City University
Ireland

Nike K. Pokorn
Professor in Translation Studies
University of Ljubljana
Slovenia

Michael Schreiber
Professor in French and Italian Linguistics and Translation Studies
University of Mainz in Germersheim
Germany

Michaela Wolf
Associate Professor in Translation Studies
University of Graz
Austria

1

Translating in towns: An introduction

Lieven D'hulst and Kaisa Koskinen

1 Translation as a local practice

Language, Alistair Pennycook has argued, is a local practice. That is, languages emerge from and are grounded in particular 'deeply social and cultural activities in which people engage' (Pennycook 2010: 1). Similarly, we argue, translation is a local practice, and translatorial practices, too, emerge through particular social and cultural activities in which people engage. It is a truism in translation studies to focus on the social and the cultural, but the discipline is yet to fully comprehend the relevance of the *local*. In this book we provide our answer to Michael Cronin's (2006: 14) call for micro-cosmopolitan thinking from below. Taking the issue of the locality of translation seriously, we ground written and oral translation to particular time and space, charting the history of local translation practices in a number of places across Europe. Our aim is to further and model the historical understanding of intermingled language and translation policies and to reconstruct patterns of negotiation between long-standing everyday practices and policies and emergent new ideologies during the European nineteenth century.

The decision to approach this broad task not from a national perspective but by focusing on local municipalities is a very conscious methodological choice. The city has long been understood as a place of language contact, attracting people from different backgrounds and with varied linguistic repertoires, and the spatial coexistence of different languages within the confined and shared urban space has made cities a popular environment for studies on linguistic variation and multilingualism. Recent research has also put forward the logical corollary idea that the city is a space of cultural exchange in which translation operates as an 'active, directional and interactional model of language relations' (Cronin and Simon 2014: 119; see also Cronin 2006 and Simon 2012). We continue this emerging spatially determined research tradition in translation studies, agreeing that one of the best possible loci to find evidence of such an interaction is the city.

As an entity below – and to an extent under the radar of – the level of the emerging nation state, the nineteenth-century city bears traces of deeply engrained habits while it is also constrained to apply or adapt, at its own level, the decisions made by the political centre. The title 'Translating in *Town*' rather than the more commonly used *city* was chosen to underline that the contributions to this volume contain evidence not only from well-known cosmopolitan cultural capitals but also from a variety of smaller towns and villages across the borderlands and heartlands of Europe. We acknowledge the varying usage and definitions of cities and towns, and the difficulty of applying them across historical periods in non-anglophone territories. What we wish to underline is the relevance of looking into language and translation policies and practices in municipalities of different size and status, applying the interactional model of everyday practices and language ideologies to entities that vary in scope, demography, location and more elements. In this way we can begin to account for both the specifics of the various locations and their similarities and common features.

Another significant contribution to the emerging 'translation and the city' research tradition comes from the decisively historical perspective employed by all our contributors, and from the unified research aim to advance our understanding of a particular period within a particular geographical area. The chosen time span, the long nineteenth century, was decisive in the building of a new social order in Europe, and language and translation issues were deeply intertwined with processes of modernization, industrialization and democratization. In looking at nineteenth-century translation policies we are therefore looking at a moving target. The European nation states were emerging, societies and municipalities were in flux, and so were also local language hierarchies, language practices and translation policies.

During the European nineteenth century, new ideas of political autonomy and cultural self-determination came to the fore, ushering in culturally oriented viewpoints that have inspired numerous historians of our time (see, for example, Hobsbawm 1992). Napoleon's defeat and the ensuing peace Congress of Vienna (1814–15) are often taken as the starting points of a new era (Duchardt 2014). Major powers such as Austria, Britain, France, Russia and to some extent Prussia, reshuffled large parts of Europe into new or modified geopolitical constructs such as the German Confederation, the United Kingdom of the Netherlands,

Switzerland, Portugal, the Grand-Duchy of Finland and even France or Austria. The new authorities of these emerging nation states facilitated and encouraged the overall spread of national feelings and ideologies via the media, public life and the many institutional and daily practices including school and education, church, administration, court, arts, monuments, theatre, historical narratives and literary genres (Anderson 1991; Leerssen 2011).

Languages became crucial vectors of national ideologies throughout Europe. Their use was partly reframed by new or rediscovered functions in addition to those of carrying information, imposing power or conveying prestige: languages received the task to bind members of national communities together and to enable them to voice this connectedness inside and outside the new nation states (Thiesse 1992). Languages originally rooted in regional and even local communities became 'national', as opposed to 'foreign' and hegemonic ones, in particular those prescribed by the Napoleonic and Habsburg regimes which they complemented, competed and eventually replaced (e.g. Weber 1976).

One nation, one language was the dominant ideology of the time, but in spite of their key premise of linguistic homogeneity, all nation states had to make complex decisions with regard to the status of the various languages used on their territory: Which one(s) would remain or become official, to be used for writing and publication of constitutions and codes, for the exchanges between the authorities and the citizens and for the representation of the state outwards? Which rights would be allotted to the speakers of the non-official languages? Fragile compromises had to be found between the major or exclusive status given to a specific language in legal and institutional domains such as law, politics, national ministries and local administration and the free or at least less constrained use of other languages in settings like religious practices, first-degree schooling, literary societies, publishing houses or written media. These compromises found many shapes: in France, for instance, regional languages were unequivocally minoritized and even banned in most domains of public life since the imposition of the *français national* (National French) by the French revolutionaries (Balibar 1985). By contrast, the Austro-Hungarian Habsburg Empire provided a *Nationalitätengesetz* (nationalities law) guaranteeing a certain degree of linguistic autonomy to an array of ethnic communities (Schjerve and Vetter 2007; Wolf 2015), while the Ottoman Empire actively sustained regional multilingualism till the twentieth century (Gawrych 1983). Of course, language practices also evolved in the course of the century, due to shifting nationalist and other policies in both the public and the private domains (see, for example, Rindler-Schjerve 2003).

Still, it would be fallacious to think that all language attitudes and language choices have undergone the same process of nationalization. On the contrary, some simply continued the usages established by former language regimes. For instance, although Finland was annexed to Russia in 1809, Swedish remained its only official language well beyond mid-nineteenth century. Similarly, the regulations of official language use by the young Belgian government largely retained the rulings imposed by the French revolutionaries, followed by Napoleon, on Belgium, the Netherlands, parts of Germany, Luxemburg and Italy. And even these hegemonic regimes had already built on earlier customized practices of language use in legislation and administration, some of which dated back to the Middle Ages. Such continued practices, one may argue, can be understood as examples of national 'indifference', by people who 'are usually not actively or consciously engaged in concerted, organized nation-building strategies' (Beyen and Van Ginderachter 2012: 10). Think of the many civil servants, clerks, secretaries and translators that survived the changes of political regimes.[1] They inherited, and transmitted in turn, language views, norms and practices over generations, as if they 'seemed on the surface to resist the momentum of modern nation-building projects' (Zahra 2010: 96). National indifference does not necessarily mean absence of national loyalty but rather loyalty to religious, social, professional and, in the case we are studying hereafter, regional and local entities, that is, a 'banal city loyalty' (Van Ginderachter 2018: 586).

At any rate, national indifference and 'hot' nationalism (Billig, 1995: 43 ff.) coexisted side by side in many of the new nation states in Europe, turning this coexistence into a truly European trend. This trend could very well be the outcome of spillover effects between more influential and less influential states. Indeed, in spite of the political independence that had been conquered by the new states, the social and cultural prestige of the hegemonic languages such as French, German or even Latin still pervaded large territories and many practices well into the nineteenth century. For example, French remained the most prominent carrier of legal thinking and writing in Europe, even in those regimes that designed their own national systems (Soleil 2017). The lingering old language regimes were also a necessity, as vernacular regional languages were only gradually developed into the kinds of usage new public domains required.

The historical study of these interconnected nationalisms with regard to language issues is still in the making, offering a striking contrast with the wealth of contributions on separate language areas and particular national language regimes (see, for example, Osterhammel and Conrad 2004). Yet many of these contributions, since they manifest a great diversity of viewpoints and methods towards nationalist language policies, lack enough shared ground to invite large-scale comparisons of the solutions offered by European governments to handle the issues of multilingualism.

The focal nineteenth-century phenomenon of the emerging nation states across Europe, with their pressing language ideological and practical needs for solving issues of multilingualism, has also foregrounded research that is based on methodological nationalism. That is, the national level has offered itself as the self-evident primary level of analysis. This has also made sense, as language regimes and practices were – and still are – often regulated at the national level. But methodological nationalism obscures lower level phenomena such as resistant local practices, unique regional realities or the fuzziness of border areas. By zooming into the level of the municipal local realities, we aim to offer a novel contribution to the study of language and translation practices during an era when Europe was radically reshaped.

2 Mapping translation policies in the making

This book investigates the intersection between nationalisms and multilingualism in Europe. The contributions take the reader through the streets, court rooms and offices in European cities big and small, central and peripheral, tracking the remaining traces of nineteenth-century written and oral translation practices. The chapters are grounded on methodological translation history work, and they offer a wealth of examples on how archival sources, in particular, can be explored to advance our knowledge on translatorial practices across time. Significantly, we also aim to show how looking into translation allows us to contribute to study beyond disciplinary borders and to bring to light new aspects of more general questions – in this case the role of multilingualism and language conflicts in the emergence of European nationalisms.

All chapters focus on (written or oral) translation practices and translation policies within a particular locale. Recent research on language policy, although in itself a domain with competing views, has considerably enhanced the potential to achieve clear and workable frameworks to deepen historical insights in this area. One well-known theoretical model to study language policies (Spolsky 2012: 5) distinguishes between three layers: language practices ('the actual language practices of the members of a speech community'), language beliefs or ideology ('the values assigned by members of a speech community to each variety and variant and their beliefs about the importance of these values') and language management ('the efforts by some members of a speech community who have or believe they have authority over other members to modify their language practice'). The three layers are closely tied up, since language management must be consistent with language practice and beliefs in order to provide real effects (Spolsky 2012: 222).

Languages have always partaken in international exchanges, which expanded considerably after the Napoleonic Wars. Any history of language policies during the nineteenth century obviously faces the necessity to observe these exchanges, as they operate at the three levels: language beliefs and regulatory practices migrate between nation states, as do language products themselves. The techniques by which these exchanges are carried out are diverse: borrowing, plagiary, multilingual writing, code-mixing and translation. In particular the last modality developed considerably during the nineteenth century, introducing policies of a new kind: while the previous hegemonic regimes mainly sustained monolingual and unidirectional translations (e.g. from French into the vernaculars of the annexed territories, cf. Schreiber 2015), a larger range of directions developed, both between the languages of a single nation state and between the latter and those shared with or pertaining to other nation states (cf. D'hulst and Van Gerwen 2018).

Clearly, the diversification of language regimes and the multiplication of translation directions are far from unconnected evolutions. They likely confirm the hypothesis that language policies are paralleled by translation policies. And so Spolsky's theoretical distinction between the three components of language policy may be tentatively applied to translation as well (Meylaerts and González Núñez 2018): both rely on some kind of regulation, legislation or set of principles; both attach a set of values or ideologies to their object; both materialize in concrete practices (for a detailed case study, see González Núñez 2016). Obviously, all these components also witness a high rate of variation, depending on the role of specified policies, their historical deployment and locus, a variation that defies generalization and turns the study of translation policies into a broad field. This emerging field is only beginning to be investigated with a historical eye. At this point, two more remarks need to be made. First, the idea of a policy as an *a priori* given does not imply that all levels are visible and elaborated: in many cases, there is simply no regulation of translation, while in other cases, views on translation are hard to reconstruct on the basis of scarce comments. It is thus necessary to understand policies as more or less elaborated constructs, depending, once again, on historical conditions. Second, the question may also arise as to whether language and translation should always be studied together, as concomitant, complementary or interdependent practices. Once again, it is the historical situation that invites for approximation or alignment of both. While it is easy to accept the idea that a language policy brings forward some translation practices, the opposite direction may very well occur as well; that is, specific translation settings may sustain a specific language policy.

Especially with regard to the European nineteenth century, similarities between translation and language policies do not imply that the former were simple derivatives of the latter nor that the two always coincided or merged. More research is needed to understand the interaction between both. For instance, in the newly created multilingual state of Belgium, language and translation policies combined intimately, with the aim of accommodating the language situations with the new principles of representative democracy and linguistic freedom inscribed in the Constitution of 1831 (Witte and van Velthoven 1999). And so translation rights had to be provided for monolingual citizens using regional or local languages when taking part in political life, accessing laws, coming to court and so on. Correlatively, regulations had to be written, translators had to be trained and recruited, and translation and transfer techniques had to be developed. Understandably, the design of translation policies always depended on the needs or expectations felt in each nation state and with regard to each specific practice or domain.

Expectations and solutions naturally differed and also evolved differently in the course of time. While Flemish turned into an official language in Belgium, while remaining de facto a target language in the official domain, nothing similar happened in France, where regional Flemish continued to be minoritized and deprived of a translation policy. In the same vein, one may wonder whether openness towards regional languages or the claim for language particularism extended to local language variants, autochthonous minorities (e.g. Sami) and nationless language groups (e.g. Roma).

With an eye on the rising nationalism of nineteenth-century Europe, it may be expected that local public life in towns and cities echoes the national debates on identity, language rights and the concomitant necessity and right to translate. In some cases, for example, in the case of bilingual Flemish cities (or the current European Union), translation between equalized languages may be given the same status as the original in all cities, small and large, central and peripheral, of a nation state, featuring what De Schutter labels 'original translations', that is, 'direct double (or multiple) renderings that at the same time appear in two (or more) languages without any of them having to be the chronological original, or without any of them having legal priority' (De Schutter 2018: 26). But it can also happen that public life bypasses such national agendas and that cities become shelter zones where the everyday practices of local communities challenge the *a priori* assumptions or ideologies that better fit the view of the nation state or the capital city or time capsules that reflect an earlier understanding of best practice. Everyday practices including professional and institutional kinds of translation may build not only on long-term strategies but also on unformulated decisions that seem to rely on a so-called 'default translation policy' (Meylaerts 2018: 222), referring to the pragmatic needs of conveying, understanding and reacting to information within a concrete communicative situation. Especially in newly established or minimally regulated institutions, where translations are made by practitioners that have not been trained or appointed as translators or interpreters, this basic understanding, coined as 'habitualized' translation (Wolf 2015: 51), seems to be widespread in nineteenth-century European translating. Its spread is probably the outcome of growing economic and social exchanges enabled by the gradual opening of national borders after the end of the Napoleonic Wars. It becomes a fascinating topic of study, when approached from an evolutionary viewpoint, featuring the birth or transformation of a policy, and revealing the intricate interaction of the three main parameters of translation policy: an ideology calling for a practice, a practice calling for a regulation, a regulation calling for changes in practice and views.

Obviously, also many more parameters need to be taken into account to describe and understand local translation policies and their evolution: the agents, the institutional contexts and frames, the actual techniques, the recipients, emerging media technologies. Such broadening of the viewpoint on translation is indispensable for studying the modernizing cities of the nineteenth century, where translation is more than ever before present in the public space, thanks to the growing literacy of the citizen, more efficient print and distribution techniques, the extended national and transnational circulation of books, magazines, people and their ideas. The spectrum of domains inhabiting translation is seemingly unlimited, as are the media that carry them: oral debate in city councils reported in the press, advertisements, translated prayer books, manuals, anthologies, novels and poetry and so on. More particularly, city and town administrations are among the best possible observatories for a detailed study of the conflicts and negotiations in the daily language practices of monolingual and multilingual citizens and officers. These conflicts and interactions make up what J. Habermas has labelled *Öffentlichkeit* (public sphere, Habermas 1962). In the context of the nineteenth century, the crucial transitional period during which the modern democratic institutions of the nation states were gradually being built, tracing the conflicts and interactions to depict a dynamic process of continuity and change as to translation views, rules and practices, provides a unique perspective into the challenges and contradictory pulls during this development.

3 Translating in European towns and cities

This book wants to be a stepping stone in the historical reconstruction of the process of nation state building and democratization. Its focus is on institutional and habitualized multilingualism and translation in a dozen of nineteenth-century smaller towns and larger cities spread all over Europe. It brings together translation historians who have thoroughly investigated materials they have discovered in local and public archives, taking stock of both the policy differences and parallels between towns and cities from North to South and East to West, from major and minor cultures, from central cultural hubs as well as borders at the outer rim of Europe. An array of historical angles is provided, covering cultural and social issues, oral and written language, translation and interpretation, print and other media, spanning broadly the long nineteenth century, that is, the period between the French Revolution and the outburst of the First World War. The main sources are previously largely unexplored data, scattered in libraries and archives all over Europe. They reveal the lasting importance of qualitative analysis, and the potential of microhistory in yielding a closer and more refined view on translating communities, translational events and translating actors.

The book is divided in four parts: the first considers upcoming language and translation policies in hegemonic regimes; the second looks at institutional translation practices and regulations occurring in border zones; the third in upcoming local nationalisms; and the fourth concentrates on translation activities in the public space. Time spans within the long nineteenth century have been chosen by each author to reflect the local realities and the research agendas of each contribution.

Decisions as to translate (or not), translation procedures, policy levels (national or local) and the status given to translation (official or not) are the outcome of complex negotiations between pragmatic views embedded in local social and cultural traditions, as well as the geopolitical constraints exerted on cities by national or transnational governing bodies. The more extreme case is no doubt that of hegemonic political regimes that seemingly strived to streamline language and translation use in occupied territories. In his opening contribution, **Michael Schreiber** allows us to delve into the complexities of local realities at an early phase of the period under study. He deals with translations of legal, administrative and journalistic texts in three Italian cities during the Napoleonic period (1796–1814). Cities at that time monitored larger political entities and handled complex or multi-layered translation policies. Milan was the capital of several states under French influence yet with changing regimes: the Transpadane Republic (1796–7), the Cisalpine Republic (1797–1802), the Italian Republic (1802–5) and, finally, the Kingdom of Italy (1805–14). Italian was the official language of the 'sister republics' and the Kingdom of Italy. In Milan, French Civil Code and the other Napoleonic codes were centrally translated into Italian. Private translation occurred in newspapers, as with writer Foscolo, but reversed the translation direction, the reason being that French was the language of literature and diplomacy in Europe, and thus an international carrier of Italian literature. In the Napoleonic period, Genoa became the capital of the Ligurian Republic (1797–1805), before the territory of this 'sister republic' was annexed by the French Empire and divided into three *départements*, one of which was Gênes (Genoa). After the annexation, the French language played an increasing role, nevertheless Italian translations of official texts were allowed and extended locally to announcements and judgements published by the local authorities in bilingual format. Finally, Turin, once annexed by the Empire, was Frenchified to the extent that French became the 'mother tongue' and monolingualism the norm of communication in public life. However, local translations of this period, especially public announcements and judgements, were rapidly made accessible in the two languages.

Michaela Wolf deals with a hegemonic regime that dated back to a remote past before turning, in the middle of the nineteenth century, into an extremely sophisticated ruling system of many nationalities. The late Habsburg Monarchy (1848–1915) covered about 50 million people with twelve different languages. Wolf's contribution focuses on the interaction between the central government in Vienna and the local governments in the crown lands. In such a context, translation served not only as a tool to enable or facilitate communication and cultural transfer but also as a way to shape the various cultures involved in that interaction. Indeed, language mediation in the form of translation and interpreting increased during that period and went hand in hand with the political conflicts that arose in the last few decades of the Empire's existence. Social, political and ideological factors merged and produced a strong effect on the institutionalization of translation, as is exemplified by the labour of the Bureau of Redaction of the Imperial Law Gazette. Wolf also looks at other regulating factors of the translation policy of the time: censorship (in its broadest sense), copyright, bookselling licensing and literary prizes. All factors helped to construct by means of translation the imperial capital of Vienna as a political and cultural centre.

Spatialities are not always clear-cut, and a particular place can host several spatial layers, with potentially conflicting statuses, ideologies and practicalities. The Swiss city of Bern, studied by **Valérie Dullion**, is is the first case of the second part that looks at upcoming local nationalisms. The Swiss federal state was founded in 1848 with a democratic, republican form of government and several official languages. At that time, Bern had been chosen as the capital, called the 'federal city'. Yet, it was also the capital of a bilingual canton within the Swiss Confederation (most of the other cantons being monolingual). Finally, Bern became host to several international organizations between the 1860s and the First World War. After the war, it was largely supplanted in this role by Geneva. Through archive research of the Federal Council's annual reports, Dullion shows us how a translation policy was developed at the pivot point between translation practice and translation management. Major questions are: To what extent did the federal administration's 'implicit or covert' translation policy reflect, qualify, contradict, supplement or shape the principles underlying the multilingual language regime? The chapter also scrutinizes the interaction and tension between the parliament, the government and the judiciary: each induced changes in translation policy, and helped not only to differentiate between the specialized fields for which translations were made (aside from the obvious overall weight given to legal translation) but also to differentiate between geographical axes of institutional translation, that is, the western, French-speaking part of the country, the Italian-speaking Ticino and Bern as the federal city, as well as an international centre. Finally, attention is turned to the figure of the translator in the federal administration, showing evidence of early professionalization tendencies.

With the help of extensive contrastive archival work in a number of border zone municipalities, **Lieven D'hulst** charts the social, cultural and political complexities of local translation practices. He looks at the slow and complex coming into being of official Flemish monolingualism in five cities of the Western province of Belgium close to the French border. This process is then compared with the use of Flemish in three cities that belong to a southern Walloon province. Crossing the border with France, the picture further changes in six cities were Flemish is lively practised: three by Flemish worker migrants and three where it is an ancient ethnic language. In Belgium, multilingual practices, as well as oral interpretation and written translation in Flemish, are tokens of a default policy designed by municipal authorities in view of ensuring citizens' and council members' access to official legal documents written in French. Conversely, from the second half of the nineteenth century on, these usages turned into a symbol of the Flemish citizens' and council members' struggle for cultural, ideological and even political emancipation of the Flemish language community. In France, however, and in the Francophone part of Belgium, Flemish was confined to social and cultural life; it was excluded from official language use.

The last contribution of the second part, by **Kaisa Koskinen**, deals with language and translation policies in the Finnish city of Tampere, more specifically at the moment when the new legislation of local governance had been issued in 1873. National revival in Finland encouraged the emergence of a more democratic language regime: while the administration had been until then almost exclusively Swedish, a new language legislation improved the status of Finnish and provided the background for new language practices in governing institutions. Locally, this change became visible in minutes of the council reporting on decisions on language policy and in the translational practices documented in them. It was also manifest in the local newspapers of the time that commented at length upon council decisions and practices. During the decade after the new legislation, the local language policy evolved through numerous translational turns from monolingual Swedish to monolingual Finnish. The chapter looks into the factors behind this rather swift change at all three levels defined by Spolsky (regulation, views, practice). It becomes clear that translation had been used as a scaffolding device, to help an underdog language move gradually into a dominant position. Putting translation in the service of Finnish was not only a language choice but also tied to a number of other societal aims such as language rights, democratization and the gradual development of civil society.

The third part is concerned with institutional translation occurring in border zones, that is, political borders between adjacent states and language communities, or a combination of these with natural borders.

Harbour cities provide a particular contact zone between the local and the global flows of commodities and people, and therefore also of commercial and social exchanges involving strong regulations and numerous language practices. **Mary Phelan** features practices of interpreting in the port of Queenstown, in county Cork in the south-west of Ireland during the period 1860–1910. At that time, a great deal of interpreting was aimed at Irish speakers, sign language users and foreigners who did not master English. Part of the latter group was made up by European migrants travelling via Ireland to the United States. In addition, interpreting activities were taken up by ship agents representing insurance companies and acting as interpreters during the loading and unloading of goods. The chapter identifies a number of interpreters, partly chosen among officially nominated consuls, vice consuls and consular agents that spoke foreign languages and bilingual or multilingual foreigners and locals appointed ad hoc. It further highlights interpreting conventions, practices and problems related to cases prosecuted or initiated at Queenstown petty sessions (the lowest courts) and including theft, assault, disputes about wages, desertion of a ship, smuggling, stabbings, disputes over salvage. Obviously, lack of written regulations and ad hoc choice of interpreters put a threat on the impartiality and accuracy of interpretation activities deployed at court, a fact largely commented upon in the local press of the time, and illustrating the centrality of normativity in interlingual practices.

By contrast, so it seems, translation and interpretation taking place in Barcelona, the mostly Catalan-speaking Spanish port on the Mediterranean and the capital city of Spain's first industrializing region in the nineteenth century, seem to benefit from a more elaborate regulation. This applies in particular to maritime or vessel interpreter brokers. **Albert Branchadell** concentrates on the latter group: who they were, from which languages they translated what, and for whom they worked under what regulations. Yet, their activity clashed with that of other brokers, including sworn interpreters who delivered also translation and interpreting services to foreign vessels, revealing thus a gap between translation management decisions and translation practice on the ground. In the longer run, this gap even provoked the collapse of the profession of vessel interpreter brokers and thus the failure of Spain's top-down translation policy in front of the changing practices and constraints of maritime trade. Again, the specifics of this case do not allow for hasty generalization, but help to identify some of the factors that may be held responsible for the success or failure of a given translational regime, in this case the dependence on language regimes, the process of de-institutionalization of translation and the world of jurisdictional struggles.

The fourth and last part views translation from the broader perspective of the public space. While institutional translation is designed and applied in specific settings or modes of interaction between more or less clearly delineated groups of producers and consumers, translation in the public space involves larger and more heterogeneous groups of consumers. The first case in this section is that of a literary journal published in Slovene in Slovenia, a nation with a long history of dependence, notably from the Austrian Empire since the early modern period. **Nike Pokorn** attempts to identify the role of translation in the cultural life of Slovenia's capital city Ljubljana in the late nineteenth century as it was reported about and manifested in the most important Slovene literary journal of the period *Ljubljanski zvon* (1881–1941). During its history, this journal reflected opposing views that saw literary translation either as a way to import new features and genres into the nascent Slovene literature or as a perilous activity that drained the creative powers of literary-gifted agents and thus ran the risk of depriving upcoming Slovene culture of the original works that these agents were supposed to write instead. The chapter identifies a number of these agents: those in particular that may be considered representative of the roles, attitudes and practices that made up translation policy and steered its effect on the emerging literary field in Ljubljana at the end of the nineteenth century.

In his contribution, **Georgios Floros** features the linguistic duality of Cyprus's capital city Nicosia. Cyprus is located at the outer rims of Europe and at the crossroads between East and West. During the nineteenth century, Cyprus was placed under Ottoman and British rule and so has played a significant role in the political and economic life of Europe, including Greece and Turkey. Neither the Ottoman nor the British rulers showed willingness to intervene in language use and translation. As a result, Cyprus emerged as a multilingual space rich in translation practice, but poor in official translation policies. This laissez-faire attitude and lack of institutionalization and regulation laid the foundations of the nationalist developments in the twentieth century, which have been perpetuated to date. The lack of intervention fuelled the continuous attachment of the two main communities of Cyprus to their respective 'motherlands', culminating in the de facto monolingual and non-translational spaces of today.

4 Where to go from here

Translating approached from a spatial, and in particular from a set of *local* viewpoints yields new insights into the historical knowledge of nineteenth-century translation, a period and a practice predominantly studied so far within national frames, and mainly devoted to types of translation other than the political, social and institutional ones that are foregrounded in this volume. Shared evolutions accompany equally shared continuities. On the one hand, translation occupies an intermediate position between the imposed monolingualism of former regimes and the often hard-won multilingualism of the new nation states: it becomes a self-reflective activity, with views and functions that are debated and yield regulations that both reproduce the national ones and create local realities. On the other hand, translation remains rooted in everyday or default language practices stretching over a longer period of time and thus escaping the influence of contemporary ideologies and any nationalist determination of language use and translation. The results published here are a first snapshot, and we hope to encourage more research to gain further insight into the conditions and constraints that explain the balance between self-reflective and default practices of translation.

As the growing body of research on translating in relation with cities has been able to reveal already, translating is closely intermingled with an array of other language practices: interpreting in the first place, but also the many forms of discursive transfer and translanguaging in addition to intermedial techniques, that is, the combination of sound and gesture, image and language by means of which non-expert translation has enabled communication between languages. Obviously, language and translation policies in the administrative domains are rarely disconnected from norms and policies designed in other domains, including the cultural and literary, as several of these chapters demonstrate. It is beyond the scope of this Introduction to look for parallels with other time-space settings. However, such parallels, as conspicuous in both historical data on formal meetings (Koskinen in this volume) and contemporary recordings of formal meetings (Koskela et al. 2017), should help to lay bare some of the presently unknown features of translatorial customs or norms inscribed in long-term interlingual exchanges by non-professionals.

Local language and translation histories are also indispensable steps for the understanding of the coming into being of our modern and contemporary views on citizenship, language and translation rights and justice as they are now being shaped in both national and supranational settings. Such cutting-edge issues challenge both abstract speculation and narrow empiricism, as well as the translatorial and other viewpoints from which they may be approached. Another option could be to look for an umbrella concept like public and social policy-making, addressing issues of design and implementation in legislation, economics, social services, in which decisions as to language and translation matters are put on the agenda. Following Hlavac et al. (2018: 83), translation policy may refer then 'to the practice of other policies that need not see translation as a goal in itself, but ... facilitate its provision as means for the achievement of any other policy goals'.

This shift of focus opens up room for a better understanding of default language and translation policies that remain seemingly deprived of regulation. Along this line, our historical concern consists less of defining and describing a proper and stable niche for translation policy next to sets of other policies than of understanding the functions of translational mediation against the backdrop of issues of access to information, inclusion and equity of citizens. In this sense, the study of self-reflective practices of translation and ensuing regulations might equally benefit from such a broadening perspective. Looking back on the tensions between official monolingualism and official multilingualism, one may raise the question whether translation has been able to achieve a closer interaction between the members of local communities or, on the contrary, whether official bilingualism should be considered one of the possible causes of their further growing apart. To answer such a question requires a more detailed and interdisciplinary modelling of translation, a major challenge for translation history.

All in all, if more history is needed, then more historical approaches are to be welcomed as well: microhistory and transnational or comparative history may help to lay bare the complementary nature of short-term and long-term viewpoints on translation. Correlatively, they may reveal parallels with habits and viewpoints carried within other social and cultural practices. Nationalisms have been both committed and indifferent. Both have made extensive use of translation. Therefore, we might hope that integrative approaches pave the way for a better understanding of the complex aggregate of historical factors that feature translating in town.

Note

1 Evidently, national indifference as perceived in the context of language use within institutional environments does not reflect the personal convictions of public officers nor their use of language in different environments: many nineteenth-century nationalists were at the same time civil servants and active in the literary and even political domains.

References

Anderson, B. (1991), *Imagined Communities: Reflections on the Origin and Spread of Nationalism*, London: Verso.

Balibar, R. (1985), *L'institution du français. Essai sur le colinguisme des Carolingiens à la République*, Paris: Presses Universitaires de France.

Beyen, M. and M. Van Ginderachter (2012), 'General Introduction: Writing the Mass into a Mass Phenomenon', in M. Van Ginderachter and M. Beyen (eds), *Nationhood from Below: Europe in the Long Nineteenth Century* 3–22, Palgrave-Macmillan: Basingstoke.

Billig, M. (1995), *Banal Nationalism*, London: Sage.
Cronin, M. (2006), *Translation and Identity*, London and New York: Routledge.
Cronin, M. and S. Simon, eds. (2014). 'The City as Translation Zone', Special issue of *Translation Studies* 7 (2).
De Schutter, H. (2018), 'Translational Justice: Between Equality and Privation', in G. González Núñez and R. Meylaerts (eds), *Translation and Public Policy. Interdisciplinary Perspectives and Case Studies*, 15–31, London/New York: Routledge.
D'hulst, L. and H. van Gerwen (2018), 'Translation Space in Nineteenth-Century Belgium: Rethinking Translation and Transfer Directions', *Perspectives: Studies in Translation Theory and Practice*, 26 (4): 495–508.
Duchhardt, H. (2014), *Der Wiener Kongress. Die Neugestaltung Europas 1814/15*, München: C.H. Beck Verlag.
Gawrych, G. W. (1983), 'Tolerant Dimensions of Cultural Pluralism in the Ottoman Empire: The Albanian Community, 1800–1912', *International Journal of Middle East Studies* 15(4): 519–36.
González Núñez, G. (2016), *Translating in Linguistically Diverse Societies: Translation Policy in the United Kingdom*, Amsterdam-Philadelphia: John Benjamins.
Habermas, J. (1962), *Strukturwandel der Öffentlichkeit. Untersuchungen zu einer Kategorie der bürgerlichen Gesellschaft*, Berlin: Luchterhand.
Hlavac, J., A. Gentile, M. Orlando, E. Zucchi and A. Pappas (2018), 'Translation as a Sub-Set of Public and Social Policy and a Consequence of Multiculturalism: The Provision of Translation and Interpreting Services in Australia', *International Journal of the Sociology of Language* 251: 55–88.
Hobsbawm, E. (1992), *Nations and Nationalism since 1780: Programme, Myth, Reality*, Cambridge: Cambridge University Press.
House, J. (2010), 'Overt and Covert Translation', in Y. Gambier and L. Van Doorslaer (eds), *Handbook of Translation Studies I*, 245–46, Amsterdam/Philadelphia: John Benjamins.
Koskela, M., K. Koskinen and N. Pilke (2017), 'Bilingual Formal Meeting as a Context of Translatoriality', *Target: International Journal of Translation Studies*, 29 (3): 464–85.
Leerssen, J. (2011), 'Viral Nationalism: Romantic Intellectuals on the Move in Nineteenth-Century Europe', *Nations and Nationalism* 17 (2): 257–71.
Meylaerts, R. (2018), 'The Politics of Translation in Multilingual States', in F. Fernández and J. Evans (eds), *The Routledge Handbook of Translation and Politics*, 221–37, London/New York: Routledge.
Meylaerts, R. and G. González Núñez (2018), 'No Language Policy without Translation Policy: A Comparison of Flanders and Wales', *Language Problems and Language Planning* 42 (2): 196–219.
Osterhammel, J. and S. Conrad, eds. (2004), *Das Kaiserreich Transnational: Deutschland in der Welt, 1871–1914*, Gottingen: Vandenhoeck & Ruprecht.
Pennycook. A. (2010), *Language as a Local Practice*, London: Routledge.

Rindler-Schjerve, R. ed. (2003), *Diglossia and Power: Language Policies and Practice in the 19th Century Habsburg Empire*, Berlin: de Gruyter.

Schjerve, R. and E. Vetter. (2007), 'Linguistic Diversity in Habsburg Austria as a Model for Modern European Language Policy', in J. D. ten Thije and L. Zeevaert (eds), *Receptive Multilingualism*, 49–70, Amsterdam: John Benjamins.

Schreiber, M. (2015), 'Nationalsprache – Regionalsprache – Nachbarsprache: Zur Übersetzungspolitik während der Französischen Revolution (am Beispiel des Sprachenpaars Französisch-Niederländisch)', in D. Dizdar, A. Gipper and M. Schreiber (eds), *Übersetzung und Nationenbildung*, 77–92, Berlin: Frank & Timme.

Simon, S. (2012), *Cities in Translation: Intersections of Language and Memory*, London/New York: Routledge.

Soleil, S. (2017), 'L'emploi de la langue française et des néologismes dans les textes juridiques étrangers du XIXe siècle', *Parallèles* 29 (1): 91–105.

Spolsky, B., ed. (2012), 'What Is Language Policy?' in B. Spolsky (ed), *The Cambridge Handbook of Language Policy*, 3–15, Cambridge: Cambridge University Press.

Thiesse, A.-M. (1992), *La création des identités nationales: Europe, XVIIIe-XXe siècle*, Paris: Seuil.

Van Ginderachter, M. (2018), 'How to Gauge Banal Nationalism and National Indifference in the Past: Proletarian Tweets in Belgium's Belle époque', *Nations and Nationalism* 24 (3): 579–93.

Weber, E. (1976), *Peasants into Frenchmen: The Modernization of Rural France, 1870–1914*, Stanford: Stanford University Press.

Witte, E. and H. van Velthoven (1999), *Language and Politics: The Situation in Belgium in a Historical Perspective*, Brussels: VUB university press.

Wolf, M. (2015), *The Habsburg Monarchy's Many-Languaged Soul: Translating and Interpreting, 1848–1918*, Amsterdam/Philadelphia: John Benjamins.

Zahra, T. (2010), 'Imagined Noncommunities: National Indifference as a Category of Analysis', *Slavic Review*, 69 (1): 93–119.

Part One

Translating in hegemonic regimes

2

Translation policies in Northern Italian cities during the Napoleonic era: The case of Milan, Genoa and Turin

Michael Schreiber

The language policy of the French Revolution and the Napoleonic era is known today especially for the imposition of French as the national language and for the suppression of the regional languages in France and of other languages in regions which were occupied by France, for example, Flemish in Belgium. This *opinio communis* may be called 'the myth of monolingualism' (Schreiber 2016). This contribution focuses on a lesser known aspect of this period: the translation policy. From 1790 onwards, several decrees stipulated the translation of national laws and decrees into France's regional languages. From the mid-1790s onwards, the translation policy was extended to other countries and regions under French influence. I will consider the case of the three cities of Northern Italy, a region which was under French influence from the beginning of the campaign in Italy until the end of the Napoleonic era. France became a model for the new states to be formed in this region, a model in the fields of politics, administration, economy, society and culture, including language. As Pillepich (2003: 157) states, French was already understood by the Italian elite of that period, who often read French translations of English and German literature. Thus, the conditions for a French language and translation policy were relatively good.

The term *translation policy* can be understood in a restricted sense (Meylaerts 2011: 163) as referring to the translation of legal and administrative texts in institutional settings. In a wider sense *translation policy* can refer to private initiatives which govern translational activities in multilingual settings, for example, in the press. This contribution will deal with the official and private translation of legal, administrative and journalistic texts in three Italian cities during the Napoleonic period (1796–1814). While *official* translations of laws, decrees, public announcements and other legal or administrative texts are published by regional or local authorities, *private* translations are published by independent authors or journalists (D'hulst and Van Gerwen 2018: 500).[1] Another distinction which is relevant especially for the translation of legal texts is the distinction between *performative* and informative *translations* (Wiesmann 2009). A performative translation of a legal text, for example, a contract, functions as a legal text in the target culture. An informative translation does not function as a legal text on its own – for example, the informative translation of a judgement for a foreign lawyer in the context of a trial. An official translation can be performative or informative, depending on the function of the target language. If a law is translated from French to Italian, the translation is performative if Italian is the official language (or one of the official languages) of the target culture and informative if French is the only official language.

According to Ködel (2014: 140-1), the Napoleonic language policy was more pragmatic than ideological. Given the huge dimensions of the Napoleonic Empire, a certain multilingualism was inevitable. From this point of view, the 'Grande nation' of the Revolution and the Napoleonic Empire can be seen as laboratories for other multilingual states in Europe during the nineteenth century.

The texts from our corpus were collected in different archives and libraries in Italy and France. Since our research on the translation policy in Northern Italy is still in an early, exploratory phase, the analysis will be restricted to a qualitative interpretation of a relatively small number of texts, the very first results of our archival research. Since most of the texts are not published and are analysed here for the first time, I will give some longer quotations to provide an impression of these historical texts.

The three cities, Milan, Genoa and Turin, were chosen because they stand as examples for different translational settings within the same historical period:

The city of Milan, the 'Napoleonic capital' in Italy (Roberti 1946/7), was, in fact, subsequently, the capital of several states under French influence: the Transpadane Republic (1796–7), the Cisalpine Republic (1797–1802), the Italian Republic (1802–5) – three so-called 'sister republics', whose political and administrative structures depended on the French model[2] (see the map on Figure 2.1) – and, finally, the Kingdom of Italy (1805–14) where the French emperor functioned as king.

In Milan, the French Civil Code and the other Napoleonic codes were translated into Italian and later transferred to other Italian regions. Local translations, that is, translations made and printed in Milan, were, according to

Translation Policies in Northern Italian Cities during the Napoleonic Era   23

Figure 2.1 Italy 1803. Wikimedia Commons.

Pillepich (2003: 157), less frequent in Milan than in other cities under French influence because Italian was the official language of the subsequent republics which had Milan as its capital and of the Kingdom of Italy. One interesting exception is the bilingual periodical *Diario Italiano*, published by the writer Ugo Foscolo in 1803, which will be presented in this contribution as an example of a private translation project.

Genoa had been the capital of the Republic of Genoa for almost 800 years until it was occupied by French troops in 1797. In the Napoleonic period, Genoa was the capital of the Ligurian Republic (1797–1805), before the territory of this 'sister republic' was annexed by the French Empire. After the annexation, the French language played an increasingly important role. I will focus on translations in the local press and will also mention some individual translations from the cultural and legal spheres and a private translation project. The choice of the texts is guided by the results of archival research.

For geographical and political reasons and for several centuries, Turin, the capital of Piedmont, had been heavily influenced by the French language and culture, much more than Milan or Genoa. In 1796, the region of Piedmont was occupied by France. In 1802, the region was annexed by the French Republic and later became part of the Napoleonic Empire. After the annexation, the French state tried to Frenchify the region completely. Most bilingual documents date from the last years of the occupation and the first years after the annexation. In my contribution, I will focus on local translations of the bilingual period, especially public announcements.

In comparing the translational settings in the cities of Milan, Genoa and Turin, I will try to answer the following questions: How was the translational activity organized? What translation procedures can be found in the translations?

1 Milan

The city of Milan was the scene of several translational activities in the context of national and regional translation policies, especially during the time when Milan was the capital of the Italian Republic (1802–5) and the Napoleonic Kingdom of Italy (1805–14).

Since the national translation policy of the French state is not the object of this contribution, I will mention here only briefly the main translations done in Milan in this context. In Milan, four Napoleonic codes were translated into Italian in order to implement the French legal system in the Kingdom of Italy: the *Code civil* (Civil code), the *Code de procédure civile* (Code of civil procedure), the *Code de commerce* (Commercial code) and the *Code pénal* (Criminal code). Since Italian was the official language of the different states under French influence which had Milan as their capital, the Napoleonic codes became valid in the Italian version. For the same reason, we can find only a restricted number of official bilingual texts, with the exception of the early Napoleonic period.[3] The *Bollettino delle leggi della Repubblica italiana* (Bulletin of the laws of the Italian Republic) and the *Bollettino delle leggi del Regno d'Italia* (Bulletin of the laws of the Kingdom of Italy) mainly contain texts in Italian (Archivio di Stato di Milano [ASM]: Atti ufficiali). Furthermore, most of the newspapers published in Milan were monolingual Italian.

An interesting but isolated example of a private translation project is the bilingual periodical *Diario Italiano* (Italian diary) published by the writer Ugo Foscolo in the end of the year 1803 (Del Vento 1999). This short-lived newspaper (only three issues were published) can be seen as the product of a local, private translation initiative with the ambition to create a 'national'[4] journal. It was completely bilingual, printed in two columns per page: the Italian text was printed on the left column and the French version (mostly translated from the

Italian) on the right column and in italics. The French texts were drafted or translated by the expatriate French writer and journalist Abbé Aimé Guillon de Montléon with whom Foscolo collaborated, although Guillon had been imprisoned in France for anti-revolutionary writings (Del Vento 1999: 230).

In the first issue of the *Diario Italiano* (12 December 1803), which is conserved in the ASM, the publisher explains the structure and the purpose of this newspaper: laws and decrees of the Italian Republic are presented, followed by international news and a section on literature (with a subsection on theatre). Foscolo enumerates three reasons why he decided to include a French translation in his newspaper: (1) French was the language of literature and diplomacy in Europe; (2) French and Italian readers should have the opportunity to study the other language; (3) Italian literature was, according to Foscolo, not well-known outside of Italy.

The first issue of the paper includes, among other things, a French translation of a part of the *Bollettino delle leggi della Republica italiana* (Bulletin of the laws of the Italian Republic) from 1802, with a report of the *Consulte de Lyon* (consultation of Lyon), where the Cisalpine Republic was transformed into the Italian Republic. This part of the newspaper reads like an official publication of the government. The second part of the newspaper, with the title *Notizie del mondo – Nouvelles étrangères* (foreign news), includes news from London (a translated article of the *Morning-Post*), Paris (a report from the Senate), Saint Petersburg, Vienna, Ratisbon and Trieste. The last part, *Letteratura italiana – Littérature italienne* (Italian literature), consists mainly of the review of an Italian translation of Tacitus's *Annals*, printed in Milan, and a subsection on local theatres, where it was announced, among other things, that the opera would remain closed until the end of the year.

The French translation of the Italian text is mostly quite literal, with some adaptations to make it comprehensible for French readers. This sort of adaptation can be illustrated by the rendering of proper names which occur frequently in the text. Proper names are normally translated, like in the following example, from the above-mentioned book review:

> Il primo Libro degli annali di Cornelio Tacito, volgarizzato da Ludovico Valeriani. Milano presso Luigi Veladini stampatore nazionale. Senza data (uscì nel corso di quest' anno).[5]
>
> // Le premier livre des annales de Cornelius Tacite, traduit par Louis Valeriani; à Milan, chez Louis Veladini, imprimeur national. Sans date (publié cette année). (*Diario Italiano*, no. 1, p. 1)

Here, not only is Tacitus's name translated (*Cornelio Tacito* – *Cornelius Tacite*) but also the Christian names of the translator and the printer (*Ludovico Valeriani* – *Louis Valeriani*; *Luigi Veladini* – *Louis Veladini*).[6]

The following example, taken from the section on theatres, shows another adaptation for French-speaking readers:

> Nulla possiam dire per ora attesa la sospensione dei teatri d'opera sino al vicino natale.[7]
>
> // Nous n'en pourrons rien dire en ce moment, vu la suspension de l'opéra jusqu'à la fin de cette année. (We cannot say anything at this moment since the opera is closed until the end of this year.) (*Diario Italiano*, no. 1, p. 4)

Here, *vicino natale* (next Christmas) is rendered by *la fin de cette année* (the end of this year). Even if this is only a local translation shift, we can interpret it as a sign of secularization, with respect to French secularism.

The second issue of the *Diario Italiano*, analysed by Del Vento (1999), has the same structure as the first issue, except for a different regional news section: the section on theatres is replaced by a section on universities (*Università* – *Universités*), dedicated to the beginning of the academic year 1803–4 at the universities of Pavia and Bologna (Del Vento 1999: 225). After three issues, the publication of the *Diario Italiano* was halted for financial reasons (Del Vento 1999: 226). Foscolo's plan to have his private initiative be supported by the government had failed.

Given the limited number of translations from Milan analysed so far, I can only give a very provisional summary: in the period under consideration, there was no systematical, official translation policy with regard to legal and administrative texts. This is underlined by the fact that a writer, Ugo Foscolo, took a private initiative to publish a bilingual journal which included such translations.

2 Genoa

In the Napoleonic period, Genoa was the capital of the Ligurian Republic (1797–1805), a relatively long-lived 'sister republic' based on a constitution which was influenced by the French constitution of 1795 (Godechot 1984: 24).[8] Since the official language was Italian, most legal and administrative texts were published in this language. From 2 to 16 December 1799, thirteen issues of a bilingual newspaper, *Petites affiches ou Mercure italien*, were published (Morabito 1973: 281–3). In 1805, Liguria was annexed by the French Empire and divided into three departments, one of which was *Gênes* (Genoa). After the annexation, the French language played an increasing role, not only because French was the official language of the Napoleonic Empire but also because all prefects, most sub-prefects and an increasing number of local officials were French (Broers 2005: 203). Thus, the main difference compared to Milan is that Genoa forms part of France from 1805 on and that French was the only official language. Given that a big part of the population did not understand French, Italian translations of official texts were allowed and often published by the local authorities. Many bilingual texts were published, for example, laws and decrees, public announcements and judgements, some of them published in the bilingual newspaper *Gazzetta di Genova* (Godechot 1984: 35). I will focus here on this newspaper and the *Mercure italien*, as well as on some separately published local announcements and judgements, mostly found in the Archivio di Stato di Genova (ASG).

The short-lived bilingual newspaper *Mercure italien* (Full title: *Petites affiches ou Mercure italien – Avvisetti ossia Mercurio italiano*), of which only one copy has been preserved (No. 13 from 16 December 1799), was founded by the Jacobite printer Canis in December 1799. According to Morabito (1973: 281), the texts were originally written in French (printed on the left side of the newspaper) and translated into Italian (printed on the right sight). The newspaper contains two parts on four pages: *Nouvelles étrangères – Notizie Estere* (foreign news) and *Nouvelles de l'Intérieur – Notizie Interne* (domestic news). The second part includes official news from the government and local news and stories from Genoa.

On the micro-level, I will again have a look on the rendering of proper names. The section on subscription details contains some personal names and place names:

> On s'abonne pour ce journal qui paroit tous les jours dans la matinée, chez le Citoyen Canis au Bureau Français et Italien à piazza de' Funghi no. 43, et chez le Citoyen Albani Libraire à la piazza Nova.[9]
>
> // Si abbona a questo giornale, che sorte [sic] tutt'i giorni nella mattina, presso il Citt. Canis, Burò della Stamperia Francese e Italiana in Piazza de' Funghi No. 43, e presso il Citt. Albani Libraro in Piazza Nova. (*Petites affiches ou Mercure italien*, no. 13, p. 52)

Here, place names and personal names (surnames) are conserved, the revolutionary form of address *citoyen* is translated: *citoyen Canis – Citt.* [i.e. *Cittadino*] *Canis; citoyen Albani – Citt. Albani.*[10]

The dates of the revolutionary calendar are converted into the Gregorian calendar throughout the text, for example, 'GÊNES le 25 Frimaire an 8.

de la République (Genoa, 25 Frimaire, year 8 of the Republic) // GENOVA li 16 Decembre [sic] 1799 (v.s.) (i.e. *vecchio stile*)' (Genoa, 16 December 1799 (old style) (*Petites affiches ou Mercure italien*, no. 13, p. 49), because many Italian readers were not familiar with the revolutionary calendar.

Since the *Mercure italien* was published by the local club of Jacobites, it can be seen as the product of a private translation policy. During the Empire, a bilingual newspaper was published which can be considered the product of an official translation policy: the *Gazzetta di Genova*. This newspaper, formally monolingual Italian, achieves the status of an official journal of the department of Genoa in June 1809 and becomes more and more bilingual, although the Italian title is retained. From No. 44 (dated 3 June 1809) on, the title of newspaper is followed by the following sentence: 'Les Actes du Gouvernement dans le Département de Gênes, insérés dans cette Feuille, sont officiels' (The governmental acts of the department of Genoa, included in this chapter, are official) (*Gazzetta di Genova*, No. 44). However, in the beginning of this phase, not all articles are bilingual. Some texts are only in French and some only in Italian. The first partly bilingual issue contains an announcement for the subscribers ('Avviso agli associati'), in Italian, which begins as follows:

> Questa Gazzetta continuerà ad uscire due volte la settimana il mercoledì e il sabato. Il privilegio d'inserirvi gli atti officiali nell'atto che la rende più interessante per gli Associati di questo dipartimento, non la renderà men pregevole per gli Esteri, giacché non resteranno punti pregiudicati nella scelta, celerità e quantità delle notizie politiche.[11] (*Gazzetta di Genova*, No. 44, 1809, p. 176)

This text shows that the newspaper is addressed to a mixed readership: local readers who are interested in local and regional news and foreign readers who are interested in international news. From the beginning of 1812, the function and the format of the newspaper changed. According to an imperial decree from 26 September 1811, which regulates the number and the structure of the official journals in the Empire, an official journal is not allowed to publish political or literary news. Furthermore, the journal of a bilingual department must be completely bilingual and printed in two columns. The introduction of the first completely bilingual issue of the *Gazzetta di Genova* contains the following explication about the usefulness of the bilingual publication:

> Noi intendiamo parlare della grande facilità che la Gazzetta stampata in due colonne è per somministrare a tutti quelli fra i nostri lettori che non sono ancora abbastanza familiarizzati colla lingua francese, con quella lingua che non è ormai soltanto necessaria a formare una buona educazione, ma che è divenuta indispensabile per chiunque vuole aspirare ad un impiego nelle amministrazioni civili o giudiziarie[12]

// Nous entendons parler de la grande facilité que la Gazette imprimée sur deux colonnes va procurer à tous ceux parmi nos lecteurs qui ne sont pas encore suffisamment familiarisés avec la langue française, avec cette langue que n'est plus seulement nécessaire pour former une bonne éducation, mais qui est devenu indispensable pour tout individu qui veut aspirer à une place dans les Administrations civiles ou judiciaires. (*Gazzetta di Genova*, no. 1, 1812, p. 1)

So, the message is clear: no French, no job with the French authorities. Although the focus of the new Gazette is on its official character, it still includes a short feuilleton with news on the local theatre (opera and ballet). This shows that translations take place also within the cultural domain. The following example is an individual translation from the same field. In January 1808, the president of the Académie des beaux arts de Gênes (Academy of Fine Arts in Genoa), C. Brack, made a speech on the occasion of the distribution of the Academy's prizes. He made his speech in Italian. It was translated into French and published by the Academy with the French target text on the left and the Italian source text on the right sight, which does not indicate the translation direction, but the political and cultural hierarchy of the languages. The text begins as follows:

> Jeunes Élèves, // Allievi Amatissimi (1) ... (Young pupils // Dearest pupils)
>
> (Footnote:)[13] (1) On a cru devoir parler en italien aux Élèves et aux Professeurs dont plusieurs n'entendent pas assez le français.[14] (AN: AD/XV/51)

This example underlines that in the cultural domain, too, translations were needed, even if there was no official translation policy in this area. The cultural dominance of the French language is marked by the layout.

Another area where there was no strict translation policy is the legal domain. Judgements, for example, were not always translated. In the ASG, we found some bilingual judgements of the Commission militaire de la 28ème Division militaire (Military commission of the 28th Military division (i.e. the region of Liguria)). It seems that especially severe judgements were published in French with an Italian translation, probably in order to have a dissuasive effect. In a judgement dated 16 April 1807, eight people were sentenced to death, five others to four months of prison and five more were acquitted. Only the death sentence is typographically highlighted in the text:

> la Commission Militaire condamne
> A LA PEINE DE MORT
> les nommés ... Antoine Bertoni, dit Rollino, de Saint-Pierre-de-Varra, et
>   Louis de la Casa-Grande ...
> Condamne à quatre mois de prison ...

> Ordonne la mise en liberté des nommés ...¹⁵
> // ... la Commissione Militaria condanna
> ALLA PENA DI MORTE
> i nominati ... Antonio Bertoni detto Rollino di s. Pietro di Varra, e Luigi della Casa grande ...
> Condanna a quattro mesi di carcere ...
> Ordina che siano messi in libertà i nominate. (ASG: Prefettura francese 550)

One thousand large-size copies of this judgement were printed and distributed in the region. As we can see, personal and place names are translated for the most part.

Finally, I would like to mention a private translation project from the period under consideration. In an undated text (probably from 1807 or 1808), found in the ASG, Joseph (Giuseppe) Crivelli, a citizen from the department Marengo and author of a manual for the local authorities (Crivelli 1806–7), announces the plan to establish in Genoa an office which would assist the local citizens in the area of official writings, including translations. The project was published in both languages and contains the following passage:

> Les occupations ordinaires du Bureau d'Agence et de Correspondance seront:
>
> 1. La rédaction des lettres, mémoires, travaux, pétitions, etc. qui pourraient être adressées aux Autorités civiles, judiciaires et militaires ...
> 2. La traduction de toute pièce, ouvrage, mémoire, compte, tableaux, etc. de la langue italienne en langue française, et vice versa ...¹⁶
>
> // Le occupazioni ordinarie del Bureau di Agenzia e di Corrispondenza saranno:
>
> 1. La compilazione delle lettere, memorie, travagli, petizioni, ec. che potrebbero essere indirizzati alle autorità civili, giudiziarie e militari ...
> 2. La traduzione di ogni genere di pezze, opere, memorie, conti, tavole, ec. dalla lingua italiana nella francese, e vice versà. (ASG: Prefettura francese 165)

We do not know whether or not this office was really established, but this private project shows that there was a need for translations of official writings for local citizens. This observation is confirmed by the fact that, according to an imperial decree from May 1807, the deadline for the obligation to draft official documents in French was prolonged for the region of Liguria. The decree itself was translated into Italian (*Raccolta delle Leggi, Decreti, ec.*, vol. 25, p. 125).

3 Turin

As I mentioned in the introduction, the region of Piedmond was occupied in 1796 and annexed by the France in 1802. Turin became the capital of the Po department. After the annexation, the French state tried to Frenchify the region completely. According to a decree dated 5 January 1802, French was to become the 'mother tongue' of Piedmont (Marazzini 1984: 135). The result can be seen in the archives in Turin that contain a decreasing number of bilingual documents and an increasing number of monolingual French documents for the period under consideration (Reinke and Schreiber 2015). Most bilingual documents date from the last years of the occupation (1800–1) and the first years after the annexation (1802–5). In the years 1801–3, there existed an official journal for the region, the *Bulletin des actes de l'administration générale de la 27ème division* (Bulletin of the Acts of the General Administration of the 27th Division) (Grilli 2012: 260-6), which included many translations. I will focus mostly on bilingual text from the beginning of the nineteenth century, especially public announcements of the local authorities because most of the texts found in the local archives belong to this category.

Public announcements often concern daily life. The first example I want to quote is an order from Trapier, the local commander of the French army in Turin. It deals with an illegal trade in bread destined for the army:

> LE COMMANDANT DE LA PLACE
> Instruit qu'il se fait un commerce indécent du Pain de Munition, même à la porte de la Manutention, que des hommes et des femmes y achetent le pain de la Troupe; voulant reprimer ce negoce contraire à tous principes, et qui fait même présumer les abus, ORDONNE:
> Que les particuliers surpris à faire ce commerce soient arrêtés sur le champ ...[17]
> // Il Commandante della piazza
> Informato, che si fa un commercio scandaloso dei Pani di Munizione alla porta stessa della Munizioneria, e che uomini e donne vi comprano il Panne delle Truppe; volendo reprimere questa negoziazione contraria a tutti i principj, e che lascia sospettare abusi, ORDINA:
> Che li privati sorpresi a fare questo commercio siano subito arrestati. (ACT: Carte periodo francese 181)

In bilingual announcements of this kind, the functions of the two languages are different. The language of the occupying power, French, is used to underline the official character of the announcement, and the language of the occupied territory, Italian, is used for communicative reasons, since many local people did not understand enough French.

The second example is an administrative order of the mayor of Turin from 28 March 1803. It concerns the office hours of the employees in the city hall and reads as follows (I quote the beginning and the end):

LE Maire
 ARRÊTE[18]
  1. Les Bureaux sont ouverts à la Mairie dés les 9 heures du matin jusqu'aux cinq du soir ...
  2. Aucun des Employés ne peut s'exempter, ou s'éloigner du Bureaux aux heures fixées, sans une permission écrite du Secrétaire en chef, chargé d'en rendre compte au Maire dans chaque décade ...
  9. Le Secrétaire en Chef de la Mairie est chargé de la surveillance générale sur tous les Employés de la Municipalité, et de l'exécution du présent Arrêté qui devra être affiché dans tous les Bureaux de la Mairie.[19]
 // 1. Le ore d'uffizio sono fissate dalle 9 alle 5 di ciascun giorno per tutti gli impiegati alla Mairie, e bureaux dipendenti ...
  2. Nissun Impiegato può esimersi, od allontanarsi dall'Uffizio alle ore stabilite, senza una permissione in iscritto del Segretario Capo, incaricato di renderne informato il Maire in ogni decade ...
  9. Il Segretario Capo della Mairie è incaricato dell'ispezione generale su tutti gl'Impiegati alle Municipalità, e dell'esecuzione del presente decreto, che dovrà stare affisso in tutti i Bureaux della Mairie. (ACT: Carte periodo francese 97)

In this announcement, some features show clearly that French is the dominant language and culture: since the French title of the text is not translated, and the official terms for mayor (*Maire*) and the city hall (*Mairie*) are borrowed from the French language into Italian, it is clear that administrative functions and structures in the annexed region are French and not Italian. Another borrowed French term is *décade*, which denotes a period of ten days in the revolutionary calendar.

Another domain where we find numerous translations in the same period is jurisdiction. In 1801, a French-type Appeal Tribunal (*Tribunal d'appel – Tribunale d'appello*) was installed in Turin, which existed until 1814 (Grilli 2012: 307). We find many bilingual texts in the context of the establishment of this tribunal. One example is a bilingual decree from 2 December 1801, which includes the rules of procedure and of document dispatch (*Arrêté concernant l'ordre des audiences et l'expédition des affaires – Decreto riguardante l'ordine delle udienze e la spedizione degli affari*). I would like to mention especially the following dispositions concerning the publication of the decree:

Le présent Règlement sera envoyé au Commissaire Organisateur pour être soumis au Gouvernement, et sera provisoirement exécuté. Il sera publié à la première audience, imprimé, et publié dans les deux langues, affichés dans les lieux accoutumés, et envoyé au Tribunaux civils, qui ressortent du Tribunal d'Appel ...[20]

// Il presente Regolamento sarà inviato al Commissario Organizzatore per essere sottoposto all'approvazione del Governo, e sarà provvisionalmente eseguito. Sarà pubblicato nel primo dì d'udienza, stampato, e pubblicato nelle due lingue, affisso a' luoghi soliti, e spedito a' Tribunali civili esistenti nella giurisdizione del Tribunale d'Appello. (AN: AD/XV/50)

The formulation *dans les deux langues* (in the two languages), without explicit mention of the languages in question, implies an enhancement of the target language, even if it is not the official language. The same formulation can be found in numerous legal or administrative texts of the period (Schreiber 2019). Here is a quotation from the announcement of a republican feast from September 1801, which ends with the formula: 'Le présent Programme sera imprimé dans les deux langues, publié et affiché. (The present programme shall be printed in the two languages, published and displayed.) // Verrà il presente Programma stampato nelle due lingue, pubblicato ed affisso' (AN: F/1a/429).

In 1803, the French minister of the interior gives the order, via the general administrator, General Menou, to the local authorities in Turin that all official documents had to be published 'in the two languages'. Ferdinand Brunot cites the original order (in French):

Je vous (i.e. Général Menou) invite ... à donner des ordres aux autorités locales pour qu'elles soient exactes à publier les Loix, arrêtés et instructions relatives dans les deux Langues.[21] (Brunot 1979: 128)

The same formulation can still be found in a decree of the prefect of the Po department from 30 April 1804:

Le présent arrêté, ainsi que celui de l'Administrateur général, du 26 germinal dernier, seront imprimés, dans les deux langues, pour être transmis dans les différentes communes du département.[22]

// Il presente decreto, come pure quello dell'Amministratore generale delli 26 germile ultimo scorso saranno stampati nelle due lingue, e transmessi in seguito in tutte le comuni del dipartimento. (ACT: Carte periodo francese 181)

This decree is signed by Hercule Ferdinand La Ville, the first Napoleonic prefect of the Po department (1802–5). His successor, Pierre Loysel (1805–8), sent the following order from 11 July 1805 to the mayors of the department, marking the way to French monolingualism for all correspondence with departmental or governmental authorities:

> Parecchie scritture che compongono la vostra corrispondenza officiale con me, devono spesse volte sommesse al governo ...; egli resta perciò indispensabile che la vostra corrispondenza sia, senza eccezione, in lingua francese, e che tutte le scritture che l'accompagnano siano compilate o tradotte in questa lingua.
> Voi avete dunque cura, signori, di uniformarvi alla regola che vi prescrivo, e ciò a cominciar dal primo termifero prossimo.
> Vi prevengo, che, dopo quest'epoca, non accetterò alcuna decisione sul vista delle lettere e scritture, nè firmerò alcun atto, che mi sarebbero presentati in lingua italiana, e avendo una data posteriore al termini stabilito dal precedente articolo.[23] (*Raccolta delle Leggi, Decreti, ec.*, vol. 19, p. 39)

It is interesting that this sharply formulated order is written in Italian, which underlines the communicative necessity to use this language on the local level, whereas French is obligatory for the communication with regional or national authorities. In public announcements or official documents, the French language becomes more and more dominant from 1805 on until the end of the Napoleonic era. The number of bilingual texts decreases. However, individual translations can be found until the end of this era. One of the latest examples in our corpus is the following announcement from 11 May 1813 which begins as follows:

> **Avis au public**
> *Maison situé à Mirafiori, Commune de Turin, à louer pour 3, 6, ou 9 ans.*[24]
> On fait savoir que le 20 mai 1813, à 11 heures du matin, dans une des salles de l'hôtel de la Préfecture du Pô, situé à Turin, place Carignan, il sera procédé, par adjudication au plus offrant au et dernier enchérisseur ... à la mise en location
> D'un corps de bâtiment situé dans la bourgade de Mirafiori, dépendant de la Commune de Turin, dit Monica, Priotta e Bellardo.
> ...[25]
> // Si notifica, che li 20 maggio 1813, alle ore undici del mattino, in una delle sale del palazzo della Prefettura del Dipartimento del Po, situato in Torino, piazza Carignano, si procederà, per mezzo d'aggiudicazione all'ultimo e miglior offerente ... all'affitamento
> Di un corpo di casa situato nella borgata di Mirafiori, dipendente dalla città di Torino, detto Monica, Priotta e Bellardo.
> ... (ACT: Carte periodo francese 181)

Since the title has not been translated, the French language dominates the text, and one important information is missing in the Italian text: the possible terms of lease. As in other quotations discussed earlier, personal names and place names are translated, but not coherently: some place names are translated (*Turin – Torino*; *place Carignon – piazza Carignano*) but others are not (*Mirafiori*; *Monica, Priotta e Bellardo*).

Last but not least, I would like to quote a curious case of language policy. In a report of the activities of the Po department in the week from 12 to 19 January 1811, I found the following remark: 'La police a enlevé le 14 au matin un placard écrit en mauvais italien qui avait été affiché dans la nuit précédente rue d'Austerlitz près de l'arsenal.' (In the morning of 14 January, the police removed a placard written in bad Italian which had been displayed in the night before in the Austerlitz Street, near the arsenal) (AST: Archivio Governo francese 1771). I cannot say what were exactly the reasons for the removal of the placard: the quality of the language (as the report states), the language itself or, perhaps, the text of the placard. In any case, poor quality of language could be an argument for such an action, which underlines the importance of the language topic.

4 Conclusion

Coming back to the questions mentioned in the introduction, I would like to summarize some main findings of my contribution: How were the translations organized? What was the role of private and official translation policies? In all three cities, we were able to find official translation policies and some private initiatives (like the *Diario Italiano* in Milan). However, little information could be found about the organization of the translation or the translators. This leads me to the conclusion that there were no professional translators, like in the national translation offices (Schreiber 2017), but that the translations were mostly done by employees or journalists for whom translation was not the only professional task.

What translation procedures can be found in the translations, especially with regard to proper names (place names and personal names)? No coherent translation strategy was found, but in many cases, proper names had been translated in order to make the text easier to understand for the readers of the target text.

What were the main differences between the translation policies of the three cities?

In Milan, Italian was the official language during the entire period. In Genoa and Turin, Italian was the official language only during the first part of the period;

French became official after the annexations of the two territories (Liguria and Piedmont). However, even during the periods when Italian was the official language of a certain region and often the source language for translations into French, French language and culture remained dominant compared to Italian – in other words, cultural dominance did not always entail linguistic domination.

Notes

1 D'hulst and Van Gerwen (2018: 500) also mention a third category: *semi-official translations*. Since the distinction between private and semi-official translations is rather fuzzy, I will not use this category in this chapter.
2 From 1795 on, more than fifteen 'sister republics' were installed in different European countries, from Ireland to Italy. These states were de jure independent, but de facto under French influence, even if the influence was less direct than in the occupied or annexed countries, such as Belgium (Soleil 2014: 160–4).
3 Recently, Sarah Hartmann discovered in Milan previously unknown translations of legal and administrative texts from 1797 to 1799, which will be analysed in a separate publication.
4 It is debatable whether the inhabitants of the Italian Republic and the Napoleonic Kingdom of Italy, both restricted to a part of Northern Italy, form a 'nation'. I will not discuss this issue here.
5 The first book of the Annals of Cornelius Tacitus, translated by Ludovico Valeriani. Milan, by Luigi Veladini, national printer. Without date (published this year). (All English translations of quotations are mine. Dates of the Revolutionary calendar in the translations are converted into the Gregorian calendar. The sign // is used to indicate a new column, the sign / indicates a new line.)
6 The translation of Christian names was not unusual at that time (see Schreiber 2001).
7 At this moment, we cannot say anything since the opera is closed until next Christmas.
8 The second constitution of the Ligurian Republic (1802) was inspired mainly by the constitution of the Italian Republic (Godechot 1984: 31).
9 The subscription for this newspaper, which appears every morning, is made by the citizen Canis in the French and Italian office, at Piazza de' Funghi No. 43, and by the citizen Albani, librarian at Piazza Nova.
10 Since the *Triennio rivoluzionario* (1796–9), the noun *cittadino* could be used in the Italian regions under French influence as universal form of address, in the same way as *citoyen* (Leso 1991: 276).
11 This gazette continues to appear twice a week, on Wednesday and on Saturday. The privilege to include the official acts, which makes the paper more interesting for

subscribers of this department, does not make it less precious for foreigners, since the choice, rapidity and quantity of the political news will not be altered.

12 We would like to speak about the easiness which the Gazette printed in two columns will provide to those of our readers who are not enough familiarized with the French language, a language which is now not only necessary for a good education but also essential for everybody who looks for a job in the civil or legal authorities.

13 The footnote is in French, under the Italian text. There is no Italian version.

14 We thought that we should speak Italian to the pupils and teachers, some of whom do not understand French adequately.

15 The Military Commission pronounces / The death penalty / against ... Antoine Bertoni, called Rollino, from Saint-Pierre-de-Varra, and Louis de la Casa-Grande. / A four-month prison sentence against ... / Sets at liberty.

16 The ordinary work of the Office of Writings and Correspondence include: / (1) The drafting of letters, memoirs, essays, petitions, etc., which could be addressed to the civil, legal and military authorities ... / (2) The translation of all writings, books, memoirs, accounts, charts etc. from the Italian into the French language and vice versa ...

17 THE LOCAL COMMANDER / Informed that an indecent trade in ammunition bread is going on even at the gate of the ammunition depot, and that there men and women buy the Army's bread; wanting to stop this trade against all principles and which presume that there will be abuses; ORDERS: / That all private individuals seen when doing this trade will be caught immediately.

18 The title has not been translated.

19 **The Mayor** / ORDERS / (1) The offices in the city hall are open from 9 o'clock in the morning until 5 o'clock in the evening ... / (2) An employee may not be absent or leave the office during the indicated hours without a written permission of the Chief Secretary, who will have to report the Mayor every ten days ... (9) The Chief Secretary acts as the general supervisor of all employees of the municipality and controls the execution of the present order which will be displayed in all offices of the city hall.

20 The present rule shall be sent via the Government Commissioner to the Government and shall be provisionally applied. It shall be published on the first hearing, printed and published in the two languages, displayed in the usual places, and sent to the Civil Tribunals which are subordinated to the Appeal Tribunal.

21 I ask you (i.e. General Menou) ... to give orders to the local authorities to be strict in the publication of the laws, decrees and regulations in the two languages.

22 The present decree, as well as the decree of the General Administrator, from 16 April 1804, shall be printed in the two languages, in order to be transferred to the different municipalities of the department.

23 Many writings which form part of your official correspondence with me have often to be submitted to the government ... So, it is essential that your correspondence is, without exception, written in French, and that all enclosed documents are written or translated in this language. / Thus, you will take care that you follow my present rule, and this from 20 July 1805 on. / I warn you that after the date mentioned in the previous paragraph, I will not accept any decision in letters or documents nor sign any act if these writings are presented to me in the Italian language and having a date later than the one that is specified in the preceding paragraph.

24 The title has not been translated.

25 **Public Announcement** / *House situated in Mirafiori, Municipality of Turin, to let for 3, 6 or 8 years* / This is to announce that on 20 May 1813, at 11 a.m., in one of the rooms of the Po prefecture, located in Turin, Carignan Place, there will be an auction with acceptation to the highest offer and last tender, in order to let / A building located in the village of Mirafiori, belonging to the municipality of Turin, called Monica, Priotta e Bellardo.

26 Archival research was done by Sarah Hartmann, Jelena Nikolic and myself, in the context of a research project on the translation of legal, administrative and political texts during the Napoleonic era in Northern Italy, financed by the *Deutsche Forschungsgemeinschaft*.

References

Primary sources[26]

ACT: Archivio Storico della Città di Torino (Historical Archiv of the City of Turin). Turin (Series: Carte periodo francese [Papers of the French Period]).

AN: Archives nationales (National Archives). Paris / Pierrefitte-sur-Seine (Series: AD/XV; F/1a).

ASG: Archivio di Stato di Genova (State Archive of Genoa). Genoa (Series: Prefettura francese [French Prefecture]).

ASM: Archivio di Stato di Milano (State Archive of Milan). Milan (Series: Atti ufficiali [Official acts]; Melzi restituito [Archive Melzi restored]).

AST: Archivio di Stato di Torino (State Archive of Turin). Turin (Series: Archivio Governo francese [Archive of the French Government]).

Secondary sources

Broers, M. (2005), *The Napoleonic Empire in Italy, 1796–1814. Cultural Imperialism in a European Context?* Houndmills: Palgrave Macmillan.

Brunot, F. (1979), *Histoire de la langue française des origines à nos jours*, vol. XI/2: Le français *au* dehors sous *le Consulat et* l'Empire, Paris: Colin.

Crivelli, J. (1806–7), *Recueil raisonné des principales fonctions devoirs et attributions des administrateurs, des communes et des hospices etc. à l'usage de messieurs les maires, commissaires de police et secrétaires des mairies*, 8 vols, Verceil: s.n.

Del Vento, C. (1999), 'Sul "Diario Italiano" di Ugo Foscolo', *Giornale storico della letteratura italiana*, 176: 222–38.

D'hulst, L. and H. van Gerwen (2018), 'Translation Space in Nineteenth-Century Belgium: Rethinking Translation and Transfer Directions', *Perspectives: Studies in Translation Theory and Practice*, 26 (4): 495–508.

Diario Italiano, no. 1, December 12, 1803, Milan: Genio Tipografico (ASM: Melzi restituito).

Gazzetta di Genova, Genoa: s.n., 1809–1814.

Godechot, J. (1984), 'La Ligurie à l'époque révolutionnaire et napoléonienne', in *Il Dipartimento di Montenotte nell'età Napoleonica*, vol. 1, 13–38, Savona: Società Savonese di Storia Patria.

Grilli, A. (2012), *Il difficile amalgama. Giustizia e codici nell'Europa di Napoleone*, Frankfurt: Klostermann.

Ködel, S. (2014), *Die Enquête Coquebert de Montbret (1806–1812). Die Sprachen und Dialekte Frankreichs und die Wahrnehmung der französischen Sprachlandschaft während des Ersten Kaiserreichs*, Bamberg: University of Bamberg Press.

Leso, E. (1991), *Lingua e rivoluzione. Ricerche sul vocabolario italiano del Triennio rivoluzionario 1796–1799*, Venezia: Istituto Veneto di Scienze, Lettere ed Arti.

Marazzini, C. (1984), *Piemonte e Italia. Storia di un confronto linguistico*, Turin: Centro Studi Piemontesi.

Meylaerts, R. (2011), 'Translation Policy', in Y. Gambier and L. van Doorslaer (eds), *Handbook of Translation Studies*, vol. 2, 163–8, Amsterdam/Philadelphia: Benjamins.

Morabito, L. (1973), *Il giornalismo giacobino genovese 1797–1799*, Turin: Associazione Piemontese dei Bibliotecari.

Petites Affiches ou Mercure italien / Avvisetto ossia Mercurio italiano, no. 13, December 16, 1799, Genoa: Imprimerie Française et Italienne des amis de la Liberté (Biblioteca Universitaria di Genova: FO.VOL.LIG.164).

Pillepich, A. (2003), *Napoléon et les Italiens. République italienne et Royaume d'Italie*, Paris: Nouveau Monde.

Raccolta delle Leggi, Decreti, ec. Turin: Davico e Picco, 1800–14 (43 vols.).

Reinke, K. and M. Schreiber (2015), 'Juristische Fachübersetzungen im Sprachenpaar Französisch-Italienisch in den Jahren 1789 bis 1814', in E. Lavric and W. Pöckl (eds), *Comparatio delectat II. Akten der VII. Internationalen Arbeitstagung zum romanisch-deutschen und innerromanischen Sprachvergleich*, 693–706, Frankfurt: Lang.

Roberti, M. (1946/7), *Milano capitale Napoleonica. La formazione di uno stato moderno 1796–1814*, 3 vols, Milan: Fondazione Treccani degli Alfieri per la storia di Milano.

Schreiber, M. (2001), 'Zum Umgang mit fremdsprachigen Eigennamen im Französischen und Deutschen (mit einem Ausblick auf das Spanische und das Italienische)', in J. Albrecht and H.-M. Gauger (eds), *Sprachvergleich und Übersetzungsvergleich. Leistungen und Grenzen, Unterschiede und Gemeinsamkeiten*, 314–39, Frankfurt: Lang.

Schreiber, M. (2016), 'Covert Multilingualism: The Case of the Translation Policy in France and Belgium during the French Revolution and the Napoleonic Era', *Across Languages and Cultures*, 17: 123–36.

Schreiber, M. (2017), 'Zur Übersetzungspolitik der Französischen Revolution und der Napoleonischen Epoche. Am Beispiel von drei nationalen Übersetzungsbüros', in H. Aschenberg and S. Dessì Schmid (eds), *Romanische Sprachgeschichte und Übersetzung*, 139–50, Heidelberg: Winter.

Schreiber, M. (2019), '*Dans les deux langues* – Zur Referenz auf Mehrsprachigkeit und Übersetzung in Texten der Französischen Revolution und der Napoleonischen Epoche', in E. Lavric and W. Pöckl (eds), *Comparatio delectat III. Akten der VIII. Internationalen Arbeitstagung zum romanisch-deutschen und innerromanischer Sprachvergleich*, vol. 2, 809–21. Frankfurt: Lang.

Soleil, S. (2014), *Le modèle juridique français dans le monde. Une ambition, une expansion (XVIe – XIXe siècle)*, Paris: IRJS.

Wiesmann, E. (2009), 'Rechtsübersetzung: Praxis – Theorie – Didaktik', in B. Ahrens, L. Černý, M. Krein-Kühle and M. Schreiber (eds), *Translationswissenschaftliches Kolloquium I*, 273–94, Frankfurt: Lang.

3

Habsburg Vienna: The institutionalization of translation in a hybrid city, 1848–1914

Michaela Wolf

1 Introduction

In the last decades of the Habsburg Empire's existence, about 50 million people were speaking twelve languages. This 'Babelian' diversity, both in linguistic and in cultural terms, is especially reflected in the censuses towards the end of the century, when the German-speaking and Hungarian nationalities formed the largest groups, followed by Czechs, Polish, Ukrainians, Romanians, Croatians, Serbs, Slovaks and Slovenes and finally the Italians, Ladins and Bosniaks.[1] The last census conducted (1910) both in Cisleithania and in Transleithania gives us the figure of 51,356,465 (see Figure 3.1).[2]

Vienna as the Imperial centre was thus continually challenged by the local governments in the crownlands to guarantee the communication between the various nationalities. From a present perspective it is not surprising that the practice of translation in all its facets assumed a major role in moulding the various cultures which made up the Monarchy.

Consequently, the central question of this chapter is, How was Vienna, as capital of an enormous, pluricultural Empire, constructed as a political and cultural focal point through translation in its varied forms? The major focus in the discussion of this construction process will be on the role of institutionalization. Methodologically, after discussing Vienna's pluricultural settings especially against the background of multilingualism, as a first step, we will thoroughly look at the production of translations from the main Habsburg languages (Hungarian, Polish, Croatian–Serbian, Slovenian, Italian) into German, the politically dominant language, first presenting the whole figures of translations published in the Monarchy and followed by the presentation of the corresponding

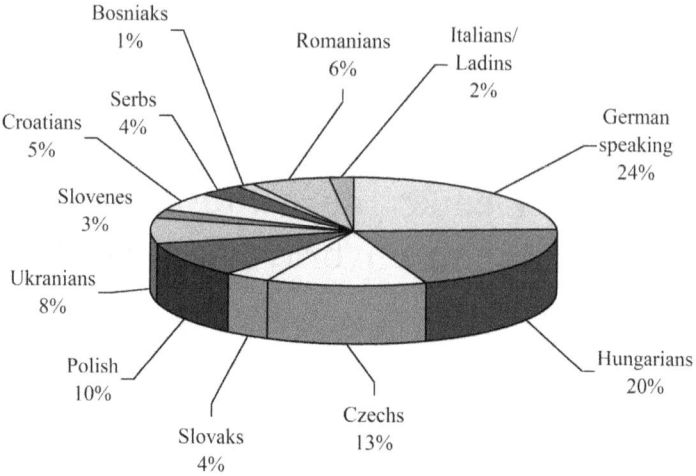

Figure 3.1 Nationalities of the Habsburg Monarchy in 1910.

data of translations published exclusively in Vienna. The translation figures will be analysed in relation to the restrictive press legislation (which substituted pre-1848 censorship laws) and the increasingly important factors governing the Monarchy's translation policy. Also, a study on the main publishing houses which were located in Vienna and which specialized in the production of translations will attempt to investigate the effects of the Empire's translation policy.

As a second step, an in-depth study will be presented, based on archival material, of the so-called *Reichsgesetzblatt* Editorial Office (*Redaktionsbureau des Reichsgesetzblattes*), which was established in 1849 and provided for the translation of all laws which were approved by the Reichstag into (nearly) all the Empire's languages. A large number of language experts were employed as civil servants in the Ministry of Justice and were working on this huge translation project, some of them for decades. The labour of this bureau makes clear the various facets of institutionalization of the translation activity and the varying impact of both general politics and language regulation.

2 Vienna, conflicting constructions of 'the other'

The so-called 'Nationality Question' was one of the major problems within the pluricultural Habsburg Empire of the nineteenth century. It became especially apparent in the crownlands after the revolution of 1848 and persisted until 1918. After the Austro-Hungarian Compromise in 1867, the Slavic peoples demanded similar privileges. The Czechs offered the most determined resistance to German-directed centralism and demanded the autonomy of the Bohemian lands. Emperor Franz Joseph rejected a 'Bohemian Compromise' in 1871 and also turned down a Polish draft outlining Galicia's autonomy (AEIOU 2016).

The ethnic, linguistic and confessional heterogeneity of the Empire, which can be regarded as one of the roots of conflicts between nationalities, has a long history and, especially in the larger cities and the capital, was fostered through migration in the eighteenth century and thickened through industrialization, even more intense migration movements, and urbanization in the nineteenth century. Most of the conflicts among nationalities took place along a wide and fractious spectrum between the legally anchored claim to equal rights and the immense regional diversity of conditions for its realization. During debates on the conflicts between nationalities, language use gradually came to be fully identified with national affiliation, as the battle for language was always a weapon in the battle for power. Actually, one of the central instruments of these conflicts was, without doubt, the language regarded as constitutive of each ethnic group. Article 19 of the 1867 Constitution aimed to secure each group's basic right to the 'preservation and cultivation of its nationality and language' and remained the foundation of nationalities legislation in the Austrian half of the Dual Monarchy until 1918 (Wolf 2015: 36).[3] In such a context, the claim raised by Cronin and Simon with reference to the urban space that 'language, itself an essential instrument and domain of the public ... is simply taken for granted' (2014: 119) is not applicable to the Habsburg Monarchy, not even for its capital – on the contrary, language and its use was a major public issue. On the other hand, translation, as will be shown, added an important dimension to this conflict.

As a consequence of migration, in the last fifty years of the Empire's existence the Imperial capital of Vienna experienced an incredible demographic increase: while in 1869 it counted 607,000 inhabitants, in 1890 it grew to 1.4 million, reaching 1.7 million in 1900 and 2.1 million in 1910.[4] Thus, within only one generation the population more than tripled (Csendes and Opll 2001: 177), a growth indebted mainly to internal migration. The immigrants mostly came from Bohemia and Moravia, the Hungarian territory, Galicia and Bukovina. Most of them found themselves occupying low social positions. They left deep marks on the everyday life of Vienna and other cities where they worked, as the following description vividly shows with reference to the Czechs:

> Damit der Wiener sein verträumtes, unpünktliches, an kleinen Freuden und Genüssen so reiches Leben führen könne, arbeitet unauffällig und still eine Präzisionsmaschine, deren rastlose und fleißige Arme die Tschechen sind. Sie

sind unsere Schneider und machen unsere schönsten Kleider; sie sind unsere Schuster und machen unsere schönen Schuhe; sie geigen und blasen unsere schöne Musik; sie kochen unser gutes, gesundes Essen; sie zimmern und polieren unsere schönen Möbel; sie kutschieren unsere schönen Equipagen ..., und die milchstrotzenden Brüste der böhmischen Ammen nähren die Wiener Kinder. (Friedländer 1948, quoted in John/Lichtblau 1993: 419)[5]

The pluricultural situation in Vienna called for measures to meet increasing conflicts between nationalities resulting mainly from the massive presence in the city of the different ethnic groups. One of the measures suggested was to split Vienna into districts according to the various nationalities; the suggestion, however, was not taken very seriously by the government. The fear of creating, with such measures, enclaves of nationalities which potentially fostered national conflicts and separation movements was succinctly articulated in 1909 by politician Michael Hainisch:

Es wäre für uns höchst unerfreulich, wenn aus Wien mit der Zeit eine Art Konstantinopel würde, in dem alle möglichen Volksstämme getrennt nach Quartieren oder getrennt durch Sprache nebeneinander wohnten. (In Csáky 2010: 135)[6]

Despite this claim, in practice, to give just a couple of examples, many Slavic, especially Bohemian, migrants lived in the district of Favoriten (1900: 25.5 per cent) while Jews lived in Leopoldstadt (1900: 36.4 per cent).

In order to conceptualize the complex multilingual and pluricultural situation of the Habsburg Monarchy, Moritz Csáky in his seminal monograph *Das Gedächtnis der Städte. Kulturelle Verflechtungen – Wien und die urbanen Milieus in Zentraleuropa* (2010) suggests viewing the city as a hybrid, urban space of communication. Accordingly, Vienna's pluriculturality can be viewed from a variety of perspectives: on the one hand, daily social life was markedly characterized by multilingualism and the crossing of different life styles which required permanently shifting processes, creating what Cronin and Simon (2014: 121) aptly called 'translation space'. On the other, the cultural sphere was significantly marked by the overlapping of different traditions, forms of expression and, of course, languages. Csáky discusses various authors who represent conjointly these various features, such as Slovene intellectual Ivan Cankar (1876–1918), who spent more than a decade in Vienna. He nearly simultaneously navigated in different cultural communication spaces: that of the poor working class of the *Vorstadt* (periphery), in the intellectual communication space of artists, writers and journalists, and in two different language spaces, writing his literature both in Slovene and German (Csáky 2010, 200). It seems obvious that translation – in whatever form – was needed to mediate between these various spaces.

3 Institutionalizing translation

As in other empires, pluriculturalism in the Habsburg Monarchy was tackled, among others, through the institutionalization of the translation and interpreting activity. Clara Reiter in her dissertation *In Habsburgs sprachlichem Hofdienst. Translation in den diplomatischen Beziehungen zwischen den habsburgischen Höfen von Madrid und Wien in der Frühen Neuzeit* (2015) delivers insights on the motives triggering the institutionalization of the translation and interpreting activity. She comes to the conclusion that at the Spanish court, which promoted the Spanish language – contrary to other European courts which at that time still practised Latin as an administrative language – both in peripheral administration units and at the central court, translation was widely adopted to handle the relationships with the court in Vienna. The increasing amount of translation practice resulting from the development of the administrative sphere in the sixteenth century led to a strong institutionalization of translation at the Spanish court, which could not be observed in such a pronounced form at the Viennese court. Also, Reiter locates a certain process of differentiation of the translatorial activities and the persons involved resulting from institutionalization (2015: 253).

By contrast, especially in the eighteenth and early nineteenth century, both the court in Vienna and certain parts of the population were characterized by widespread multilingualism.[7] Only the post-1848 call for equal rights for all the Empire's nationalities led to a clear decrease of multilingual practice and subsequently to an increase of language mediation in the form of translation and interpreting. Multilingualism as well as monolingualism are thus the result of social, political and ideological orders. Therefore, Reine Meylaerts is right when she claims that 'as an institutional phenomenon, translation has a very ambivalent function in multilingual societies: it both allows and annihilates multilingualism' (Meylaerts 2006: 3). Against this backdrop, language policy and translation policy can be seen as guiding the cultural practice of translation into particular channels, thus having at least an indirect impact on the final outlook of a translation.

Translation policy is thus closely connected to the institutionalization of translation. Generally, institutionalization is understood as a process intended to regulate societal behaviour within organizations or entire societies. It is a human activity that installs, adapts and changes rules and procedures in both social and political spheres, thus affecting the interactive behaviour of individuals and organizations as well as of political entities (Keman 2018). In the area of translation studies, in the wake of the gradual establishment of sociological approaches to translation, the idea of 'translation as institution' has been developed. A strong argument in favour of viewing translation as institution is delivered by Theo Hermans who underscores the 'public face' of translation: its presence in daily life, its codification in dictionaries, and its professional (translators and interpreters) and organizational (translators' and interpreters' associations) representation (Hermans 1995: 5). The author also mentions the importance of the high number of people involved in the translation process, like clients, translators and interpreters, translation agencies, publishing houses or readers, whose expectations generate a series of norms and conventions referred to the translation (Hermans 1995: 9). Thus, the institutionalization of translation and interpreting can be understood as a process which results from the continuous negotiation of the norms governing an institution or organization in the context of which translation is practised. Additionally, it is engendered as a cultural practice within a certain community. In such a view, the main features of the institutionalization of the translation and interpreting practice can be identified, first, in the presence of a mediating figure, then, in the participation of a series of agents who accomplish a variety of actions and, finally, in the negotiation of norms. Furthermore, the interaction with other fields of social life is an important aspect.

Within the realm of this chapter, the focus will not be on the (individual) practice of translation and interpreting but on larger translation projects promoted and enacted by the central government, on the one hand, and by the expanding publishing sector, on the other. Both endeavours represent the gradual institutionalization of the translating and interpreting activity and are strongly connected with aspects of language and translation policy. The next few paragraphs will thus shed light on the main traits of this policy, which guided the production of translation and interpreting in the last few decades of the Empire's existence.

3.1 Language policy in the late Habsburg Monarchy

The Dual Monarchy's linguistic diversity was regulated by a complex body of central and provincial laws. The major points of this legislation map out the landscape within which translation took place and show how closely the 'language question' in the multi-ethnic state was associated with the activity of translation. Article 19 of the Constitution enacted on 21 December 1867 remained the foundation of nationalities legislation until the end of the Monarchy:

> Alle Volksstämme des Staates sind gleichberechtigt, und jeder Volksstamm hat ein unverletzliches Recht auf Wahrung und Pflege seiner Nationalität und Sprache. Die Gleichberechtigung aller landesüblichen Sprachen in Schule, Amt und öffentlichem Leben wird vom Staate anerkannt. In den Ländern, in welchen mehrere Volksstämme wohnen, sollen die öffentlichen Unterrichtsanstalten derart eingerichtet sein, dass ohne Anwendung eines Zwanges zur Erlernung einer zweiten Landessprache jeder dieser Volksstämme die erforderlichen Mittel zur Ausbildung in seiner Sprache erhält. (Artikel 19, RGBl. 142/1867)[8]

Although the law gave primacy to no single language, German in effect took priority over all the other languages. In the decades that followed, repeated attempts were made to challenge this pre-eminence of German, resulting in bitter disputes in parliament. None of these plans bore fruit, and Crown Prince Franz Ferdinand, too, failed to achieve his goal of having German codified as the *Staatssprache* (state language) (see Stourzh 1980: 1041–3).

In these discussions, a distinction was made between an 'external' and an 'internal' official language (*Amtssprache*). The 'external official language' was that used between government authorities and the public, in other words for everyday communication in the state's offices both orally (for interviews, hearings and so on) and in writing (lawsuits, official decrees, judgements). The 'internal official language' was used for communication within the administration, for example, in correspondence, file notes or minutes not designed for public circulation (Rumpler 1997: 505). Kasimir Felix Badeni (1846–1909), minister of the interior of Cisleithania, in 1897, enacted an ordinance which regulated the linguistic qualification of civil servants in the crownlands. The ordinance referred to the 'internal official language' and resulted in the legally binding regulation that all civil servants had to have a command in both German and the respective *Landessprache* (language of the land), which meant the language used by at least 20 per cent of the population of a crownland. From 1 July 1901 onwards all applicants for the civil servants had to know both languages (Hugelmann 1934: 177–81).[9] The reaction to this ordinance was extreme violence, as in practice it would have meant that civil servants from the crownlands would have largely gained priority over those coming from the German-speaking parts of Cisleithania. Badeni's successors withdrew the ordinance, and the 'language question' found no solution until the dissolution of the Empire. Yet, the national(ist) conflicts experienced an enormous acceleration through these events.

The legal determinations of language policy affected translation in many different ways. The place of translation activities in the domain of the Habsburg administration was therefore exposed to the meandering course of language-related legislation. As soon as bilingual official business was permitted, a drop in demand for translation was likely to result. In some cases this was probably, at best, accompanied by increased verbal communication between speakers of different languages for the sake of optimizing everyday work processes.

3.2 Translation policy in the late Habsburg Monarchy

Much less evident than language policy and thus more difficult to identify were the measures related to a Habsburg translation policy. Actually, despite its importance in the production of cultural heterogeneity, translation policy was never carried out explicitly but through the filter of other cultural policy regulations. Yet, it can be assumed that in its different forms, translation policy was felt at every stage of the translation process. It is often officially or semi-officially described (or, perhaps, disguised) as 'cultural policy', 'publishing policy' or simply an 'economic' measure. Whatever the designation, the practice of translation, especially literary translation, is always subject to the ups and downs of economic cycles and sets of interests, depending on the particular text type involved. Regarding the translation policy of the Habsburg Monarchy, the focus will be first on three regulating factors: (1) censorship, and the publishing legislation that continued to shape literary production after censorship was abolished; (2) copyright regulations of the Habsburg book market; and (3) the state licensing of booksellers. With a stronger reference to cultural policy, I will then turn to discuss the state promotion of the arts and, especially, to the literary prizes that were awarded in the Habsburg Monarchy between 1848 and 1918 (see also Wolf 2015: 134–46).

Generally speaking, censoring institutions' claim to regulate the public sphere leads to massive conflicts especially in the area of culture and art. Jürgen Habermas has placed this in a historical context, locating the call for freedom from censorship within the eighteenth-century bourgeoisie's growing self-confidence (Habermas 1989). The gradual commercialization of literary life and the industrialization of the press led to a structural transformation of culture that culminated in a differentiation of the organization, distribution and consumption of literature. Literary production was now larger in scale, more professional and addressed new classes and groups of readers; print products were theoretically open to everyone whose literacy qualified him or her to read them (Habermas 1989: 37). This utopia of an unrestricted public sphere of readers, in turn, provoked attempts at political control. In the Habsburg context, until the revolutions of 1848, the pertinent laws provided for a particularly rigorous form of censorship, which left deep marks on intellectual life even after 1848.

Although the revolutionary events of March 1848 – which were the product of social and political tensions after the 1815 Congress of Vienna – put a temporary stop to Metternich's feared censorship apparatus, the relative process of liberalization promptly led to reinstating restrictions on the freedom of the press. Every printed work now had to be deposited with the authorities three days before publication while every periodical had to be handed in one hour before publication (see Ogris 1975: 540–1). Little had thus changed since pre-1848 days, until the press law of 1862 (*RGBl.* 6/1863) decreed genuine changes, restricting control to periodicals. The index of books banned in Austria, as compiled by Anton Einsle (1896), lists approximately 3,800 banned works, including 119 translations (about 3.15 per cent) (Bachleitner and Wolf 2010: 34). The now practised post-publication censorship encroached severely on the process of literary production and distribution and affected the relationships between authors or translators and their publishers: authors increasingly practised preemptive 'self-censorship' to avoid the confiscation of books already printed, and publishers watched even more vigilantly than before over the content of works they planned to publish, for post-publication confiscation produced a risk of great economic losses.

Another area of cultural policy impacting critically on translation was copyright legislation. For a long time, the Habsburg state showed little interest in modernizing copyright law. An Imperial Patent of 1846 protected literary and artistic property against unauthorized publication and reproduction. The new copyright law of 1895 gave a more concrete form to the idea of a unitary copyright title, but it did not fundamentally expand the protection of literary and artistic work. Regarding translation rights, after only eight years, translations could be made and sold without the slightest recompense to the original author (Gerhartl 2000: 215). Although the Habsburg Monarchy signed copyright treaties with several individual countries (e.g. Italy in 1890 or Spain in 1912), it did never subscribe to the Berne Convention of 1886.[10] This meant that many Austrian publishers began to market their books in the other German-speaking countries.

Beside censorship regulations and the issue of copyright, the obligation on booksellers to obtain a state license is a further indication of the Monarchy's attempts to control the literary market. It impacted crucially on the distribution of books in general and thus also of translations. Legal regulations in 1806 expanded the control over bookselling, determining that licenses could now only be issued by provincial governments, and bookstores could operate only in provincial or district capitals; the result was a drop in the number of bookstores and a temporary stagnation in the book trade more generally. Only about fifty years later did the sector gradually begin to draw benefit from the longer-term economic growth. As in other countries, bookselling and publishing was increasingly driven by market criteria, and the new commercial regulations of 1859 considerably reduced state influence. Linked with the improving economic situation, the various legislative measures led to a spectacular rise in the number of bookstores towards the end of the century – in Vienna alone, the number of bookshops rose from 39 in 1859 to 115 in 1891 (Bachleitner, Eybl and Fischer 2000: 171–85).

State promotion of culture and literature is another important step in the institutionalization of translation. It appears that the Ministry of Culture and Instruction, established in 1848, played only a minor role in art and literature, as many of the pertinent institutions were privately owned or the responsibility of local administrations. The Vienna court opera and the court theatre, both of which used numerous translated works, also fell outside the ministry's remit. Regarding literature, the institutionalization of state-managed support started in 1867, when a permanent committee was appointed to advise the ministry on the arts. Support for (also translated) literature focused on grants and state-funded prizes or on Christmas relief for writers in distress. Later this support was extended to cover institutions, subsidizing literary societies such as the *Wiener Goethe-Verein* or the *Literarischer Verein in Wien* (Wolf 2015: 138).

Literary prizes form a nexus between production, distribution and reception of literature and are important factors in the cultural policy of a country. Although the literary prizes awarded in the late Monarchy never specifically honoured translations, both the recipients and the juries included several people also known as *translators*. There are records of nine literary prizes established in the Habsburg Monarchy between 1859 and 1910, eight of them in Vienna and one in Jetřichovice, Bohemia, as can be seen in Table 3.1.

One of the most prominent prizes of the time was the Bauernfeld Prize. In 1912 Siegfried Trebitsch (1868–1956) was among the prizewinners and received 1,000 crowns. Trebitsch was a poet, author and dramatist, but never achieved

Table 3.1 Literary prizes in the Habsburg Monarchy, 1859–1918

Prize	Year founded	Place founded
Schiller Prize, Vienna	1859	Vienna
Grillparzer Prize	1872	Vienna
Raimund Prize	1895	Vienna
Bauernfeld Prize	1894	Vienna
Prize of the Kanka Foundation	1899	Jetřichovice
Prize of the Fröbel Foundation	1900	Vienna
Volkstheater Prize	1905	Vienna
Lower Austrian Provincial Authors Prize	1908	Vienna
Prize of the Ebner-Eschenbach Fund	1910	Vienna

Source: Dambacher 1996

great fame through his original writing, rather his reputation rested on his translations of George Bernard Shaw. Shaw made Trebitsch his sole authorized translator and agent, and shared all the income from his German editions and performances on a 50:50 basis. Reviewers soon attacked Trebitsch's translations as defective, wooden and 'unperformable'. Trebitsch was actually well aware of his shortcomings as a translator and had declared himself willing to pay for the corrections out of his own pocket (Mendelssohn 1970: 413–15). The Bauernfeld Prize also honoured some writers who, unlike Trebitsch, were highly respected as translators, for example, Marie Herzfeld (1855–1940). Herzfeld spent most of her life in Vienna and was best known for her translations from Scandinavian languages; she also translated from Italian, French and English. Her work in the mediation of literature was accompanied by prolific literary criticism and writing of her own, documented in extensive correspondences with fellow writers including Hugo von Hofmannsthal, Rainer Maria Rilke and Marie von Ebner-Eschenbach.

Otto Hauser (1876–1944), a Bauernfeld Prize recipient in 1916, also spent most of his life in Vienna. He was considered an exceptional figure in literary circles because he spoke around forty languages and translated from most of them. His work as a writer and critic was dwarfed by his translation activities, which were, however, far from uncontroversial as he was repeatedly accused of using 'vulgar Austrianisms'. Hauser's importance as a literary mediator is undeniable despite his strong racism in later years. It seems clear that his outstanding profile in the sphere of translation was at least part of the reason for him being awarded the prize.

The juries of the literary prizes also included translators. One was Alfred von Berger (1853–1912), professor of aesthetics at the University of Vienna, director of the *Deutsches Schauspielhaus* in Hamburg and the *Hofburgtheater* in Vienna, and editor of the *Österreichische Rundschau*. Among other languages, Berger translated from Italian, especially in the field of drama. A deputy of the Bauernfeld Foundation, Berger also belonged to other juries such as that of the Grillparzer Prize or the Raimund Prize. Max Kalbeck (1850–1921), too, can be regarded as a classic multifunctionary. An art and music critic, the author of an important biography of Brahms, a journalist for the *Neue Freie Presse* and the *Neues Wiener Tagblatt*, and the translator of numerous opera libretti, he was also a respected member of the Bauernfeld and Raimund Prize juries.

Generally, the factors regulating cultural policy as discussed in this section testify not only to a conflicted field in which the agents struggle for recognition via their cultural products/translations but also to visible signs of institutionalization of the translation activity. In order to meet the Empire's increasing pluricultural realities especially in the wake of 1848 revolutions, which – through legal regulations – prompted the diminution of multilingualism in favour of a certain increase of translation and interpreting, the institutionalization of these activities experienced considerable consolidation. Accordingly, translation policy in its different shapes gained momentum and was enacted through various instruments such as censorial measures through publishing legislation which tried to keep cultural production immune against change, through copyright regulations which aimed at compensating for the refusal of the Berne Convention and through state licensing of booksellers which met gradual liberalization towards the end of the century. Additionally, literary prizes enabled through state promotion shaped the cultural landscape regulated by selective measures. The institutionalization of language mediation thus took place on various levels and, not least in view of the growing nationalities conflicts, was dependent on legal regulations, economic situations and the overall response to the upcoming national problems.

4 Vienna: Translating (in) the urban space

The Imperial capital of Vienna was without doubt at the centre of the various stages of institutionalization and can be considered the crossing point of multiple translation processes. To illuminate these Babelian conditions and to better reveal how institutionalization was implemented, I will take a closer look first at the translation flows from the main 'Habsburg languages' into German, and then examine the work of the *Reichsgesetzblatt* Editorial Office.

4.1 Translation flows

The more general discussion of the impact translation policy had on the production of translations in the Habsburg Empire will first be tested against the translation flows to the Imperial capital.

The figures in Table 3.2 refer to translations into German in the period between 1848 and 1918 and fully reveal the problems related to any statistics: highly divergent bibliographical procedures and the varying availability of data prevent the statistics from being reliable in every detail. The high number of translations from Bosnian–Croatian–Serbian, for instance, might owe to the fact that about 75 per cent of the entries in Lauer's bibliography (1995) appeared in periodical publications, while these are excluded from most other bibliographies. These data are mirrored in the production of translations from the main Habsburg languages published in Vienna (Figure 3.2), which comes to no surprise: as Figure 3.3 shows, Vienna was undoubtedly the centre of publishing activities in the Empire's territory.

The high percentage of translations from Italian are, similar to those from Bosnian–Croatian–Serbian, partly due to the increasing number of periodicals published in Vienna, while the quite high number of translations from Hungarian tendentially refers to the increase in Hungarian originals after the 1867 Compromise which was paralleled in an increased translation of these new works.

Looking at the number of publishers based in the three most important places of publication (Figure 3.3), Vienna once again tops the list with 168 publishers, followed by Budapest with 56 and Zagreb with 21.

The strong position of Zagreb in the publishing field raises the question of how the occupation of Bosnia-Herzegovina in 1878 (and its annexation in 1908) affected the production of German translations of Bosnian–Croatian–Serbian

Table 3.2 Translations into German 1848–1918 by language, numbers (Habsburg Monarchy)[11]

Habsburg source languages	Translations
Bosnian–Croatian–Serbian	992
Hungarian	403
Italian	306
Polish	142
Czech	40
Slovenian	29
Total	**1,912**

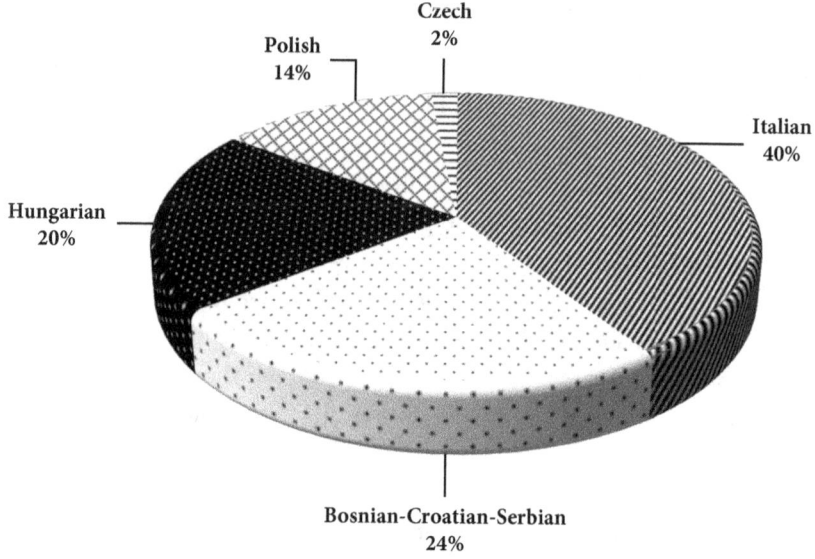

Figure 3.2 Translations into German 1848–1918, published in Vienna.

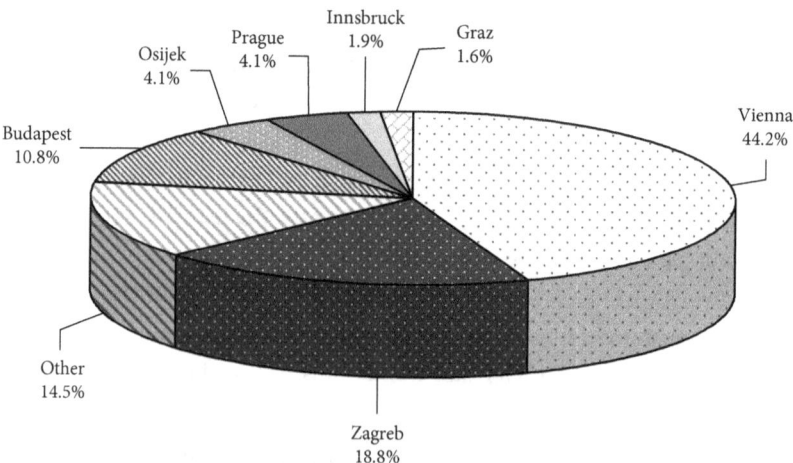

Figure 3.3 Place of publication, 1848–1918.

works, or whether Zagreb may be regarded as a kind of transmission belt for all the literature coming out of Bosnia-Herzegovina.

As Figure 3.4 shows, the number of publishing houses located in Vienna is particularly high. In the last seven decades of the Monarchy's existence, more than fifty publishers provided for the publication of translations from the six Habsburg languages under investigation.

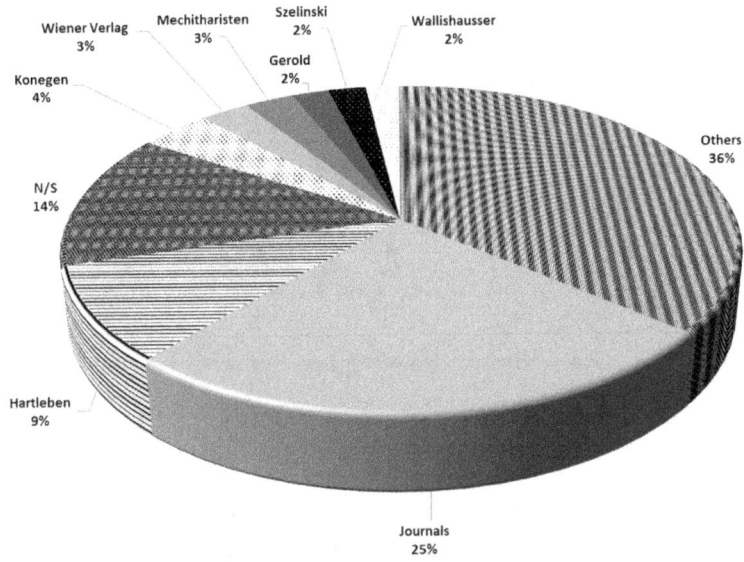

Figure 3.4 Publishing houses in Vienna, 1848–1918.

Hartleben was by far the most significant publisher, not only in terms of quantity (with 9 per cent of the total production of translations in the period) but also in terms of diversity. Actually, it published all kind of translated genres, with a special focus on novels, drama and travel accounts from most European languages into German. Hartleben was indeed the only Austrian publisher which could stand up to the German early nineteenth century's 'Übersetzungsfabriken' ('translation factories'), as Norbert Bachleitner (2000) reminds us when he points to the widespread critical opinion that translations were being made too eagerly with no regard for quality. One of the activities related to this concern was the foundation of the series *Belletristisches Lesecabinet der neuesten und besten Romane aller Nationen in sorgfältigen Uebersetzungen* (*Book cabinet of the latest and best novels of all nations in accurate translations*), founded in 1846 and continued up until 1879 which clearly reflects the publisher's policy to foster the production of translation: in the thirty-three years of its existence 1,008 volumes were published as translations from most European literatures, produced by more than fifty different translators (2000: 324).

Similarly, Konegen, founded in Vienna in 1877, followed a very clear publishing policy, bringing out mainly philological works and fiction,[12] after 1920 with a special series of children's books. Besides some Italian and Polish translations, Konegen put its emphasis on Hungarian literature and literary

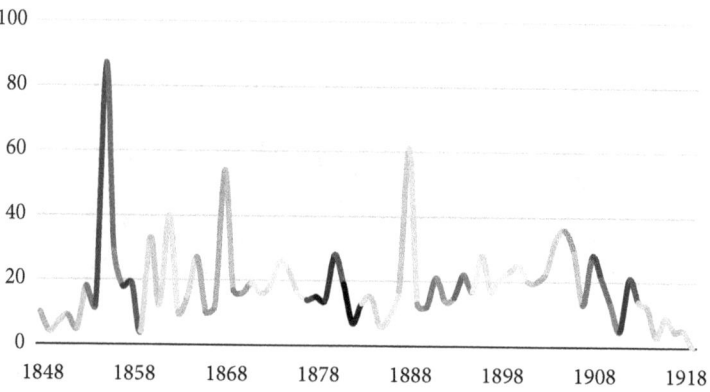

Figure 3.5 Translation production over time, 1848–1918.

criticism, publishing translations from works by Jenő Heltai or Lajos Hevesi. A few other publishers like Gerold or Wallishausser over the years developed an explicit publishing profile, mostly based on a long tradition of focus areas, be it the translation of literary works or on academic publications.

A short glance at the translation flows in Vienna over the various decades shows a sharp increase in the production of translations in the 1850s which might be due to new commercial regulations in that period, but is counteracted by the subsequent decrease and ensuing oscillation in the translation production (see Figure 3.5).

Although we can observe several peaks over the years – these are mainly due to the publication of anthologies of lyrical texts – the translation production in Vienna during the period under investigation remains quite stable.

To sum up, the regulating factors, which indicate whether we can identify a translation policy in this period, and thus also indications for a process of institutionalization of translation, are quite scarce in the investigated field: on the one hand, press legislation, especially the press law of 1862, was not as strict as to yield drastic changes in the translation production. On the other hand, bookseller licensing enabled a radical increase of bookstores in Vienna in the last decades of the century; yet, despite certain peaks not least due both to economic growth and to the founding of new journals and newspapers towards the turn of the century, we cannot observe a corresponding growth of a public demand for translations which would result in a clear quantitative increase. Translations produced in publishing houses thus to some extent elude measures deducible from a translation policy. This is not the case in the second study which explores the *Reichsgesetzblatt* Editorial Office.

4.2 The *Reichsgesetzblatt* Editorial Office

The *Redaktionsbureau des Reichsgesetzblattes* was founded in March 1849 to handle the translations of laws and ordinances for publication in ten languages in the *Reichsgesetzblatt* (Imperial Law Gazette).[13] The labour of this bureau clearly illustrates the various institutional stages of the translation activity and the varying impact of general politics and language regulation. Minister of Justice Alexander von Bach wanted one translator-cum-editor to be appointed per language, with good knowledge of the language and a legal background, alongside with a second person as 'Kontrollredakteur' ('checking editor'). While its first decade was the heyday of the Editorial Office, especially with respect to staffing, the number of translators later fluctuated considerably, not least because of the shortage of skilled candidates qualified to carry out such complex work. Accordingly, in 1853, the lowest-grade salaries were raised in the hope of acquiring staff with high competence in languages and law. The institutional development of translation was thus in full swing.

With the Imperial Patent of 27 December 1852, the German text of Habsburg laws was made the only authentic version. Although the *Reichsgesetzblatt* now began to appear only in German, translations into the languages of the crownlands were still carried out centrally in Vienna. The only difference was that these translations would appear in the various provincial government gazettes alongside the German texts. The justification given for maintaining the central Editorial Office in Vienna was primarily that the close collaboration between its translators was favourably influencing the development and standardization of the written forms of the various Slavic languages. However, the Imperial Patent of 1 January 1860 made the Imperial Gazette – in German only – the organ for the publication of all laws and abolished the institution of the provincial government gazettes in which the translations had been published since 1853. Now only selected laws would be translated, as determined by the central authorities on a case-by-case basis. This patent thus considerably diminished the value accorded to translation work.

The impact of politics on the Editorial Office is further proved by consequences the Austro-Hungarian Compromise of 1867 had on its functioning. From now on, the Ministry of the Interior – to which the Office had been shifted in the meantime – would publish the *Reichsgesetzblatt* in all the languages of common use (*landesübliche Sprachen*) in the Empire's lands. The editions in all languages were to appear simultaneously. The new law thus tried to fulfil the principle of equality between the nationalities that had been decreed in the already mentioned Article 19 of the 1867 Constitution. Also, the events of the First World War impacted dramatically on the production and punctual circulation of the *Reichsgesetzblatt*, and there were additional printing problems caused by the growing difficulty of sourcing paper.

Institutionalization of the Editorial Office's translation activities was further promoted by increasing quality requirements. As early as 1851, an examination with sample translations was introduced to test candidates' skills in legal language. In 1869, four new translators/editors were to be appointed, for Italian, Polish, Romanian and Ruthenian (= Ukranian). Franz Wagner, director of the Editorial Office, argued for publicly advertising the posts with the following words:

> Nach den bisherigen Erfahrungen halte ich nämlich die Berufung von Translatoren ohne deren früher [eingereichte] Befähigung für das Übersetzungsgeschäft nicht für nützlich und bin der Meinung, dass in der Regel die Translatoren aufgrund des Erfolges und von den selben abgelegten schriftlichen und bewährten Sach- und Sprachkundigen beurteilten Concursarbeit angestellt werden sollten. (AVA, II.A.5, ct. 14, no. 16796/869)[14]

Wagner's claims were put into practice by the introduction of a much more severe entry examination than practised until then. Now, the candidates had to translate several difficult laws from German into the other language and vice versa (AVA, 40/1, ct. 2788, no. 10546/911). Using translations as a means of testing language knowledge is of course an important factor in assessing the linguistic aptitude of the applicant with the attempt to guarantee high(er) translation qualities. These attempts, however, remained quite fragile as of the Office's 28 'systemisierte' ('systematized', that is, effectively permanent) translators/editors ten worked there more than twenty years, with one of them having worked for forty years and four having worked for between thirty-one and thirty-three years; the average length of service across the entire period was around fifteen years. Quality requirements were thus rather limited to newcomers. The main reason for this continuity is the fact that these were civil-service posts and thus predicated on life-long service. In any case, the profile of the state-appointed translators of the *Reichsgesetzblatt* corresponds with the practice, current well into the twentieth century, of giving priority to subject competence (law) over translation competence, although of course the particular case of translating laws and ordinances clearly did necessitate a legal background. The institutionalization of the post ('systematized translators') thus did not necessarily fully correspond to that of the translating activity.

4.3 Translation between 'distancing' and 'furthering'

Drawing on Sherry Simon's concern to depict cities as dynamic sites of translation, in the following discussion my emphasis is on her concepts *distancing* and *furthering*. While the first refers to translation as a bridge that both separates and joins cultures, postulating mediation as a technique 'aimed at managing difference but not disturbing the categories from which these differences issue' (Simon 2012: 13), the latter rather reflects a translation form related to a loosening of boundaries, through mingling and contamination, thus allowing for the potential to create hybrid forms (Cronin and Simon 2014: 123).

The two case studies involve different forms of translation *skopoi*: The translation flows embrace the potential of all kinds of *skopoi* imaginable, depending on the text genre, the language involved, the period explored, the agents participating in the translation and distribution process. The quite institutionalized work of the Editorial Office, on the other hand, necessarily followed a clearly defined *skopos* resulting from the explicit legislative mandate to allow for each 'national' group the basic right to preserve and cultivate its nationality and language (Article 19, *RGBl.* 142/1867). Yet, both areas of translation practice can be labelled as *distancing*, as both use language as 'privileged markers of conflictual identity' (Cronin and Simon 2014: 122), accentuating the differences that exist between languages and cultures. As the translation flows indeed reveal, *distancing* is activated through selection of texts, of translators, of paratexts, and they are widely supported by censorship or press legislation. Therefore, all measures related to translation policy can be seen as the practice of *distancing* rather than *furthering*. Especially in times when nationalities conflicts tend to gain the upper hand in the political sphere, the cultural sphere does not remain untouched; consequently, literatures in late Habsburg Monarchy are widely perceived as 'national literatures' impacting on the translation activity which accordingly is often called to support or undermine national claims.

Furthering rather implies an activity that encompasses the productive effects and engagements of translation with the perspective of 'broadening horizons' (Simon 2012: 16) and recalls the idea of one language infusing another 'with influences, alterations and combinations' (Cronin and Simon 2014: 122). Thus, it is not directly applicable to the case studies presented in this chapter. However, as processes of *furthering* might arise out of the displacements of (im)migration and diasporic culture, the concept fully applies to those kinds of translation which elsewhere I have called 'habitualized translation' (Wolf 2015: 51). This communication form was widely used in the Habsburg Monarchy and refers to the bilingualism or multilingualism that made the speakers of the various languages within the

Monarchy switch between linguistic and cultural contexts in order to perform the daily labour of communication arising from their class-specific, professional and personal situations. *Habitualized translation* was practised by a series of occupational groups, including servants, craftspeople, teachers, officers or judges.

Both concepts, *distancing* and *furthering*, in the form of various translation and communication practices contributed to shaping the urban face of Vienna, simultaneously forging together and keeping apart the various heterogeneous elements which made up the city's cultural and linguistic complexity.

5 Conclusion

When Sherry Simon states in her *Cities in Translation* that 'to speak of the multilingual city is to call up an image of simultaneous, parallel conversations taking place across urban terrain' (Simon 2012: 2), this is certainly true for Habsburg's Vienna. The various constituents which moulded the city's multilingual and pluricultural space have their origin both in increasing nationalities conflicts which fostered the institutionalized variant of translation, while considerable migration movements from all over the Empire to the Imperial capital triggered the necessity of translation forms which gave rise to a distinct hybridized communication space.

Translation policy played a vital role in shaping this space by promoting institutionalization. Also, the analysis of the translation flows to Vienna and the Editorial Bureau of the *Reichsgesetzblatt* showed that individuals were less effected by institutionalizing procedures than their products. The translation figures can be rather regarded as hybridized subjects, located at the borders of cultures who, habitually according to the pronounced and unpronounced expectations of a reading public, oscillated between *distancing* and *furthering*, either fostering or counteracting – not least through institutionalizing processes – politically and ideologically motivated tendencies which simultaneously coexisted, bearing the potential of triggering new translation movements.

Notes

1 Jews were not regarded as a separate nationality, so that Yiddish, the thirteenth language, does not appear in the list of possible 'languages of common communication'. In the census of 1910, Yiddish was subsumed under German as

a German 'dialect', so that Yiddish-speaking Jews were counted as Germans (Wolf 2015: 39).
2. Cisleithania was the unofficial but quite common denotation of the northern and western part of the Dual Monarchy of Austria–Hungary created through the Compromise of 1867. It has to be distinguished from Transleithania, that is, the Hungarian Lands east of the Leitha River.
3. Whereas Article 19 assumed that all the Monarchy's peoples enjoy equal rights, and thus also the right to use their own mother tongue, Article 44 in the Hungarian half of the Empire followed the Jacobin tradition of a unified nation state, and gave Hungarian the status of an official language.
4. In 2018, the population of Vienna amounts to 1.9 million.
5. For the Viennese to lead his dreamy, unpunctual life, so rich in little joys and pleasures, a piece of precision machinery has to work quietly and discreetly. Its indefatigably industrious arms are the Czechs. They are our tailors and make our most beautiful clothes; they are our cobblers and make our beautiful shoes; they play our beautiful music; they cook our good, healthy food; they build and polish our beautiful furniture; they drive our beautiful carriages …, and the milk-filled breasts of the Bohemian nurses nourish Viennese children (Translation Kate Sturge).
6. It would be highly unpleasant if Vienna turned into a kind of Constantinople, where all imaginable *Volksstämme* (ethnic groups) live separately in different quarters or separated according to their language.
7. The importance attributed to multilingualism in daily social life, in political routine and also in the academic world is attested by the fact that the president of the Imperial Academy of Sciences, renowned orientalist Joseph von Hammer-Purgstall (1774–1856), on occasion of the quinquennial existence of the Academy in 1852 explicitly dedicated his ceremonial address to the topic of 'multilingualism' (Hammer-Purgstall 1852).
8. All the state's ethnic groups [*Volksstämme*] are equal, and each has an inviolable right to preserve and cultivate its nationality and language. The state recognizes the equality of all languages current in a region [*landesübliche Sprachen*] within schools, administration and public life. In those lands which are home to various ethnic groups, the institutions of public education shall be organized in such a way that each of these groups receives the means to be educated in its own language, without being forced to learn a second regional language (Article 19, *RGBl.* 142/1867).
9. For details on legal regulations of language issues in the Empire see Fischel 1910.
10. The Berne Convention for the Protection of Literary and Artistic Works is an international agreement governing copyright. It was founded in Berne, Switzerland, in 1886. Officially, the main reason for avoiding the Convention was that especially the Slavic nationalities feared that joining the Convention would jeopardize their production of cheap translations (Wolf 2015: 136).
11. This analysis necessarily applies the concept of 'national literatures' because they are treated as such in the respective bibliographies – the sources available impose this

notion of literature or culture due to the assumptions of the bibliographers, authors and other agents concerned. To move beyond that nationally oriented viewpoint, it would be necessary to investigate in detail, for each language, the full complexity both of the bibliographies themselves and of the roles of the various mediators involved in the translations' production. For an attempt to accomplish this claim, see Wolf 2015: 169–233.

12 The same applies to the renowned Wiener Verlag, which published many translations from the Italian (famous authors such as later Nobel laureate Grazia Deledda, or Antonio Fogazzaro, Matilde Serao and Giovanni Verga), and fostered the translation activity with its series *Bibliothek berühmter Autoren* (Library of famous authors).

13 This section is primarily based on the Austrian Administration Archive fascicle on the history of the Editorial Office from 1849 to 1870 (AVA, 40/1, ct. 2788, no. 10546/911). For further details, see Wolf 2015, 83–96, and especially the excellent dissertation by Aleksandra Nuč (2017).

14 Judging by previous experience, I believe that it is not useful to appoint translators without their having presented qualifications in the business of translation, and it is my opinion that as a rule translators should be employed on the basis of their successful completion of competition tasks which are evaluated by trusted legal and linguistic experts.

References

Primary sources

AVA *Verwaltungsarchiv, Innenministerium* (*Administration Archive, Ministry of the Interior*), Vienna.

Einsle, A., ed. (1896), *Catalogus Librorum in Austria Prohibitorum. Verzeichniss der in Oesterreich bis Ende 1895 Verbotenen Druckschriften* (*Registry of Works Banned in Austria by the End of 1895*), Vienna: Verlag des Vereines der österreichisch-ungarischen Buchhändler.

Fischel, A. (1910), *Das Österreichische Sprachenrecht. Eine Quellensammlung* (*The Austrian Language Right: A Collection of Sources*), 2nd ed, Brünn: Irrgang.

RGBL, *Reichsgesetzblatt* (*Imperial Law Gazette*).

Secondary sources

AEIOU (2016), 'Nationalitätenfrage', in *AEIOU Austria-Forum, das Wissensnetz*. Available online: https://austria-forum.org/af/AEIOU/Nationalitätenfrage (accessed 20 December 2018).

Bachleitner, N. (2000), 'Übersetzungsfabrik C.A. Hartleben. Eine Inspektion', in K. Amann, H. Lengauer and K. Wagner (eds), *Literarisches Leben in Österreich 1848–1890*, 319–9, Vienna: Böhlau.

Bachleitner, N., F. M. Eybl and E. Fischer (2000), *Geschichte des Buchhandels in Österreich*, Wiesbaden: Harrassowitz.

Bachleitner, N. and M. Wolf (2010), 'ÜbersetzerInnen als "gatekeepers"? (Selbst) Zensur als Voraussetzung für die Aufnahme in das literarische Feld der späten Habsburgermonarchie', in M. Wolf, D. Merkle, C. O'Sullivan and L. van Doorslaer (eds), *The Power of the Pen: Translation & Censorship in Nineteenth-century Europe*, 29–54, Vienna: LIT.

Cronin, M. and S. Simon (2014), 'Introduction: The City as Translation Zone', *Translation Studies*, 7 (2): 119–32.

Csáky, M. (2010), *Das Gedächtnis der Städte. Kulturelle Verflechtungen – Wien und die urbanen Milieus in Zentraleuropa*, Vienna: Böhlau.

Csendes, P. and F. Opll, eds (2001), *Wien: Von 1790 bis zur Gegenwart. Vol.3*, Vienna: Böhlau.

Dambacher, E. (1996), *Literatur- und Kulturpreise 1859–1949. Eine Dokumentation*, Marbach am Neckar: Deutsche Schillergesellschaft.

Gerhartl, S. (2000), '"Vogelfrei": Die österreichische Lösung der Urheberrechtsfrage in der zweiten Hälfte des 19. Jahrhunderts', in K. Amann, H. Lengauer and K. Wagner (eds), *Literarisches Leben in Österreich 1848–1890*, 200–49, Vienna: Böhlau.

Habermas, J. (1989), *Strukturwandel der Öffentlichkeit. Untersuchungen zu einer Kategorie der bürgerlichen Gesellschaft*, Frankfurt am Main: Suhrkamp.

Hammer-Purgstall, J. von (1852), 'Vortrag über die Vielsprachigkeit', in *Die Feierliche Sitzung der Kaiserlichen Akademie der Wissenschaften am 29. Mai 1852*, 87–100, Vienna: Kaiser-Königliche Hof- und Staatsdruckerei.

Hermans, T. (1995), 'Translation as Institution', in M. Snell-Hornby, Z. Jettmarová and K. Kaindl (eds), *Translation as Intercultural Communication*, 3–20, Amsterdam: John Benjamins.

Hugelmann, K. G. (1934), *Das Nationalitätenrecht des alten Österreich*, Vienna: Braumüller.

John, M. and A. Lichtblau (1993), *Schmelztiegel Wien – einst und jetzt*, 2nd ed, Vienna: Böhlau.

Keman, H. (2018), 'Institutionalization: Social Process', in *Encyclopædia Britannica*. Available online: https://www.britannica.com/topic/institutionalization (accessed 20 December 2018).

Lauer, R., ed. (1995), *Serbokroatische Autoren in deutscher Übersetzung. Bibliographische Materialien (1776–1993)*, Part 1, Wiesbaden: Harrassowitz.

Mendelssohn, P. de (1970), *S. Fischer und sein Verlag*, Frankfurt am Main: S. Fischer Verlag.

Meylaerts, R. (2006), 'Heterolingualism in/and Translation: How Legitimate Are the Other and His/Her Language? An Introduction', *Target*, 18 (1): 1–15.

Nuč, A. (2017), 'Slowenische Translatoren treffen auf Asklepios. Die Übersetzungen des Reichsgesetzblattes ins Slowenische', doct. dissertation, University of Graz.

Ogris, W. (1975), 'Die Rechtsentwicklung in Österreich 1848–1918', in A. Wandruszka and P. Urbanitsch (eds), *Die Habsburgermonarchie 1848–1918. Band II: Verwaltung und Rechtswesen*, 538–662, Vienna: Verlag der Österreichischen Akademie der Wissenschaften.

Reiter, C. (2015), 'In Habsburgs sprachlichem Hofdienst. Translation in den diplomatischen Beziehungen zwischen den habsburgischen Höfen von Madrid und Wien in der Frühen Neuzeit', doct. dissertation, University of Graz.

Rumpler, H. (1997), *Österreichische Geschichte 1804–1914. Eine Chance für Mitteleuropa. Bürgerliche Emanzipation und Staatsverfall in der Habsburgermonarchie*, Vienna: Ueberreuter.

Simon, S. (2012), *Cities in Translation: Intersections of Language and Memory*, London: Routledge.

Stourzh, G. (1980), 'Die Gleichberechtigung der Volksstämme als Verfassungsprinzip 1848–1918', in A. Wandruszka and P. Urbanitsch (eds), *Die Habsburgermonarchie 1848–1918*, 975–1206, Vienna: Verlag der Österreichischen Akademie der Wissenschaften.

Wolf, M. (2015), *The Habsburg Monarchy's Many-Languaged Soul: Translating and Interpreting, 1848–1918*, trans. Kate Sturge. Amsterdam: John Benjamins.

Part Two

Upcoming local nationalisms

4

Bern in the nineteenth century: Emerging institutional translation in a multilingual state

Valérie Dullion

1 Introduction

In the political landscape of nineteenth-century Europe, Switzerland had several peculiar features that make its 'capital' an interesting case for this volume. The modern federal state was founded in 1848 with a democratic, republican form of government and three official languages: German, French and Italian, spoken as a mother tongue by 71.4, 21.4 and 5.7 per cent of the population, respectively, according to the first statistics from 1880 (see *HSSO* 2012). Romansh, a language with five different varieties whose native speakers formed 1.4 per cent of the population, had no official status at the time. The constitution included mechanisms of semi-direct democracy (popular referendums and initiatives) that were initially very limited in scope but then extended from 1874 onwards. In the course of the nineteenth century, the country (known as 'the Swiss Confederation') developed its own model of linguistic pluralism (Weerts 2015: 115–227). Since it was out of step with the ideology of a monolingual nation state prevailing in Europe, national narratives had to be constructed accordingly (Walter 2016: 362–9). Bern had been chosen as the capital, called the 'federal city'. It was additionally the capital of a bilingual canton (German-speaking, with a French-speaking minority). The cantons were the member states of the Swiss Confederation and remained sovereign in all matters but those transferred to the federal power by the new constitution. Finally, Bern became host to several international organizations between the 1860s and the First World War, before being largely supplanted in this role by Geneva.

While the history of Swiss language policy is well researched (see inter alia Weilenmann 1925, Widmer et al. 2005), institutional translation practices at the federal level seem much more complex than is suggested by the fiction of a state communicating in three languages. A diachronic approach to these practices over the nineteenth century can be expected to shed light on how they were established, particularly as regards processes and degrees of 'institutionalization' (Koskinen 2014: 489). This approach will be adopted here for the period 1848–1914 on the basis of one main type of archival source, the Federal Council's annual reports. This official publication will be used to gain a general picture, from the point of view of the federal executive power, of how Bern set out to handle translations. Although the study will thus explore only one layer of Bern's translation policies as a local, cantonal, federal and international 'hub', it will also show how this activity was part of a more complex translation landscape due to the city's unique role (see Figure 4.1).

How did federal translation policy interact with the principles underlying the country's multilingual language regime, and to what extent did the former reflect, qualify, contradict, supplement or shape the latter? (On the potential discrepancies between translation policy and language policy, see D'hulst and

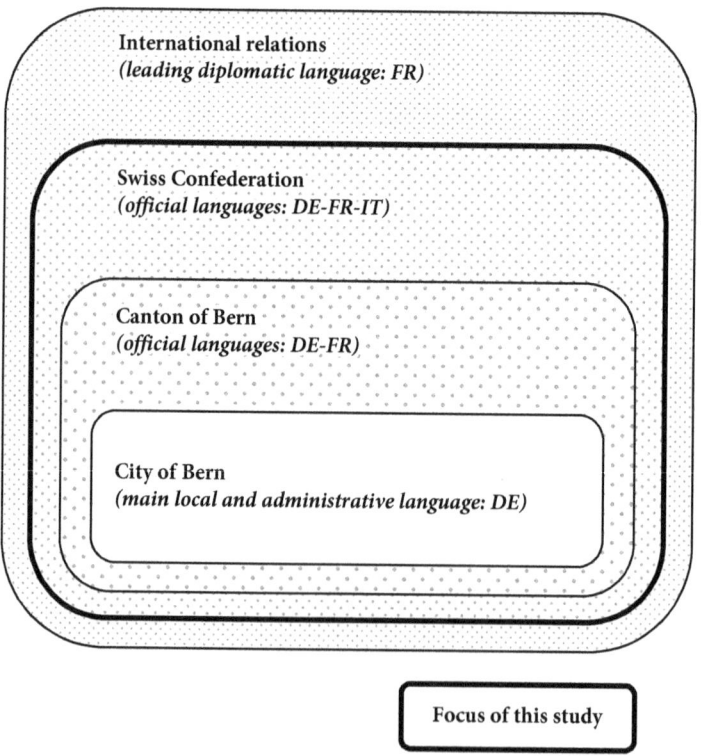

Figure 4.1 Bern as a capital city between 1848 and 1914.

Schreiber 2014.) Until far into the twentieth century, Swiss language policy relied on few statutory provisions and was largely based on customary and case law. Accordingly, the 'explicit or overt' part of translation policy consisting of codified rules and regulations with various levels of legal force (which can be referred to as 'translation management', see González Núñez 2016: 92) was limited. To find more signs of a translation policy, one must look at the translation practices of the federal administration, that is, its 'implicit or covert' translation policy.

Although a few studies have touched upon the history of multilingual institutions and translation in Switzerland (Adam 1995, Bürki-Gyger 1996, Comment 2016, and especially Pini 2017), the federal archives have not yet been explored from a translation studies point of view. The archives potentially contain sufficient material for a large-scale research project that could use a combination of perspectives, such as those of parliament, the government and the judiciary. Tensions between the powers would be particularly worth investigating, as it seems that changes in translation policy are in many cases a result of pressure from parliament. The archives would make it possible to conduct research for each perspective with varying degrees of detail.

Since this study aims to provide a dynamic overview of translation policy as it was emerging, a general and digitized source was chosen so as to approach the topic from the government's perspective through a systematic analysis covering several decades: the annual reports of the Federal Council (*Geschäftsberichte des Bundesrates / rapports de gestion du Conseil fédéral* – abbreviated here as 'AR'), which the government is constitutionally required to submit to the Federal Assembly. In a context in which there seems to be little codification of translation practices, the way these practices are reported by the government, as regards the federal administration at large, opens an interesting window into the history of Bern's translation policy at the precise place where translation practice turns into translation management (González Núñez 2016: 92).

2 Data and method

The study covers the period between the beginning of the federal state (1848) and the First World War. During that time, key developments took place that extended and consolidated the modern institutional framework (see Section 3.2). For the purpose of this study, the Federal Council's annual reports were analysed from a thematic and diachronic perspective, paying special attention to divergence, tension and change in translation policy in all its aspects.

The method for data collection and analysis was defined considering two well-known difficulties. Firstly, what may be of interest to today's translation studies is not always labelled a 'translation' in sources from the past. Secondly, it is not advisable to study translation policy without relating it to other aspects of language policy. As Meylaerts and du Plessis (2016: 272) state, 'For TS [translation studies] it is important to realize that T&I [translation and interpreting] is bound up in a large continuum of language and translation practices and that it makes no sense to isolate T&I from them.' Another factor had to be taken into account: the Federal Council's annual reports from the nineteenth century are themselves bilingual parallel documents resulting from translation. They are available in German and French with approximately the same length and content (while they were not available in Italian until 1996, as a result of the fragmentary publication policy towards this minority language). Language quality is good in both versions. Although it can be assumed that the bulk of translations were from German into French, the most usual translation direction in the federal administration, both versions share the status of 'original' text. For practical reasons, the French version served here as the main material and the German version was referred to, where useful.

The annual reports are available in pdf format with optical character recognition, enabling a systematic keyword search. After several tests, the following strings were used to identify and mark relevant passages:

- 'tradu*';
- 'langue*';
- 'en allemand', 'en français', 'en italien', 'en rhét*', 'en roman*';
- 'édition*', 'publication*', 'rédaction*', 'texte*', 'version*'.

The results of this first stage are summarized in Table 4.1.

Table 4.1 Data Collection – First Stage

67 AR (1848–1914)	Minimum	Maximum	Average
Number of **pages per AR**	23 (1849)	891 (1900)	607
Number of **marked passages per AR**	0 (1849)	37 (1891, 1892, 1894)	19

In addition to the relevant passages, the sections on the Federal Chancellery (present each year) and on the *Repertorio di giurisprudenza patria* (present from 1883, see Section 6.1) were read in each report.

The marked passages were then sorted according to the thematic categories listed below, with bold font for those that provided the richest data:

1. **managing multilingualism in general,**
2. translation and transfer,
3. non-translation,
4. **what is translated,**
5. multilingualism and official publications,
6. **multilingualism in the legislative process,**
7. **communicating with the cantons,**
8. Italian and Romansh as special cases,
9. **multilingualism in foreign affairs,**
10. **profile and status of translators,**
11. constraints and costs of multilingualism,
12. paying for translation,
13. problems with translations,
14. benefits from translations,
15. approaches to intertextual divergence.

Some of the categories were partly predefined on the basis of previous reading and research (especially Pini 2017 for categories 5 and 8, and Dullion 2017 for 2 and 3), while others (7, 9 and 12) emerged during the study.

The resulting data were analysed and, where necessary, supplemented with other sources to be interpreted. The main weakness of the annual reports is that they often provide scattered information, without elaboration or arguments: the Federal Council's discourse leaves much unsaid. However, rich secondary sources are available regarding the history of language policy and the most visible ('management') part of translation policy (Weilenmann 1925, Widmer et al. 2005, Weerts 2015). These were referred to for contextualization, and thus helped to '[tease out translation policies] from regimes of practices around communication and documentation' (Koskinen 2014: 484). An overview of the results is presented in this chapter after a short introduction to the history of Bern (see Section 3). Considering the 'spatial' perspective adopted in this book, the focus will be on categories 1–9 listed earlier, which all contribute to mapping the areas and flows of translation: results are presented in Sections 4–6, aiming to situate institutional translation in its environment, measure its scope and uncover its external interactions. For categories 10–15, directions for further research suggested by the data are outlined in Section 7.

3 Bern in the nineteenth century

3.1 From city state to bilingual canton

The city of Bern was founded in 1191 by Berthold V, Duke of Zähringen, and was granted imperial immediacy – a privilege of autonomy from local lords within the Holy German Empire – in the early thirteenth century (for a detailed chronology, see Bähler et al. 2003: 352–63). It then made alliances with other cities and signed treaties within the emerging Swiss Confederacy, a structure that was gradually gathering together members with various statuses and political systems in the geographical space that came to be known as 'Switzerland'. The members of this structure (which historians refer to as the 'Old Swiss Confederacy') came to be called 'cantons'. (This name is still used today for the member states of the post-1815 Swiss Confederation, although the extent of their sovereignty has changed with time.) Some of these members were cities that had established control over large rural territories and thus ended up ruling over 'city states'. During the fourteenth century, Bern began to follow this pattern: by the fifteenth century, the Republic of Bern, dominated by the city, had become one of the largest and most powerful city states north of the Alps, which it remained until the end of the eighteenth century. At that time, the city of Bern was the capital of a Protestant canton which was one of the leading states of the Old Swiss Confederacy. Political authority was in the hands of an urban aristocracy consisting of patrician families. The canton had a German-speaking population and had acquired a few territories in French-speaking regions (in particular the *pays de Vaud* in 1536). These territories, which had a subservient status, were governed in the local language according to a model which Weerts (2015: 71–6) describes as a 'juxtaposition of languages'. French was also spoken in aristocratic circles in Bern, like in many other European cities, which meant there was a certain amount of bilingualism in economic and administrative matters (Werlen 2000: 37–8).

From 1798 to 1813, Switzerland experienced two political regimes that drastically changed the relationship between the regions that made up the Old Swiss Confederacy and, incidentally, the language situation for Bern. Walter (2016: 215–16) stresses the strong 'anti-urban' dimension of these political changes, since they were directed against the leading circles of the city states, among others. In the wake of the French Revolution, the constitution of the Helvetic Republic (1798) set up a unitary state subordinate to France which was based on equality between citizens and recognized – ideally, if not always in practice – three official languages (German, French and Italian). The Act of Mediation (1803) took a step back towards a federative regime, which nevertheless remained a client state of France. The de facto bilingualism, with German as the dominant language, that had prevailed since 1800 was maintained and even increased. New cantons were created, including a *Canton de Vaud* that became independent from Bern: as a result, Bern no longer had a significant linguistic minority within its territory. The Congress of Vienna (1814–15) had to address Swiss affairs as part of the restructuring of the European geopolitical landscape after the end of the French Revolution and Napoleonic Wars. Following the Congress, the Federal Treaty adopted in Switzerland in 1815 marked the beginning of the Restoration and formed the constitutional basis of the Swiss Confederation until the foundation of the modern federal state in 1848: Switzerland had returned to being an alliance of fully sovereign states and their pre-1798 political systems were re-established. German became the only official language again (as it was before 1798) in the – limited – field of the Confederation's affairs. Detailed accounts of Swiss language policies for the period between 1798 and 1848 can be found in Weilenmann (1925: 178–202, 288–93) and Weerts (2015: 97–112, where the successive policies are related to the French revolutionary model of a single 'national language').

At the Congress of Vienna, the French-speaking territories of the former Prince-Bishopric of Basel (Jura region) had been allocated to the canton of Bern to compensate for the loss of other territories, including the *pays de Vaud*. (As mentioned earlier, this former subordinate territory had become an autonomous canton in 1803.) The presence of a francophone minority in the western part of its new territory (see Martig 2011: 69–73) led the canton of Bern to recognize two official languages in its constitution (1831). This happened in the context of changing political conceptions and structures: the movement known as 'Regeneration' resulted in the adoption of liberal constitutions throughout the Swiss cantons. (Symbolically, the demolition of the fortifications that separated the cities with their aristocracies from the surrounding land started mainly in the 1830s – see 'Ville' in *DHS* 2018.) In Bern, the status of French changed slightly along with the later constitutions of the nineteenth century (1846 and 1893) but did not yet reach parity with German in legislation (Weilenmann 1925: 211–12, 293–4; Werlen 2000: 162–8). Tensions between the government of the predominantly

German-speaking and Protestant canton and the French-speaking and partly Catholic Jura region arose on various occasions, especially regarding church organization, education and civil law. Over the course of the nineteenth century, bilingualism also became an issue in the city of Biel, which had been incorporated into the canton of Bern at the same time as the Jura territories. Biel initially had a German-speaking population, but starting in 1842, French-speaking workers, especially watchmakers, settled in the city: its population experienced rapid growth and included 29.1 per cent native French speakers in 1900 (Werlen 2000: 79–82). At that time, cantonal language policy consisted essentially of (unequal) bilingualism in legislation combined with a territorial approach to the application of laws and regulations (Weerts 2015: 217–20).

When the federal state was founded in 1848, the choice of Bern from a couple of candidates for the role of federal city was mainly due to the fact that it had been the capital of one of the leading cantons under different political regimes. Secondarily, this choice had to do with Bern's profile as a city mediating between linguistic regions, as has been shown by research into the political debate of the time (Widmer et al. 2005: 99–104). It should be noted here that mediation was thus conceived as implying only the two main languages of the new federal state, which was imagined as a *bi*lingual (not *multi*lingual) country (Widmer et al. 2005: 104). Italian and Romansh were scarcely visible in this construction and were to remain so for a long time in language and translation policy.

3.2 After 1848: The federal city and language mediation

The first constitution of the federal state (1848, Art. 109) recognized three 'national' languages (this term was actually understood in a rather practical way, as meaning 'official' languages – see Widmer et al. 2005: 56–82). However, the multilingual regime at this level was combined with the right of each canton to determine, within its jurisdiction, its own official language(s) and language policy. The canton of Bern, where bilingualism remained in force, became one of the few exceptions in a national landscape where monolingual entities were the rule. In Meylaerts's (2011) classification of linguistic and translational regimes used by authorities to communicate with their multilingual populations (743), post-1848 Switzerland can be classified under the fourth category, that is, 'institutional monolingualism at the local level [combined with] institutional multilingualism with multidirectional mandatory translation at the superior (e.g., federal) level' (752). In this context, the city of Bern's new status in the federal state brought an additional layer to its role as linguistic mediator.

From the beginning, the language policy of the federal state (Weilenmann 1925: 203–21, 295–8) entailed publishing legislation in three languages. It should nevertheless be stressed that the Confederation at that time had very limited power. After an unsuccessful attempt in 1872, the federal constitution was revised in 1874: the Confederation's remit was widened, the Federal Supreme Court established on a permanent basis, and democratic rights extended towards semi-direct democracy (Walter 2016: 342–8). A further step was taken in 1898, when the Confederation was granted authority in civil and criminal law. This opened the way to the adoption of common codes that came into force in 1912 and 1942, respectively. To a large extent, language policy during the nineteenth century rested on informal principles, with the notable exception of Article 107 of the 1874 constitution, which ensured that the three languages would be represented in the Federal Supreme Court (Weerts 2015: 171–5). From the 1890s, some tensions arose between language groups (Widmer et al. 2005: 127–32). During that same period, measures were taken at the federal level to improve the quality of institutional texts in French, including the appointment, for the first time in 1896, of a second vice chancellor in charge of checking the French texts of government decrees (Pini 2017: 28–9). Official publications in Italian remained largely incomplete until 1918, when the first issue of a – partial – Federal Gazette in this language came out (Pini 2017: 41–61). As for Romansh, it was not until 1938 that it was finally recognized as a national – but not official – language.

In the political evolution underlying these legal and institutional changes, the constitutional revision of 1874 is considered a turning point. In 1848, the focus had been on the relationship between the Confederation and the cantons as well as on equality among the latter, which were pre-existing political entities (Weerts 2015: 147–53). Equality among citizens identified according to linguistic criteria (rather than religious denominations, for instance) had not really been an issue at the federal level (see also Widmer et al. 2005: 11–15, 31–126). By 1874, the federal state was moving towards more centralization and more democracy. There was greater concern for individuals as citizens taking part directly in the affairs of the federal state (Weerts 2015: 171–5). On this ground, a model of linguistic pluralism gradually took shape and a language regime was elaborated around the principles of personal freedom and equality between languages and linguistic territoriality. However, it was not codified into constitutional law until much later (the second half of the twentieth century) (Weerts 2015: 231–6).

In addition to federal institutions and agencies with their multilingual staff, some of the first international (intergovernmental and non-governmental) organizations' offices were housed in Bern, starting with the International Telegraphic Bureau established in 1868 (Bähler et al. 2003: 295–316, Martig 2011: 123–31). From the beginning of the twentieth century, however, Bern's position in the new networks of international diplomacy was challenged by other cities such as Brussels and Geneva.

3.3 A city and its landscape

The status of federal city was initially both a burden and an honour. In 1875, Bern was relieved of the costs associated with being the seat of the federal authorities (Bähler et al. 2003: 295–7). The federal administration had a very modest size at the beginning: it started with about fifty civil servants (Walter 2016: 344) and had about one hundred in 1910 (Bähler et al. 2003: 323 – on the federal state as an employer, see Martig 2011: 369–72). The economical and sociological impacts of public service departments on the city therefore remained rather low until the twentieth century, contrary to its cliché as a 'city of bureaucrats' (Bähler et al. 2003: 94–6; 'Berne (commune)' in *DHS* 2016). Moreover, some of the federal institutions were located elsewhere, for example, the Federal Institute of Technology and the National Museum in Zurich (1855 and 1891) and the Federal Supreme Court in Lausanne (1874). Economically, Bern did not become a capital city either, even though it housed the headquarters of the main federal state companies, for example, in the transport and communication industries (Bähler et al. 2003: 323). It was connected to the railway network in 1857, with its station building inaugurated in 1860. With the Gotthard railway, a north–south line across the Alps was opened in 1882, linking the Italian-speaking canton of Ticino to the German-speaking part of the country. Although Bern was centrally located, it remained a medium-sized city (Bähler et al. 2003: 317–28) in a country that, despite growing urbanization, was paradoxically building an identity revolving around images of mountains and countryside (see 'Ville' in *DHS* 2018). Its function as a federal and international city nevertheless marked the urban landscape (Bähler et al. 2003: 97, 296–7) through the construction of the Federal Parliament House (1852–1857 and 1888–1902) and other large official buildings (e.g. the Federal Archives) from 1890 to 1910.

In 1910, 91.43 per cent of the city's population spoke German as a mother tongue (with a diglossia between standard German and an Alemannic dialect – *Bärndütsch*), 5.02 per cent French, 2.29 per cent Italian and 1.26 per cent another language (see 'Berne (commune)' in *DHS* 2016). In other words, Bern was both a translating city and a relatively monolingual city. Most of its translating activity was directed towards the outside, with targets at different distances (see Section 6). In a 2003 book on the city's history, Bähler et al. (369) note the lack of literature on the institutional, economical and sociological impact of the role of federal city. It seems that their remark remains valid.

4 The environment of institutional translation

4.1 Think before translating: A key to managing official multilingualism

In the federal state founded in 1848, multilingualism could obviously be a problem not only for enacting new common rules but also for ensuring their uniform application, especially at the local level where the employees in charge were not always federal staff. This had implications not only for translation, of course, but also for staff recruitment (e.g. linguistic profiles of factory inspectors, AR 1898: 406–7) and training (e.g. promoting individual multilingualism in the post office, AR 1911: 599, or organizing parallel sessions about forestry in different linguistic regions, AR 1877: 149–51). As pointed out by Wolf (2015: 26–9, 239–43), one of the characteristics of officially multilingual spaces is that translation strictly speaking, which involves an agent in charge of explicit mediation between languages, coexists with the kind of 'institutionalized translating' that is simply part of daily 'polycultural communication' in institutional contexts. The army and the Federal Institute of Technology emerge from the annual reports as two institutions constantly in search of the right combinations between organizational structures and recruitment criteria during the period under study – they questioned whether joint multilingual activities were a better choice than parallel monolingual ones, and wondered at what levels individual multilingualism should be required (see, among others, AR 1876: 513 and 1885: 54).

As regards translation, numerous occurrences in the annual reports suggest that the federal administration was particularly anxious to maintain the following principles: do not translate everything; do not translate everything in full; and if translation is necessary, think about who (the Confederation, a canton, the private sector, etc.) is responsible for it operationally and/or financially. Beyond the core of official publications (see 5.1), criteria such as the target audience or the importance of an issue (AR 1892: 215) were commonly used to decide what deserved to be translated. The rationale behind multilingual publication was then mostly an intent to unify procedures through common reference documents (e.g. in post offices, customs or registry offices) or to disseminate up-to-date information as broadly as possible (e.g. in efforts to modernize agriculture, fight against epidemic or epizootic diseases, or promote technical progress in the field of telegraphs). The reports regularly refer to national or international language policy rules according to which there was no obligation to translate, using them as an argument to refuse funding (AR 1914: 75) or to prevent cantonal authorities from unnecessarily requiring translated documents from citizens or charging them for a translation (AR 1888: 393).

4.2 Translation and transfer experiments

During the analysis of the annual reports, it was possible to identify or reconstruct a number of different ways to combine languages in the production of written texts. They include translation to a variable extent, along with other forms of linguistic and cultural transfer, in a context where the notions of source, target and directionality can only be assumed (see D'hulst 2012: 140–3). Instead of there being a couple of set methods, various strategies can be observed throughout the period under study:

1. documents on the same topic written separately in different languages;
2. a single document with (untranslated) sections in different languages and multilingual paratexts;
3. a document written in one main language but including some (fully) bilingual sections;
4. a monolingual document summarized elsewhere in another language;
5. a multilingual document with some sections summarized (rather than fully parallel) in one or more of the languages;
6. a document published in several, fully parallel language versions (after a process of unidirectional or multidirectional translation);
7. a document in several language versions bound in the same volume.

Some departments (e.g. the Statistical Bureau) seem to have used several formats not only based on the potential use of the document but also for more mundane reasons such as the cost of paper or typesetting. As the list shows, there were three main variables: the number of separate documents, the relationships between different language versions (translation, summary or looser thematic connection) and the extent (partial or full) to which these relationships were applied to the document.

Legislation should be mentioned as a special case. In this field, the combination of languages was part of complex processes involving discussions within committees and the production of intermediary documents at various stages. These procedures became particularly important in the last quarter of the nineteenth century: in a semi-direct democracy, reaching a political consensus early in the legislative process was key to preventing any failure that could result from a referendum held after a statute had been passed (Walter 2016: 360). The annual reports show that French was already part of the legislative process in the early years of the federal state (AR 1850: 28), through the translation of drafts and the presence of French-speaking experts in committees – at least for large projects that the Federal Council found worth mentioning. Italian was integrated much later on: the translation of some preliminary documents is attested for large projects starting in the 1880s (AR 1880: 396–7).

5 The scope of translation

5.1 At the heart of state authority: Official publications

Official publications belong to the well-researched part of Swiss language and translation policy. Since the foundation of the federal state, statutes have been published in German, French and Italian in the Official Compilation; preliminary and explanatory documents (among others) have also been published in German and French in the Federal Gazette (an Italian edition did not appear until 1918, as already noted). Statistics for these publications are given in each issue of the annual report, in the section on the Federal Chancellery. A recurring question during the nineteenth century concerned the publication of reports of parliamentary proceedings, which had initially been left to the press. The Official Bulletin of the Federal Assembly first came out in 1891 (Comment 2016). Annual reports from 1870 to 1881 provide interesting insight into previous attempts, particularly the interplay between the government and parliament with regard to financial aspects.

Furthermore, reports from the 1860s contain detailed information about one of the large-scale projects carried out in all three official languages so as to offer, on the periphery of official publications, a compilation of administrative and judicial decisions at the federal level (known as the 'Ullmer' Compilation). In this case again, interinstitutional and financial aspects are particularly interesting, as are questions of scheduling and recruitment (with remarkable differences between the two target languages). Finally, it should be noted here that case law produced by the Federal Supreme Court from 1874 onwards was never officially translated but instead disseminated through translations published in private legal journals (Dullion 2017).

5.2 Subject areas, text genres and target audiences

Although the Confederation had been given limited responsibilities in 1848, the annual reports show that subject areas for translation rapidly expanded to include topics necessary for technical and economic modernization. The 1874 constitution added new responsibilities, increasing the scope and volume of institutional translation (Bürki-Gyger 1996: 17). The gradual extension of the subject areas mentioned in the annual reports is represented in Figure 4.2. The 1850s and 1910s correspond to the beginning and the end of the period covered by this study, while the 1890s were chosen because, during this decade, there is a significant increase in the occurrences mentioning specialized translations in the data collected.

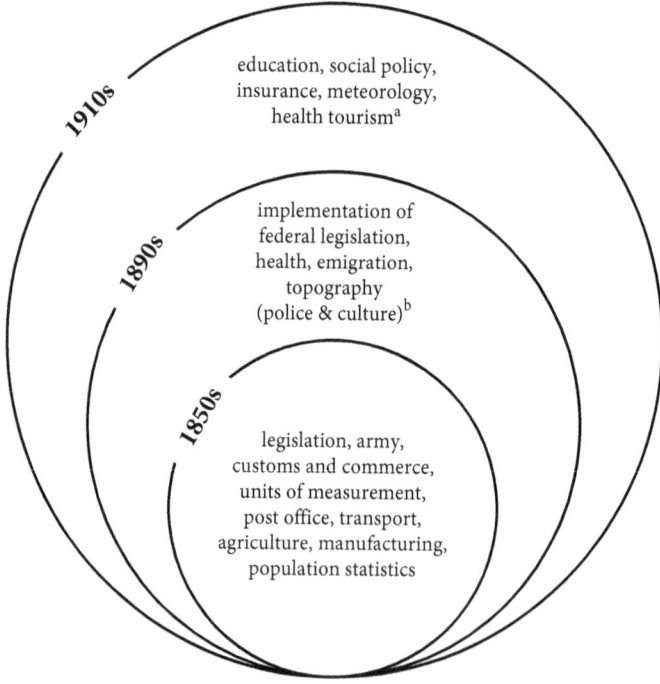

[a] With (rare) examples of translation into English
[b] One occurrence each

Figure 4.2 Areas of specialized translation.

Table 4.2 Typology of texts

Genres	Main potential target audience
Legislation, regulations and decisions	Legal and administrative circles
Practice-oriented administrative documents concerning implementation: lists, tables, indices, tariffs, instructions, manuals, guides and collections of forms	Legal and administrative circles (e.g. registrars at the cantonal level)
Technical documentation: technical books and journals, experts' reports, statistics, atlases and exhibition and fair catalogues	Professional circles
Documents needed in international relations: birth, death or marriage certificates, arrest warrants, diplomatic correspondence and treaties	Foreign countries
Popular information: posters, notices and brochures	Ordinary people

This rich list points in the same direction as Pini's review (2017: 53–5) of books available on the shelves of the Federal Chancellery, some of which date back to the nineteenth century.

As regards textual typology, the categories emerging from the annual reports are presented in Table 4.2.

As in Figure 4.2, Table 4.2 suggests that translators were required to be very versatile and flexible, which raises questions about recruitment and training. These points should be noted here with a view to analysing the data on translators (see Section 7.1).

6 The geographical axes of translation

The thematic analysis carried out in this study shows that in the federal government's view, Bern's translation role was not simply to establish a direct link between the Confederation and citizens – it was also a way to connect to other areas. Particularly rich data highlight how institutional translation was shaped by the specific position of Bern as a capital city in a federalist environment where the cantons had their own official language(s), and in a context of developing international relations.

6.1 Between Bern and the Swiss cantons

Within the federal framework established in 1848 and tightened in 1874, institutional translation from Bern towards the cantons mainly aimed at ensuring the uniform implementation of new federal rules by cantonal authorities. However, the cantons often appear in the annual reports as benefiting from translated information, and even claim so (e.g. AR 1866: 253): translated documents helped them to perform their duties towards both the Confederation and their own population. There are also traces of federal support to intercantonal projects involving the publication of multilingual documents (AR 1914: 167). In another respect, many comments found in the annual reports show that the government ensured the rules of the 'linguistic game' were being followed, whether they concerned the right of the cantons to determine their own official language(s) (AR 1912: 225), their obligation to take account of official languages at the federal level (AR 1888: 393), or the languages to be used for communicating with foreign countries in legal procedures (see Section 6.2).

Tension over translation issues arose principally in Ticino, where Italian was the only official language at the cantonal level (e.g. AR 1881: 35). Its minority-language status, difficulties recruiting native-speaking experts, and isolated location south of the Alps contributed to the risk that the region would stay on the sidelines, separated from the rest of the country by a widening gap. During the nineteenth century, despite the legal status of Italian in the Confederation, institutional translation into this language left a lot to be desired compared with the situation for French: it had a more limited scope, usually came later (e.g. AR 1879: 484–5) and was more dependent on alternative solutions. From 1883 until after the First World War, it relied heavily on an 'external network' (Pini 2017: 56–9): a federal subsidy was granted on a regular basis to the *Repertorio di giurisprudenza patria*, a private legal journal founded in Ticino in 1866, whose editorial team published federal legal texts translated into Italian and provided translators for many projects (see also Dullion 2017: 82–3). In addition to the statutes published in Italian by the Confederation itself in the Official Compilation, Italian-speaking legal, administrative and political circles could find in this journal, among other text genres, the decisions of federal authorities, legislative drafts and explanatory materials. The federal support granted in 1883 was instrumental in keeping a language minority informed of the lawmaking process and enabling its participation therein, which had become particularly important in the post-1874 constitutional framework. The 1886 annual report (180) explicitly states that publication in the *Repertorio* was intended to replace a Federal Gazette in Italian. In other words, the Confederation was outsourcing the translation of institutional text genres belonging to 'maintenance' and 'regulation', that is, the 'core' activities in 'the art of government' (Koskinen 2014: 488).

As for Romansh, it had no official status for most of the nineteenth century, even in the south-eastern, alpine canton of Grisons where it was spoken: it was recognized at the cantonal level in 1880, beside German and Italian. There have been a few exceptional times when translation policy went beyond the requirements of official language policy: the Civil Code was translated (AR 1909: 10) with co-funding from the canton of Grisons; and in 1872 and 1874, the draft constitutional revisions were translated before being submitted to popular vote (Widmer et al. 2005: 133; Weerts 2015: 172–3). However, when the government of Grisons asked in 1877 (AR 31–2), at the request of its parliament, for statutes submitted to popular vote to be translated into one of the Romansh language varieties at the federal government's expense, the federal answer was negative. In other words, the introduction of semi-direct democracy, which established a direct relationship between Bern and Swiss citizens, did question translation management but did not change it when a language still lacked an official status at the level of language policy.

6.2 Between Bern and foreign countries

The annual reports mention many cases where the Confederation, which was in charge of foreign affairs, had to act as an intermediary between other countries and cantonal authorities, which had extensive powers in the fields of justice and civil status registration. Disagreements or misunderstandings on language matters are reported especially from the mid-1880s in relations with the authorities of the German and Austro-Hungarian Empires. The Federal Council often refers to a combination of Swiss and international principles as a reminder that cantonal authorities cannot be expected to communicate in German in all cases (AR 1886: 353). Ironically, it appears the Federal Council was strongly committed to the use of French as a *lingua franca* in international affairs (AR 1899: 242).

Being a multilingual country was a clear advantage when setting up the emerging international organizations: local staff, including translators, could be used as a resource, particularly to launch the new publications of these institutions (e.g. the *Journal télégraphique*, AR 1870: 125–33).

Many instances of communication with foreign countries on matters of immigration and emigration are mentioned in the annual reports. For example, it can be assumed that many language questions arising in relations with Italy (with regard to civil status, mutual legal assistance, work accidents, etc.) concern Italian immigrants or refugees. The interventions reported by the Federal Council usually support communication in Italian, reiterating that it is an official language of the Confederation (e.g. AR 1892: 18–19). However, it should be noted that nineteenth-century Switzerland was foremost an emigration country. Departures from mountain regions (including Ticino and Grisons), mainly to North America, reached their highest level during the 1890s (Walter 2016: 378–9). The difficulties and poor living conditions of its nationals when they arrived at their destination gave the Confederation cause for concern. The annual reports from 1889 to 1904 provide details about the information policy that was then conducted in all three official languages: it included statistics, public meetings, notices to be posted in agency offices, a Swiss emigrant's guide to the United States, and translations of US laws restricting immigration.

7 Staff and resources

Beyond mapping where translation is (not) found, what kinds of texts it applies to and towards which targets it is directed, the data collected for this study shed light on how translation was performed from a practical point of view, especially by whom and with what resources. This opens up avenues for further research in combination with other types of data.

7.1 Translators

In 1895 (AR: 266), '2 chambres pour les traducteurs' ('two rooms for the translators') were planned in the new building of the Federal Parliament House, on the first floor. The annual reports provide a wealth of information on the different types of translators working for the Confederation in various capacities. This should be analysed in connection with other sources: directories and vacancy announcements for translation positions could be retrieved from the archives, for example (on the use of institutional documents to approach the notion of a 'translator' in a historical perspective, see Paloposki 2016: 21–3). The main topics that stand out from this study as deserving further exploration are professional profiles, questions of status and personal backgrounds.

Whereas translation positions are mentioned since the very beginning of the period at the Federal Chancellery and in parliament, institutional translation was only partially centralized: various departments of the federal administration had their own translators, many of them with hybrid job profiles. References to language combinations suggest that despite the clear dominance of German as a source language, translation was performed from and into all three official languages. As for the translator's background, law is at the top of the list. Employed and contract translators often came from federal judicial and political circles. Additionally, experts from various fields participated in the collective production of multilingual – notably legislative – documents, doing translations and revision as part of this activity. In the 1892 annual report (207), delay in work on the *Pharmacopoea Helvetica* is explained as follows:

> Malgré la meilleure volonté, le président n'a pas pu empêcher ce retard, les traductions en question nécessitant le concours de spécialistes et de pharmaciens versés dans la pratique du métier, lesquels, outre des connaissances scientifiques parfaites, doivent posséder à fond au moins deux langues. Les quelques personnes chargées de ce mandat sont les unes propriétaires d'une pharmacie, les autres revêtent un emploi et elles ne pouvaient négliger les obligations imposées à leur profession et à leur emploi au profit de travaux sur la pharmacopée.[1]

The whole spectrum from permanent positions to contract or even volunteer work is represented in the annual reports. As regards employees, a job classification system was introduced in the federal administration at the very end of the nineteenth century. Translation positions, notably at the Federal Chancellery, were integrated into this framework (*Message du Conseil fédéral à l'Assemblée fédérale concernant l'organisation de la Chancellerie fédérale* 1919). Career mobility would be particularly interesting to study. Finally, it should be noted that hybrid positions that include translation vary from the bottom of the ladder (clerk-translator) to senior ranks (translation and revision were part of the job for the second vice chancellor appointed in 1896 and for secretaries of emerging international organizations).

The annual reports often mention where translators come from. Some regions (Neuchâtel and Jura) seem to be over-represented, but further research would be needed in order to reach conclusions. For individual translators (or even translator families), tracking personal and career paths may be relevant. The careers of Elie Ducommun and Albert Gobat, who were awarded a Nobel Peace Prize in 1902 for their work at the bureau of the Inter-Parliamentary Union, may be illustrative of the intersections between Swiss politics, emerging international organizations and institutional translation.

7.2 Cost or benefit?

Starting with the annual reports, the costs and benefits (in the broadest sense) of institutional translation may be explored along various lines. Firstly, they may be explored as part of the overall implications of multilingualism. Translation costs are often mentioned in the annual reports as costs for publication and multilingualism in general, including travel expenses and the very material aspects of written communication (indeed, typesetting, paper and printing seem to have been a greater source of worry than translation). Ingenious solutions were attempted to rationalize multilingual publication: for example, attempts were made to generate economies of scale by offering cantonal governments the option to reuse the page layout of the Official Compilation in their languages for their own compilations (AR 1863: 176).

A second interesting topic would be how translation was paid for. In addition to translators' salaries and fees, a whole range of ways to finance translation emerge from the annual reports, including subsidies, book subscriptions and co-funding with cantonal governments. These could be studied further with the help of budgetary documents available in the archives. In fields where there was an obvious interest in disseminating information, the Confederation actively supported the translation or printing of multilingual works (e.g. AR 1894: 511, about Bertillon's anthropometric identification system). This happened already in its early years, partly through subsidies to federal societies.

Translation is also part of the 'costs' of multilingualism as a source of problems. The main types of problems mentioned in the annual reports are delays (a recurrent situation for Italian) and discrepancies between language versions. The latter appear in the reports principally in the last quarter of the century. Measures to address quality concerns expressed by parliament are reported during the same period (AR 1874: 172, 179; 1880: 397).

As the annual reports record some decisions of the federal executive authorities on appeals involving the application of federal law, they give an idea of how discrepancies were approached in this context and how the new federal state was learning to live with divergence. The reports show that there was still some indecision at the end of the nineteenth century: priority to the source text and more complex interpretation methods were applied alternatively. Furthermore, cases are reported in which multilingual parallel texts were used as a resource to resolve ambiguity (AR 1890: 233–7).

8 A picture of partial institutionalization

During our stroll through nineteenth-century Bern, we have come across a series of interesting phenomena: a government promoting a 'think before translating' approach; large-scale projects running over years in order to translate several-volume collections of legal texts, but also hastily produced multilingual public notices warning against the dangers of emigration; instances of outsourcing, delocalization, exploitation of synergies and cost optimization; and clerk-translators, translators with a Nobel Peace Prize, and pharmacists who helped out with multilingual drafting in their spare time. Beyond these anecdotal encounters and the intermediate conclusions of Sections 4–7, what can be learned from our archival source when approached from an institutionalization perspective?

Some of the features of translation policy in the nineteenth-century federal administration, as it is presented by the executive power in its annual reports to the legislative body, are no surprise. The scope of translation activities grew between 1848 and 1914, in line with transfers of powers from the cantons to the Confederation. Some processes became standardized or even codified (in fields such as legislation and official publications). Some measures were established to ensure quality. Translation positions were created early on, yet many job profiles remained hybrid at the end of the period. In many respects, translation practice turned into translation management. However, other features are more unexpected. Despite signs of institutionalization, many questions continued to arise as to what was supposed to be translated at what level – and this within a federal framework that remained subject to change: since language policy was largely addressed at the cantonal level, the federal state did not take it for granted that translation work was its responsibility in all cases. Another interesting finding is the resourcefulness in the use of ad hoc solutions (e.g. outsourcing and ways to recruit experts in a given domain) throughout the period under study, which made it possible to manage large-scale and relatively long-term projects in spite of the limited means.

The 'institutional translation centre' developed by Bern in the nineteenth century in its capacity as federal city looks more like a loose network than a neat architectural structure. It is multidirectional but clearly unbalanced in favour of French. Tellingly, the translation of official texts into Italian on behalf of the Confederation was largely performed not in Bern but beyond the Gotthard, the mountain range that separates Ticino from German-speaking Switzerland. Finally, as an international city hosting intergovernmental organizations, Bern was able to take advantage of the bilingual resources of the federal city in the same way that being the capital of a bilingual canton had been an asset in 1848 for becoming the seat of the federal authorities, but with the notable difference that French was both a minority language inside Switzerland and a *lingua franca* of international affairs.

9 Conclusions

Nineteenth-century Bern was thus a city with several layers of language mediation. In this chapter, the focus has been on translation policy at the federal level. Given the characteristics of the Swiss political system in the European landscape of that time, this has involved addressing questions related to how federalism and democracy evolved in the country.

A striking feature of institutional, federal translation in nineteenth-century Switzerland is that a key element of translation policy lay in a selective approach where not everything was intended for translation, coupled with a partial institutionalization that left room for unconventional resources. In contrast to other cases addressed in this volume, this approach does not appear to be very ideological or self-reflective. This may be due to the specific political framework in which the institutionalization process was taking place. In post-1848 Switzerland, multilingualism and official translation did not have to struggle with a 'one nation, one language' ideology, but rather developed within a federal framework which had been established so that territories with equal autonomy – and that happened to have their own languages – could coexist. One of Bern's functions was to guarantee the stability of this framework.

However, the federal city's translation policy was discussed and challenged with the shift towards semi-direct democracy, as it entailed increased and unmediated participation of citizens in the political space of the Confederation itself. The extension of initiative and referendum rights from 1874 onwards is certainly a relevant landmark insofar as incomplete access to draft legislation and other pre-legislative documents, particularly in Italian, was then felt to be in contradiction to the official language policy and became a matter for repeated demands. Indeed, the drawback of a 'pragmatic and flexible' translation policy may be vagueness and inequality. At the beginning of the twentieth century, arrangements that went beyond alternative or improvised solutions had to be found for Italian, driven by political pressure.

The study presented in this chapter provides a thematic and diachronic analysis of one type of archival source covering more than six decades, which allows for a 'mapping' approach. The study was designed as a prerequisite for further research on more specific topics, such as how translation activities were funded and paid for. By diversifying the sources, it would be possible to gain a multi-perspective view of the development of institutional translation. Of course, translation policy at the cantonal and local levels, and in emerging international organizations, would also be worth exploring. Such research may create opportunities for examining, at a later stage, the influence of institutional translation on the construction of professional identity in multilingual countries like Switzerland and contribute to studies on professionalization (see Sela-Sheffy 2016).

Note

1 Despite best efforts, the chairman could not prevent this delay, as these translations necessitated the collaboration of experts and accomplished pharmacists who have perfect scientific knowledge and full command of at least two languages. Of the few people in charge of the task, some own a pharmacy, the others are employed, and they could not neglect the duties of their professions or jobs in favour of working on the pharmacopoeia.

References

Primary sources

Geschäftsberichte des Bundesrates / Rapports de gestion du Conseil fédéral, 1848–1914, Schweizerisches Bundesarchiv (Bern) / Archives fédérales suisses (Berne), Online-Amtsdruckschriften / publications officielles numérisées (Annual reports of the Federal Council, 1848–1914, Swiss Federal Archives (Bern), digitized official publications), https://www.amtsdruckschriften.bar.admin.ch (abbreviated here as 'AR').

Message du Conseil fédéral à l'Assemblée fédérale concernant l'organisation de la Chancellerie fédérale (du 21 février 1919), *Feuille fédérale* (Dispatch of the Federal Council to Parliament on the organization of the Federal Chancellery (21 February 1919), *Federal Gazette*), 1919 (I.8): 287–93.

Secondary sources

Adam, E. (1995), 'La Chancellerie fédérale dans l'histoire : aperçu sur les origines d'une institution bientôt bicentenaire', in M. Klaus (ed.), *Quelle chance pour nos institutions?* 163–97, s.l.: s.n.

Bähler, A., R. Barth, S. Bühler, E. Erne and C. Lüthi (2003), *Bern – die Geschichte der Stadt im 19. und 20. Jahrhundert: Stadtentwicklung, Gesellschaft, Wirtschaft, Politik, Kultur*, Bern: Stämpfli.

Bürki-Gyger, E. (1996), 'Stellung und Aufgaben der Bundeskanzlei im Bundesstaat von 1848. Analyse der Jahre 1848–1900', unpublished typescript, Diplomarbeit 7. Höherer Lehrgang für das Bundespersonal, Bern.

Comment, F., ed. (2016), *125 Jahre Amtliches Bulletin der Bundesversammlung*, Bern: Parlamentsdienste.
DHS (*Dictionnaire historique de la Suisse*), 'Berne (commune)', 'Ville'. Available online: http://www.hls-dhs-dss.ch/textes/f/F209.php (dated 29 September 2016), http://www.hls-dhs-dss.ch/textes/f/F7875.php (dated 1 February 2018).
D'hulst, L. (2012), '(Re)locating Translation History: From Assumed Translation to Assumed Transfer', *Translation Studies*, 5 (2): 139–55.
D'hulst, L. and M. Schreiber (2014), 'Vers une historiographie des politiques de traduction en Belgique durant la période française', *Target*, 26 (1): 3–31.
Dullion, V. (2017), 'La traduction des décisions de justice dans les revues juridiques suisses : développement d'un régime de traduction privée (1853–1912)', *Parallèles*, 29 (1): 74–89.
González Núñez, G. (2016), 'On Translation Policy', *Target*, 28 (1): 87–109.
HSSO (Historical statistics of Switzerland Online) (2012), 'Resident Population by Mother Tongue', Tab. B.44. Available online: https:hsso.ch/2012/b/44 (accessed 22 August 2018).
Koskinen, K. (2014), 'Institutional Translation: The Art of Government by Translation', *Perspectives*, 22 (4): 479–92.
Martig, P. (2011), *Berns moderne Zeit: Das 19. und 20. Jahrhundert neu entdeckt*, Bern: Stämpfli.
Meylaerts, R. (2011), 'Translational Justice in a Multilingual World: An Overview of Translational Regimes', *Meta*, 56 (4): 743–57.
Meylaerts, R. and T. du Plessis (2016), 'Multilingualism Studies and Translation Studies: Still a Long Road Ahead', in Y. Gambier and L. van Doorslaer (eds), *Border Crossings: Translation Studies and Other Disciplines*, Amsterdam: Benjamins.
Paloposki, O. (2016), 'Translating and Translators before the Professional Project', *JoSTrans*, 25: 15–32.
Pini, V. (2017), *Anche in italiano! 100 anni di lingua italiana nella cultura politica svizzera*, Bern: Federal Chancellery / Bellinzona: Casagrande.
Sela-Sheffy, R. (2016), 'Profession, Identity, and Status', in C. V. Angelelli and B. J. Baer (eds), *Researching Translation and Interpreting*, 131–45, Milton Park: Routledge.
Walter, F. (2016), *Une histoire de la Suisse*, Neuchâtel: Alphil-Presses universitaires suisses.
Weerts, S. (2015), *La langue de l'État : Proposition d'un modèle de pluralisme linguistique à partir de l'étude comparée des droits belge et suisse*, Brussels: Bruylant.
Weilenmann, H. (1925), *Die vielsprachige Schweiz: eine Lösung des Nationalitätenproblems*, Basel: im Rhein-V.
Werlen, I. (2000), *Der zweisprachige Kanton Bern*, Bern: Haupt.
Widmer, J. et al. (2005), *Die Schweizer Sprachenvielfalt im öffentlichen Diskurs: eine sozialhistorische Analyse der Transformationen der Sprachenordnung von 1848 bis 2000*, Bern: Lang.
Wolf, M. (2015), *The Habsburg Monarchy's Many-Languaged Soul: Translating and Interpreting, 1848–1918*, trans. K. Sturge, Amsterdam: Benjamins.

5

Mediating Flemish: Local language and translation policies on the French–Belgian border

Lieven D'hulst

1 Language borders in and around Belgium

Belgium is a small country with a long and complex history of multilingualism. Today, two of its three official languages occupy two areas that are comparable in size (the Flemish[1]-speaking North or Flanders and the French-speaking South or Wallonia), while the capital city Brussels and its surrounding municipalities are bilingual.[2] Belgium shares its official languages with its four neighbours: French with France and Luxemburg, German with Germany and Luxemburg, and Dutch with the Netherlands. Until the early twentieth century, Flemish was also a well-established spoken language in France: since the second half of the seventeenth century, it was commonly spoken in the rural areas of the northern part of the County of Flanders, also called French Flanders, which were annexed by France; from the mid-nineteenth century to the First World War, it was used by Flemish migrant workers in French municipalities and cities of the same county or department, close to the Belgian border.

This chapter deals with the history of mediation between Flemish and French for almost a century (roughly between the founding of Belgium in 1830 and the end of the First World War), a period that witnessed changing language laws, changing language practices and emerging views on democratic representation and cultural identity. More in particular, I will focus on mediation through translation, and will view the latter through the lens of the language and translation policies of fourteen municipalities close to the Belgian–French border: eight of them are located in the Western province of Belgium, the other six in the Northern department of France. Cities and municipalities are complex loci of language exchange. During the nineteenth century, they witness a growing awareness of language diversity and the need to regulate communication between the municipality, the province and the state, as well as between the citizens and the local authorities. The birth of democratic regimes and their mode of public representation marks a strong shift away from the long-term customs of debate and report in private settings.

After 1830, Belgian municipalities and their governing bodies offer, more than ever before, meeting ground, conflict and compromise between languages and by extension between legal constraints and local practices. Indeed, citizens and authorities cannot but comply with the law, even if the latter does not fit standing practices, or language demands of its population. In this respect, mediation through translation can be considered as a way of supporting democratic claims of monolingual citizens and elected representatives. It can also be understood as a hidden 'tactic' turning into a 'strategy' of resistance against official monolingualism, as underpinned by linguistic domination. In concordance with de Certeau's (1984/1974) understanding of tactic as a practice set in time and determined by specific constraints of daily communication, translation and other forms of interlingual mediation may emerge occasionally, without adhering to a particular hierarchy or preference. Later on, they can evolve into tools of a more conscious strategy, adopting a recurrent or even systematic character shared by a larger group of elected members, with one practice favoured over the other.

Be that as it may, all fourteen municipalities have remained blind spots as far as the study of translation is concerned, which is in itself surprising. Why has translation, though crucial to interlingual mediation, remained the orphan child of historical research on languages in nineteenth-century Belgium and France?

A first reason is that the Belgian language history has been mainly studied from the point of view of cultural nationalism that pervaded large parts of Europe from the end of the eighteenth century onwards. Adhering to this ideal, the young Belgian nation, and Flanders in particular, fostered a Romantic and Herderian vision on language as a vector of cultural identity. However, as in many other multilingual nations, Flanders had to share its cultural identity with a larger national one. This dual connection turned into a tension between a non-dominant ethnic identity and its language, on the one hand, and a dominant national identity expressed by another language, that is, French, on the other. Histories of the domination and later emancipation of Flemish in Belgium have been written from an array of angles, that is, by legal historians (see a.o. Van

Goethem 1990; Clement 2003), language historians (Willemyns and Daniëls 2003) and political historians (Witte and Van Velthoven 1998; Wils 2001).

A second reason is the common language view that is wedged in methodological nationalism,[3] featuring each nation state as a kind of 'container' (Darquennes 2014: 78) of one or more individual languages and language communities: 'a view of languages and speech communities as bounded entities, so-called segregational linguistics' (Pietikäinen & Kelly-Holmes 2013: 2). Approaching languages as interactive would help to shift the emphasis towards instances of code-mixing and code-switching, as well as numerous other mediation modes especially aiming at monolingual citizens who do not master the socially necessary codes of the other language. Court interpreting, community interpreting and translation, next to summaries, paraphrases or adaptations are among the most prominent techniques of interlingual mediation.

Last but not least, the study of translation is hindered by the latter's poor visibility: views and comments on Belgian translation were rarely phrased in an explicit way, translation itself was not always noticeable or marked as such, translators remained in the shadow of authors and politicians, etc. Nevertheless, interpreting and translation were everywhere, as practices as natural as single language use, intimately connected with the many social, political and cultural elements that turn its study into a rich yet difficult undertaking.

In the two following sections, I will provide a sketch of the general translation activities and regulations in Belgium, followed by an overview of translation and multilingual practices in a set of Flemish municipalities located in the most Western province of Belgium, that is, West-Flanders. The last part looks at the fate of Flemish and its mediation in a set of French municipalities of the Northern department close to the border with Belgium.[4]

2 Translation regulation in Belgium

As in other multilingual nations, laws and instructions with an impact at the national, regional and local levels addressed more explicitly language use than translation. However, both were interwoven and reflected the numerous conflicts and compromises that feature the language history in Belgium. The newly independent Belgium inherited its translation views and practices between French and Flemish from its recent past, especially the so-called French (1795–1815) and Dutch (1815–30) regimes or periods: the first had imposed French in law and administration, while providing translations into Flemish (D'hulst and

Schreiber 2014); the second reversed the translation direction from January 1823 on, in accordance with a royal order of King William (15 September 1819): in Flanders, all administrative, financial and military authorities had to use Dutch or Flemish only. After the Belgian Revolution of 1830, this trend was changed again, as made explicit in the Belgian Constitution of 1831:

> Art. 23. L'emploi des langues usitées en Belgique est facultatif; il ne peut être réglé que par la loi et seulement pour les actes de l'autorité publique et pour les affaires judiciaires.[5]

However, such a general formulation opened room for interpretation. On the one hand, it laid down the language freedom of the citizen, as opposed to the previous regimes. On the other hand, it restricted that freedom. The expression 'actes de l'autorité publique' (acts of public authority) referred not only to the government or the king but also to the provincial and municipal councils, the mayors and governors and even to civil servants. In other words, the local authorities and their officials were free to decide which language they used in their relations with the citizen, even if that citizen benefited from the same right. But for decades citizens were not in position to exert that right. In fact, the politicians had from the start the unambiguous intention to impose French as the only official language (Clement 2003: 85). The law of 19 September 1831 (Article 2) confirms this interpretation: 'Les lois seront insérées au *Bulletin officiel*, aussitôt après leur promulgation, avec une traduction flamande ou allemande pour les communes où l'on parle ces langues; le texte français demeurant néanmoins seul officiel.'[6] French was the elite language, the language of legal thinking and writing, and the international reference language par excellence (Soleil 2017). The result was a far-reaching Frenchification of government agencies, and more specifically of the administrative system in Flanders, even though that Frenchification was symbolically contained by the principle of language freedom.

Against this background, an intense translation activity of French and French–Belgian official texts was initiated,[7] while French-speaking Belgium in-translated considerably less from (Netherlandic) Dutch and Flemish. Legal texts were made available in published form, among others in bilingual versions, such as the *Bulletin officiel/Staetsblad* (Belgian official journal, 1831–45) and the *Recueil des lois et arrêtés royaux / Verzameling der Wetten en Koninklijke Besluiten* (Collection of laws and royal decrees, 1845–1972). In addition, countless translations were made by the administration for internal use, for communication with the public, for use in education, in courts, for the police, for ministries, etc.; they were sometimes printed and published, but mostly they were unpublished and handwritten translations.

All in all, the presence of translations was more than substantial: a rough estimate amounts to circa 100 million printed words in the administrative and legal domain for the period 1830–1914 (D'hulst and Van Gerwen 2018). In addition to these 'intranational' translations from French into Flemish, international ones, although less numerous, need to be reported as well, for example, those imported from France and Germany. At this point, it is impossible to compare the volumes of translated and non-translated texts in Flemish that are printed or distributed, except for the legal domain, where translation must be close to 50 per cent. The unknown pervasiveness of translation is a strange paradox that needs further investigation.

When looking more closely, one cannot but observe that legal and administrative translations were not always unbiasedly welcomed. As the century advanced, they started to face more and more criticism and even resistance. In fact, from the early 1840s onwards, Flemish politicians increasingly strove for the recognition of Flemish as an official language. They realized that the fragile compromise between language freedom and official French did not guarantee steady access to legal information for the citizen. When claimed by both administrators and citizens, language freedom rather became a barrier to exchange. New initiatives emerged, such as the 'Flemish petition' of 1840 asking for the use of Flemish in administration, justice and education. Nevertheless, it took several decades before Flemish demands were granted.

The 1878 law (22 May) implemented a territorial language principle and installed bilingualism in Flanders (Clement 2003: 198). However, bilingualism meant in fact that extensive minority rights were given to Francophones in Flanders (Clement 2003: 199). Did that push translation into the background? If the term is not mentioned as such in the law, the practice seems to have been tolerated. However, it should not be forgotten that Article 23 of the Constitution still guaranteed freedom of language use for all, including civil servants in their communications with the citizens. In Belgium, it seems, new language laws always aimed at tightening the loopholes of previous ones.

3 Locating practices

Obviously, language laws were incomplete, maintained a certain abstraction, and said nothing about values, form requirements and functions granted to languages. As to the concrete language practices in administration, a few trends have been laid bare by recent research, a.o. on the basis of language use in municipality councils and aldermen colleges in Flanders in the nineteenth century (a.o. Vanhecke 2004; Vanhecke and De Groof 2007). These studies both reveal significant differences between cities and municipalities, and a general trend for Flanders: in 1840 French reaches a peak; in 1860 Flemish returns in smaller cities and towns; in 1880, larger cities follow, before Flemish becomes the exclusive administrative language in most Flemish town halls around the turn of the century (Vanhecke 2004: 59). Variation occurred when there was a higher degree of urbanization (French-speaking elites were stronger in larger cities), in towns in the vicinity of Brussels, and in towns close to the language border (Wils 2008: 124–5).

What about the concrete practice of translation within the Flemish municipal administration? It remains a terra incognita: whether translations existed, where and when, how they were carried out, by whom and for whom, how they were presented (beneath or next to the source text, or separately) and treated (separately from the original or in a comparative and interactive way) are still open questions, not in the least because they were rarely discussed in public, as if every single administration had to decide on the issue. To uncover and describe in detail this decision process needs more than a reference to the previously mentioned official argument, that is, translation as a resource for monolingual citizens. Cultural and political parameters should be taken into account, especially when debates on language use were put on the agenda of council meetings, figured in the reports or were commented upon in the local press. As the century advances, Flemish-speaking councillors grew in number, creating a firmer public representation of their particular group of constituents.

The Belgian law on the municipalities of March 1836 stipulated that every inhabitant had the right to access the minutes of the meetings (*Loi communale*, art. 69). Access to the meetings themselves was also provided in a number of cases (Art. 70 and 71). Debates on language entered thus the public space and became even tokens of representative democracy. It is there that translation has unobtrusively nestled, exerting important but ambivalent roles: as a mediating instance between conflicting positions, but likewise as a carrier of Flemish as a legitimate language of political representation[8].

The following paragraphs explore administrative translations in fourteen border towns and municipalities located within and close to the Belgian province of West-Flanders, where Flemish was primarily interacting with French. As we will see, regulations, practices and beliefs in particular not only followed a general trend but also showed a remarkable degree of variation, turning Flemish translation space into a quite diversified landscape (Figure 5.1).

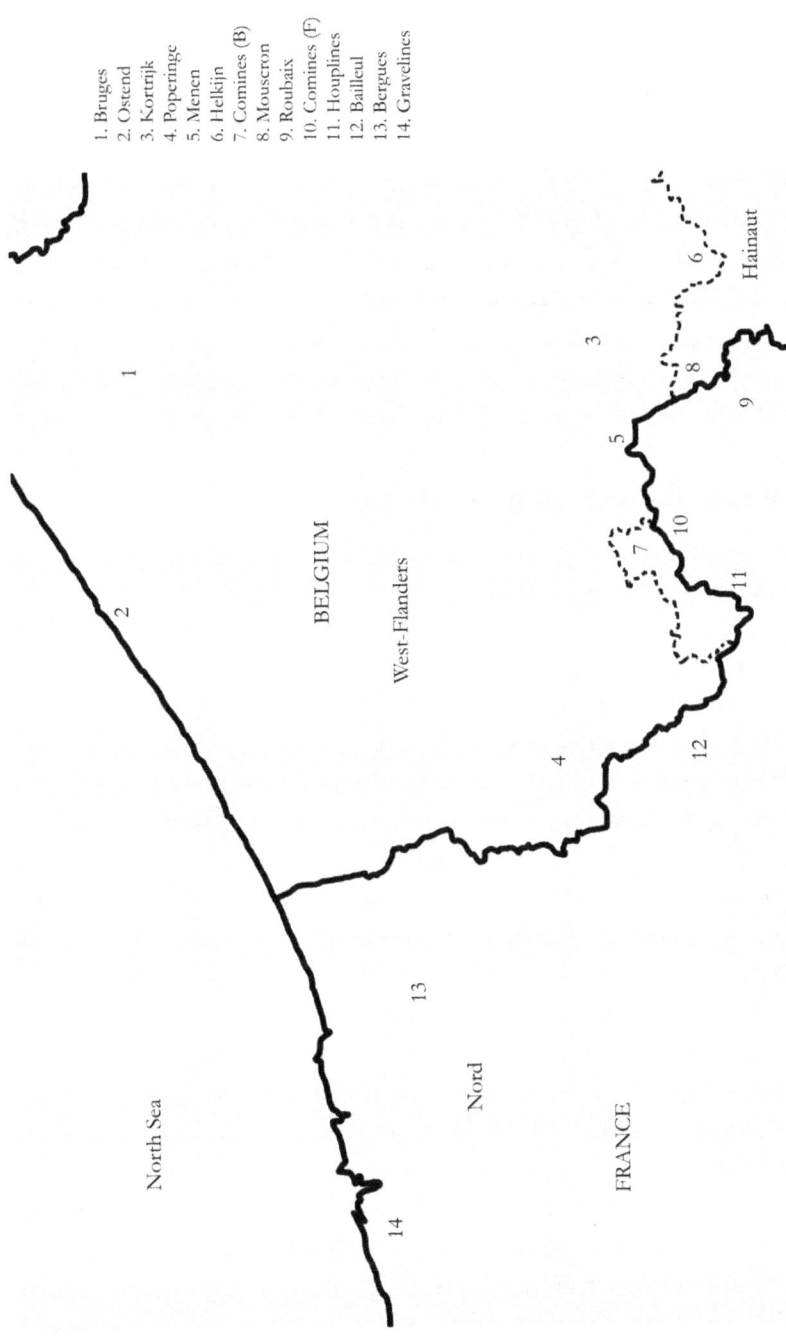

Figure 5.1 Source: Map data © 2018 Google.[9]

These towns and municipalities are allocated to one of the three following areas: West-Flanders, where Flemish was the spoken and written language of the majority of the people (1–8); the southern part of the French Nord department, where it was the language of a Flemish migrant group (9–11); the northern part of the same department, where it was the language spoken by an ethnic minority (12–14).

The local municipalities' published and handwritten minutes of council meetings, which are mostly filed in the archives of the municipalities in question,[10] show that the status of Flemish as well as the mediating activities between Flemish and French were a frequent subject of debate in West-Flanders but that they do not seem to have been an overt issue in France. The following section starts with West-Flanders, from north to south (1–8). It continues with a glance at the French municipalities of the Nord department: the first ones (9–11) are close to the Franco-Belgian border, the last ones (12–14) are located in the heart of French Flanders.

3.1 Meandering through West-Flanders

The Western province of Belgium offers the only Flemish border zone with France and draws a border with French-speaking Wallonia.

Bruges (1)*

Bruges was (and is) the capital of the province, with the highest number of inhabitants (51,000 in 1900, of which 61 per cent were literate, 73 per cent monolingual Flemish, 2 per cent monolingual French, 24 per cent bilingual[11]). As one of the major Belgian cities, Bruges has attracted the attention of sociolinguists, who have shown that debates in the city council revealed pragmatic language views together with a defence of French ('a prestige marker and a tool for social exclusion in the domain of political decision-making', Vandenbussche 2004: 44) and, later on, of Flemish.

French being the official language since 1830, the minutes, printed as yearbooks from 1840 on, remained indeed monolingual French till the mid-1870s, when Flemish started to be used occasionally by councillors.[12] In 1885, the latter group complained that Flemish interventions were not stenographed during the council meetings, while the French were. Moreover, the French texts were then literally transcribed, sent to their authors, who corrected them, the corrected version being finally registered and printed in the minutes. Technical files were given in French only, or translated partially, as were the street names: councillors pointed out that these were always translated literally from French

---

* Numbers in parenthesis in headings refer to the numbers on the map (see Figure 5.1).

into Flemish, in a 'slavish, stupid' way ('letterlijk, slaafs, dom', *Bulletin communal* 1885: 479), the new names becoming palimpsests of French originals that had already lost their link with the old Flemish names.

More generally, councillors criticized the language of translation, because it featured non-Flemish words and expressions and false sentences. In short, translations were miserable gibberish, as unintelligible as Volapük[13] ('zit vol onvlaamsche woorden en uitdrukkingen, vol valsche zinnen, in een woord 't is eene nieuwe ellendige war- of brabbeltaal zoo onverstaanbaar als Volapük', Brugge 1885: 489). Flemish deserved a better treatment, and should become the first language of debate. Yet, when councillors plead for the reversed translation direction, that is, from Flemish into French, they subtly recalled a lasting risk factor: 'le traducteur rendrait-il fidèlement notre pensée?' (Would the translator render faithfully our ideas?, 1885: 478). Obviously, demands for more and better and reverse translations became scarce; they were even openly challenged, a.o. by the Francophone mayor, who argued that councillors should focus less on the quality of language issues than on the quality of the deliberations and decisions taken (1885: 494). Besides, he added, an exclusive use of Flemish would entail political criticism if not harassment on behalf of the central administration in the capital Brussels (1887: 161).

Nevertheless, French withdrew as the main language of the minutes towards the end of the century (e.a. Brugge 1896: 228), while oral bilingualism as practised during the sessions was maintained. This discrepancy yielded criticism, because it rendered translation imperative: Why translate oral French into Flemish in the minutes of the council, instead of directly speaking and writing in Flemish? The perennial answer: Article 23 of the Constitution guarantees freedom of language. Some councillors argued then in favour of a 'translation on demand' of documents written in French (1896: 230) while others advocated anew the sole use of Flemish, in their view the most simple solution (1896: 284–5). Yet, such pragmatism was steadily superseded by the argument of administrators' freedom. At last, Flemish was confirmed as the exclusive language of the minutes around 1912.

Although it was a provincial capital, Bruges did not set the norm for views and practices in West-Flanders: each town had to invent a balance between centrally imposed laws, local conventions and expectations, as well as appropriate tactics to face the unpredictable problems of everyday communication.

Ostend (2)
Ostend is a seaside town, at a distance of some 23 kilometres from Bruges. It had 39,000 inhabitants in 1900, of which 66 per cent were literate, 71 per cent

monolingual Flemish, 2 per cent monolingual French and 28 per cent bilingual.[14] During the second half of the century, local politicians put much effort to convert Ostend into a transit harbour to England, and brought to the fore openness and accessibility as values to be promoted. But local views on language and translation did not reflect this evolution. As in Bruges, the meetings of the council were bundled and printed as yearbooks, starting in 1864 in monolingual French. The use of Flemish was usually limited to contracts, formal specifications, or quoted letters sent to the administration (all formal specifications had to be bilingual from 1892 on, see *Bulletin communal* 1892: 196). Translation and multilingualism were rarely commented upon in these years: in 1886, the council's secretary reported that the mayor congratulated citizens in Flemish, but paraphrased the mayor's speech in French (1886: 243). Interventions by Flemish councillors were ordinarily translated in French, without entailing discussion.

This situation altered towards the end of the 1890s. During the session of 26 January 1897, a councillor required bilingual versions of the distributed documents as well as of the minutes of the meetings. The mayor refused, invoking the arguments of cost and uselessness (since all councillors understood French). In 1899, the same councillor requested the reading in Flemish of a report on taxes; the mayor replied that he would give 'necessary explanations' in Flemish after reading the French report. And so, a set of transfer techniques developed side by side: code-switching was used by different members; paraphrase became a popular tool, while translation proper of interventions by the mayor or council members became less common, unless requests were made to translate official documents. Bilingual posters became compulsory. One could interpret these mediating techniques as a token of linguistic democracy or at least as a sign of growing and shared courtesy towards both language groups. But they did not last long.

In 1904, newly elected council members took the oath: nine in French, eight in Flemish. A small majority attested thus to be Francophone. In 1912, the order reversed: nine oaths in Flemish, five in French. On 1 January 1912, a strong plea was made in favour of an increased use of official Flemish in towns: Ostend should follow the example of the 'three sister towns' Ghent, Antwerp and Bruges (1912: 29). Later in the same year, subtle strategies aimed to push the boundaries further. A councillor asked for a vote on both the Flemish and French versions of a regulation, compelling the mayor to admit that the Flemish version was in fact a translation, and therefore deprived of an official status. Defending the current practice, the mayor qualified translations as dangerous: in Brussels they were made with great care, whereas in Ostend, the quality of translations inspired defiance and required more control. Be that as it may, the councillor insisted: Why not consider the original and translation as two originals as stipulated by the Equality Law of 1898, and endow them with the same value?

Concessions were made, and the successive reading and voting of both texts seemed to be acceptable to all parties, yet also inspired mistrust: Were the two texts 'identical'? Was the translation well made? (1913: 486). Such awareness, as well as reading and voting, invited frequent, if not systematic, comparisons of two texts. All this tipped the scales in favour of French as the main language of the minutes, as well as of the exchanges.

The year 1914 was pivotal: the war introduced the language of the German occupier, who governed most areas of Belgium, including Ostend. Local German *Kommandanturen* (governors) imposed new regulations, including military control on translations into and from German made by public officers. The following case is exemplary of a changed language and translation policy. In early 1915, the *Bulletin communal* reported an embarrassing incident: the German city commander of Ostend, Bittinger, accused the mayor and the head of administration of having deliberately mistranslated in Flemish and French the German text of a placard, by rendering 'Flämisch (Niederdeutsch)' as 'Vlaamsch (Nederlandsch)' and as 'Flamand (Néerlandais)'. 'Niederdeutsch' or Low German suggested common roots for German and Flemish, and expressed a dismissal of the Netherlands remaining neutral during the war. The head of administration was sentenced to eight days of prison, yet argued that his translation had been altered afterwards by the college of mayor and aldermen. Bittinger then sentenced the secretary of that college, even though the latter was deprived of voting rights, to three days of prison.

The same year, the governor of the province strategically informed the Ostend administration that all epistolary exchanges with other administrations should occur in Flemish. In 1917, the *Bulletin communal* turned monolingual Flemish; however oral bilingualism during meetings was tolerated. After the war, French briefly returned in administration, and as a consequence translation and bilingualism again became the subject of heated debate, especially in 1919. While Flemish was imposed from August 1921 on, French was still used as a translating language from Flemish (e.g. 1925: 198). French source texts immediately induced translations into Flemish (e.g. 1926: 336). Flemish won the battle at the end of the 1920s, when translation disappeared as an explicit tool of language mediation.

Kortrijk (3)

Kortrijk is a town located some 10 kilometres from the French border. It had approximately 33,000 inhabitants (1900 census) of which 61 per cent were literate, 69 per cent monolingual Flemish, 1 per cent monolingual French and 30 per cent bilingual.[15] From 1831 until the end of the century, French was the only language in council meetings. Monolingualism got under pressure around 1900, while translation and other mediating techniques came to the fore. For instance, during a meeting on 4 August 1902, a member claimed the use of a single language in order to ensure maximum participation of members and the public, yet the mayor refused to provide an oral translation of French documents and gave instead an 'explication', that is, a paraphrase, in Flemish, as a token of courtesy towards the Flemish council members. The discussion went on until the mayor – albeit reluctantly – agreed to have this French text translated in the minutes, again in order to satisfy a group of councillors. Obviously, we are dealing here with a conflict between a private representation on the side of the French-speaking mayor and a desire for public representation on the side of the Flemish council members.

At the start of the meeting of 30 May 1904 a councillor rocked the boat again and asked for translations to be included as well as approved in the minutes. The mayor subtly pointed out that only reports could be approved, and not the translations of reports, since translations had no official value. So the question arose as to the choice of the language to be used for the report. If Flemish was chosen, then many texts on the basis of which decisions had to be made needed to be translated from French: a technically demanding task, for which a special employee had to be hired, only with the aim to please a small number of councillors that mastered French anyway. Nevertheless, the mayor's strategy evolved, be it slowly and implicitly. During a session of early August of the same year, the mayor addressed his colleagues in Flemish: a fine example of courtesy achieved by the use of the second language. Other 'concessions' followed, such as the recourse to paraphrase in Flemish upon request. But a few years later, the discussion on 'the issue of Vlaamsch' arose again, in particular during the meeting of 10 January 1913. Several Flemish councillors rejected all transfer modes, including translation, which they subordinated to full bilingualism, in line with the Equality Law of 1898. But they also asked for monolingual oral communication in Flemish, reversing the current situation. After the First World War, monolingualism became the norm.

Poperinge (4)

Poperinge is located some 40 kilometres from the French border. In 1900, the town had approximately 11,000 inhabitants (of which 66 per cent were literate,

79 per cent monolingual Flemish, 20.8 per cent bilingual[16]). The language of the minutes was monolingual French between 1830 and 1895 (although the minutes registered decisions only, not the exchanges between council members). In 1895, Flemish took over, yet not without debate. In 1896, it was decided that both the exchanges and the written report should be in Flemish. And so Poperinge embarked on a trend initiated by the closer and more influential city of Bruges (see Section Bruges (1)). Curiously enough, during and after the war (till 1919), French reappeared together with a temporary commission of dignitaries taking over the administration of the town, which was largely destroyed. A sense of urgency seemed to move the language issue to the background; but it was also an attempt to reinstall French as the language of exchange with both the Belgian and the international authorities.

3.2 Moving South: Translating in Belgian border municipalities

Menen (5)

It may be assumed that border proximity yields enhanced bilingualism of council members and less translation. But has that been the case? Menen is a border town located less than 2 kilometres from the French border, as well as from the Francophone province of Hainaut. According to the 1900 census, it had a population of 18,000 inhabitants (56 per cent of them were literate, 62 per cent monolingual Flemish, 1 per cent monolingual French, 37 per cent bilingual[17]). French was the language of the minutes for the longest part of the nineteenth century. In 1890, Flemish made its appearance, in a quoted contract notice on building a fence around the cemetery. The discussion that followed was still rendered in French only. Few years later, in 1895, a couple of newly elected council members took their oath in Flemish. From 1896 on, bilingualism made its appearance while Flemish translation was required for French documents. Yet changes were slow and far from systematic. Even after the First World War, between March 1918 and March 1921, the minutes were still rendered in French only. It took two more years to see a new bilingual format in two columns (French–Flemish) make its appearance (with a changed order Flemish–French in 1928). After 1932, the reports were monolingual Flemish.

And so, Menen may very well be the West-Flemish town that resisted the dismissal of translation the longest. One may venture several hypotheses to explain why: the vicinity of the border with monolingual France, the pragmatic strength of local traditions, the weight of Francophone council members, the resistance against central language policies and trends in major Flemish cities.

Helkijn (6)

Helkijn (or Helchin) is a small border municipality south of Kortrijk and located at some 11 kilometres from the French border. In 1900, there were 1,300 inhabitants, of which 68 per cent were literate, 5 per cent monolingual French, 15 per cent monolingual Flemish and 76 per cent bilingual.[18] Few language discussions are registered, excepting the regular demand of the council to become part of the Walloon province of Hainaut. As elsewhere, there was a transition from monolingual Flemish to monolingual French in January 1830. Occasionally, during the 1830s, Flemish was used, notably when elected Flemish members took the oath. Yet, it was French that dominated throughout the century. On 8 June 1920, with reference to the upcoming law on compulsory use of Flemish in the administration of West-Flanders, the council called for respect for the claims of its inhabitants, that is, the right to use French in administrative matters, and the recognition of its identity as a 'commune wallonne' (Walloon municipality).

Comines Belgique (7)

Comines Belgique offers a similar picture to Helkijn: a smaller border municipality (6,000 inhabitants according to the 1900 census, of which 59 per cent were literate, 36 per cent monolingual French, 19 per cent monolingual Flemish and 45 per cent bilingual[19]), but located on the French border as well as on the language border with Hainaut in Wallonia (in 1963, it is transferred to the latter province). Meetings of the municipal council were invariably held in French (information is lacking before 1868). From 1920, several requests were addressed to the Senate and the Chamber of Representatives in order to be considered as a 'commune wallonne' (e.g. 10 June 1920, 17 August 1920, 15 October 1920). In response to the law of 31 July 1921, the council decided on 4 August to reject all received letters written in Flemish.

Mouscron (8)

Mouscron is also a border town, comparable to Menen with respect to demography (18,900 inhabitants), of which 56 per cent were considered literate, 14 per cent monolingual Flemish, 41 per cent monolingual French, 44 per cent bilingual[20]). During the French period (1795–1815), the council meetings were in French only. Under Dutch rule (1815–30), Flemish became the norm in 1823, while from later in the same year the council produced either monolingual Flemish versions or bilingual versions Flemish–French in two columns (with only the Flemish version being signed by the council members). Curiously, the order changed in 1825: French on the left side, Flemish on the right, the latter being official. From 1830 onwards, French controlled the scene, apparently without giving rise to much controversy.

Obviously, as the previous examples have shown, public debate on language and translation had a higher bet in cities or towns than in municipalities. In the first case, it seemed to mimic trends that occurred elsewhere, as well as in other major cities in Flanders and the National Parliament in Brussels (Nouws and Meylaerts 2018). Conversely, Flemish border municipalities adhered less than central ones to the provincial and national strategies of 'Flemishification', stressing on the contrary their kinship with vicinal language communities – France in the case of Menin, Hainaut in the last three cases. In this respect, both towns and municipalities seem to have elaborated different networks.

4 Crossing the national border: The dismissal of Flemish

The French border crosses a Flemish language community dating back to the Middle Ages. Since the Revolution, the history of that community has followed a specific track: a number of language functions (communicative as well as patrimonial) were tolerated, but strictly separated from the official domains, such as education, administration, justice and army (see a.o. H. Ryckeboer 1997). The decree of 2 Thermidor of year II (20 July 1794) and the consular decree of 24 Prairial year XI (13 juin 1803) imposed the use of French only. From then on, translation policy in the administrative domain was poorly developed and few words are needed to describe the regulation on transfer between French and regional languages during the nineteenth century. Nevertheless, official monolingualism no doubt continued to go hand in hand with 'covert multilingualism' (Schreiber 2016), that is, an array of oral and written transfer modalities between French and Flemish. One may assume that these modalities occurred more frequently in oral than written genres, but remained banned from institutional practices that were at the heart of the French language policy: a perfect mastery of French was concomitant with exemplary Republican citizenship, to the extent that the law on municipalities of 1855 prohibited public sessions of the city councils (Art. 22).[21] Correlatively, the minutes and other documents remained silent on language mediation during council meetings.

By way of comparing France and Belgium, I will briefly look at language practices in a small number of French cities, towns and municipalities. They belong to two areas: the first one is an industrial one, located south of the

Northern department; it groups three places accommodating Flemish migrants that did not acquire French citizenship; the second one is a rural area, inhabited by Flemish-speaking and bilingual French citizens.

Roubaix (9)

Roubaix was by far the largest city of this group and even of this overview (18,000 inhabitants in 1830, but 124,000 in 1900[22]). The increase was due to massive immigration from Belgium, and more specifically from Flanders. French was the only language used by the administration, in spite of the many issues in which decisions had to be made by the municipality with regard to the Flemings living and working on its territory. As a consequence of this language policy, the administration did not provide translation or interpretation. Also, Belgian councillors were excluded following the law on municipalities of 1884 (councillors had to be French citizens living on the territory of the municipality). In contrast, the cultural and social domains allowed for code-switching, code-mixing and the use of foreign languages, albeit to a limited extent in the written domain and within lower genres such as popular songs or theatre (Declercq 2012). This duality also applies to the two following migrant towns.

Comines France (10)

Comines France is separated from its counterpart Comines Belgique by a bridge over the river Lys. It is a small municipality, inhabited by many Belgian, including Flemish, migrants; as a consequence of this influx, the number of citizens grew from 5,300 in 1830 to 8,000 in 1900.[23] However, this growth and ensuing changed balance between Belgian and French inhabitants did not impact on language use or translation: French has been, since the eighteenth century, the dominant and later on the exclusive language of the council minutes and quite probably also of the oral exchanges (Duvosquel 1973).

Houplines (11)

Houplines is a similar case: it is close to the Belgian border, and its population similarly expanded considerably due to Belgian immigration (from 2,000 in 1830 to 7,800 in 1900[24]). Deliberations of council meetings were monolingual French, while occasional references were made to Belgian inhabitants, mostly named 'étrangers' (strangers), that is, non-citizens. Yet, French administration did not only deprive the latter from language rights, as many small but intriguing decisions make clear. For instance, on 18 November 1885, the council decided to deny a grant to a boy wanting to pursue secondary school at the college of Armentières, the argument being that the boy's father was Belgian. Also, on 10 July 1890, the council decided to distribute meat among the poor at the occasion of the 14 July *Fête nationale*: however, only the 'familles françaises seules' (French families only) could benefit from this charity. On 8 December 1899, help was exclusively provided for French families with infants ('seules les familles françaises').

Bailleul (12)

Bailleul is located on the border of French Flanders, where cultural localism and attachment to ethnic Flanders and its language, as well as the transmission of patrimonial customs and artefacts, were strongly put in the forefront for many centuries. French citizenship did not contradict, however, 'overlapping identities with Belgian West-Flanders' (Baycroft 2004: 196) throughout the nineteenth and twentieth centuries. It paralleled the awareness of a cultural unity across geopolitical borders. This awareness inspired a short-lived cultural movement in favour of the Flemish language, and local cultural bilingualism. However, due to a lack of political support, the latter declined rapidly, giving way to a more vague and disorganized sort of cultural regionalism within the shared nation state. Bailleul is a good example of this evolution. During the nineteenth century, it was a larger municipality inhabited by autochthonous French Flemings (its number of inhabitants increased from approximately 10,000 in 1830 to 13,000 at the end of the century[25]). French was nevertheless the sole language of the minutes of the council meetings between 1881 and 1900 (the only years preserved in the local archives).

Bergues (13)

In spite of its past as a prominent Flemish town, Bergues's official language became French in 1797. Similar to Gravelines in its demography[26] and belonging to the same Nord department as the Southern municipalities, it did not face immigrant population like Roubaix, Comines or Houplines. Council minutes were monolingual French throughout the century.

Gravelines (14)

Gravelines is located at the seaside (the number of its inhabitants grew from 4,200 in 1830 to 6,200 in 1900[27]). The council minutes were monolingual French, as they were in Dunkerque and other coastal towns, all massively Frenchified since their annexation by France in the course of the eighteenth century.

5 Conclusion

The purpose of this chapter was to examine and compare the modalities, functions and evolutions of administrative translation between official French and non-official Flemish in a number of Belgian and French border municipalities. In very general terms, one can say that the fate of Flemish in Belgium and France oscillated between two translatorial regimes: the Belgian one imposing 'institutional monolingualism and translation into the minority languages' (Meylaerts 2011: 750) and the French one imposing 'complete institutional monolingualism and non-translation' (Meylaerts 2011: 747). Looking more closely at Flanders, one needs to distinguish between policies deployed in the official domain at the national, regional and local levels.[28] Indeed, translation and multilingualism being inscribed in laws, there was no doubt a close interaction between central policies and local ones, the latter being inspired by ideologies and practices that were prevalent in national governmental bodies (van Gerwen et al. 2017). In turn, debates in major cities and towns may have helped to put translation on the agenda of the national parliament and government. Conversely, we also see how smaller municipalities developed more specific and adaptive tactics that fitted the internal usages of the representative bodies, the spatial position and transborder relations and probably more factors that need further nuance.

Obviously, depending on the focus that is put on language or translation one is tempted to interpret in more than one way the evolution of language and translation issues in the Flemish context of the nineteenth century. For instance, was the 'slow' 'Flemishification' of the administration due to political resistance, to cultural and social resistance, to the lack of language standardization or to the steering role that French as a language of administration had been given nationally as well as all over Europe? More research and more parameters are needed to answer these questions: the role of prominent agents (e.g. simultaneously active as local councillor and national deputee) and special events[29] and the array of transfer modes accompanying the complex process that has run from monolingual Flemish reports till 1830, to mediated French–Flemish ones throughout the century, back to monolingual Flemish ones (with or without translations in French) during the first decades of the twentieth century.

From a translational point of view, one could suggest, in turn, that institutional translations had a mainly pragmatic function in a first phase, acting as a necessary tool for accessing the laws and the administration. Later on, translation was given cultural and social functions that not only facilitated the transition to administrative bilingualism but also shaped the Flemish language of administration. Paradoxically, towards the end of the century, these functions seem to have become an obstacle for the emancipation of the 'own' language: if translations contribute to national unity, they were also felt as a threat for the equal treatment of the language communities. Why? Was it because the quality of translations left much to be desired? Was it because the idea of translation itself carried too many negative connotations? Was it because the actual bilingualism as accomplished through the existing systematic translation of legislative texts was but a small step from achieving equal rights for the two languages? Was it because nationalism was essentially deemed incompatible with multilingualism? Or was it for some other reason?

Each linear explanation mechanism is simplistic and incomplete: this holds equally for the translational viewpoint. Not only is it likely that different translation beliefs overlapped, there remain undoubtedly more translation features and transfer procedures to be identified and taken into account, not to mention the specific political or social features of each municipality, as this overview has been able to illustrate. Understanding and modelling the varying interwovenness of cultural, social and institutional aspects of translation policies is a major challenge for future histories of translation in Belgium.[30]

Notes

1. I will use the term 'Flemish' to qualify Southern Dutch: it is the term used by most actors in the nineteenth century.
2. A small German-speaking community (less than 1 per cent of the population) lives close to the German border.
3. 'Historians usually study the impact of nation-building through the nationalist gaze. By that I mean that they tend to rely on the discourse of the active brokers of nationalism in government and civil society' (Van Ginderachter 2018: 590).
4. This chapter is part of a larger interdisciplinary project at KU Leuven (Belgium) on the emergence and evolution of translation policies in Belgium (1830–1914). I am grateful to Heleen van Gerwen for her careful language revision.
5. Translation: The use of the languages employed in Belgium is free; it can only be regulated by law and only with regard to acts of public authority and legal matters.
6. Translation: The laws will be published in the *Bulletin officiel*, immediately after their promulgation, with a Flemish or German translation for the municipalities where these languages are spoken; the French text only is official.

7 That translation direction extended to the non-official domains of science, religion, economy and literature, be it that the reverse direction (Flemish–French) gained a foothold during the first decades after independence (D'hulst and Van Gerwen 2018).
8 On emerging representative democracy in the nineteenth century, see a.o. Ankersmit (1997).
9 I am grateful to Tim Piceu for his generous assistance in drawing this map.
10 See full references in the bibliography. It should be noted that the municipal archives often hold incomplete files of the minutes and that local newspapers also record some of the debates.
11 Source: http://www.lokstat.ugent.be/vt1900_alfabetisme.php?key=407&naam=Brugge. Accessed on 4 September 2018.
12 Regulations for schools, the police, funerals or the fire brigade were bilingual.
13 Volapük (meaning: world language) is an artificial (or constructed language) created in Germany in the late 1870s with the purpose of replacing national languages. It is a predecessor of Esperanto.
14 Source: http://www.lokstat.ugent.be/vt1900_gemeenten1.php?key=1988&naam=Oostende. Accessed on 4 September 2018.
15 Source: http://www.lokstat.ugent.be/vt1900_nationaliteit.php?key=1368&naam=. Accessed 4 September 2018. For an initial account of language use, see XX.
16 Source: http://www.lokstat.ugent.be/vt1900_alfabetisme.php?key=2143&naam=Poperinge. Accessed on 4 September 2018.
17 Source: http://www.lokstat.ugent.be/vt1900_alfabetisme.php?key=1705&naam=Menen. Accessed on 8 September 2018.
18 Source: http://www.lokstat.ugent.be/vt1900_alfabetisme.php?key=1083&naam=Helkijn. Accessed on 4 September 2018.
19 Source: http://www.lokstat.ugent.be/vt1900_alfabetisme.php?key=508&naam=Comines. Accessed on 4 September 2018.
20 Source: http://www.lokstat.ugent.be/vt1900_alfabetisme.php?key=1824&naam=Mouscron. Accessed on 4 September 2018.
21 Among the arguments advanced is the mastery of the language: '[Certains] commettraient des fautes de langage ou sortiraient des bornes de la moderation' (Taillefer 1868: 248). Translation: Certain councillors would commit language errors or would speak immoderately. The sessions became public in 1884 (Art. 54 of the new law on municipalities of 5 April 1884). This contrasts with the more lenient view towards correctness of French and Flemish as used in Belgian council meetings.
22 Source: http://cassini.ehess.fr/cassini/fr/html/fiche.php?select_resultat=29736. Accessed on 4 September 2018. In 1866, almost 50 per cent of the population was Belgian, of which the majority was monolingual Flemish (Declercq et al. 2009).

23 Source: http://cassini.ehess.fr/cassini/fr/html/fiche.php?select_resultat=10030. Accessed on 4 September 2018.
24 Source: http://cassini.ehess.fr/cassini/fr/html/fiche.php?select_resultat=17327. Accessed on 4 September 2018.
25 Source: http://cassini.ehess.fr/cassini/fr/html/fiche.php?select_resultat=2412. Accessed on 4 September 2018.
26 Source: http://cassini.ehess.fr/cassini/fr/html/fiche.php?select_resultat=3751. Accessed on 4 September 2018.
27 Source: http://cassini.ehess.fr/cassini/fr/html/fiche.php?select_resultat=16094. Accessed on 4 September 2018.
28 It would be interesting to enquire whether the intense migration flows of Flemish workers to industrial Wallonia in the nineteenth and early twentieth centuries have led to an increase of multilingualism and translation in the municipal administrations of the steelmaking and coalmining areas.
29 For example, 11 July commemorations, notably in 1902 and 1912, of the famous Battle of the Golden Spurs (1302), by then a symbol of the struggle for resistance against foreign rule and cultural domestication of Flanders.
30 It is beyond the scope of this chapter to look for parallels with other time-space settings. However, such parallels, as conspicuous in both historical (Koskinen in this volume) and contemporary formal meetings (Koskela et al. 2017), should help to lay bare some of the unknown features of translatorial customs or norms inscribed in long-term interlingual exchanges by non-professionals (see also the Introduction to this volume).

References

Primary sources

Brugge (B): Stadsarchief, Bulletin Communal/Gemeenteblad, https://www.archiefbankbrugge.be, 1815–1900 (Local government bulletin of Bruges, 1815–1890)
Comines (B): Hôtel de ville de Ploegsteert, Registre des délibérations du Conseil communal de Comines, 1868–1914 (Register of deliberations of the municipal council of Comines, 1868–1914)
Helkijn (B): Rijksarchief Kortrijk, Notulen van de Gemeenteraad van Helkijn, 1828–1921 (Minutes of the municipal council of Helkijn, 1828–1921)
Kortrijk (B): Modern stadsarchief, Verslagen van de Gemeenteraad, 1815–1914 (Minutes of the city council of Kortrijk, 1815–1914)
Menen (B): Stadsarchief Menen, Notulen van de Gemeenteraad van Menen, 1821–1932 (Minutes of the town council of Menin, 1821–1932)

Mouscron: Archives de la ville de Mouscron, Registre aux délibérations du conseil communal, 1818–1895 (Register of deliberations of the municipal council of Mouscron, 1818–1895)

Oostende (B): Archief van de stad Oostende, Bulletin communal, 1869–1913 (Local government bulletin of Ostend, 1869–1913)

Poperinge (B): Archieven van de stad Poperinge, Notulen Gemeenteraad, 1831–1919 (Minutes of the town council of Poperinge, 1831–1919)

Bailleul (F): Mairie de Bailleul, Délibérations du Conseil municipal de Bailleul, 1881–1900 (Deliberations of the municipal council of Bailleul, 1881–1900)

Bergues (F): Mairie de Bergues, Délibérations du conseil municipal de Bergues, 1839–1914 (Deliberations of the municipal council of Bergues, 1939–1914)

Comines (F): Maison du patrimoine de Comines, Registre des délibérations du conseil municipal, 1854–1909 (Register of the deliberations of the municipal council of Comines, 1854–1909)

Gravelines (F): Archives municipales, Fonds moderne, Délibérations du Conseil municipal, 1811–1865 (Deliberations of the municipal council of Gravelines, 1811–1865)

Houplines (F): Centre culturel Jean-Charles Bringuez, Registre des délibérations du Conseil municipal de Houplines, 1885–1914 (Deliberations of the municipal council of Houplines, 1885–1914)

Roubaix (F): Archives communales de Roubaix, Délibérations du Conseil Municipal, Bibliothèque numérique de Roubaix, https://www.bn-r.fr/, 1881–1914 (Deliberations of the city council of Roubaix, 1881–1914)

Secondary sources

Ankersmit, F. (1997), *Macht door representatie. Exploraties III. Politieke filosofie*, Kapellen: Kampen.

Baycroft, T. (2004), *Culture, Identity and Nationalism: French Flanders in the Nineteenth and Twentieth Centuries*, Woodbridge: The Boydell Press.

Certeau, M. de. (1984/1974), *The Practice of Everyday Life*, Berkeley: University of California Press.

Clement, J. (2003), *Taalvrijheid, bestuurstaal en minderheidsrechten. Het Belgisch model: een constitutionele zoektocht naar de oorsprong van het territorialiteitsbeginsel en de minderheidsrechten in de bestuurstaalwetgeving*, Antwerpen: Intersententia.

Darquennes, J. (2014), 'Macrosociolinguïstisch onderzoek naar historische taalminderheden in tijden van globalisering – pleidooi voor een vernieuwing van binnenuit', *Us Wurk – Tydskrift foar Frysistiek*, 63 (1/2): 73–92.

Declercq, E. (2012), *Migrants belges en France. Une histoire revisitée à travers la chanson populaire (1870–1914)*, Gent: Academia Press.

Declercq, E., M. Depaepe, L. D'hulst, W. Kusters, S. Vanden Borre and T. Verschaffel (2009), 'Belgische migratie naar Noord-Frankrijk (1850–1914): interculturele identiteiten in grensregio's', *De Franse Nederlanden / Les Pays-Bas français. Jaarboek 2009*, 109–24, Rekkem: Ons Erfdeel.

D'hulst, L. and Schreiber M. (2014), 'Vers une historiographie des politiques des traductions en Belgique durant la période française', *Target*, 26 (1): 3–32.

D'hulst, L. and van Gerwen, H. (2018), 'Translation Space in Nineteenth-Century Belgium: Rethinking Translation and Transfer Directions', *Perspectives: Studies in Translatology*, 26 (4): 495–508.

Duvosquel, J.-M. (1973), 'L'emploi des langues à Comines et Warneton du Moyen Âge à nos jours', *Mémoires de la Société d'histoire de Comines-Warneton et de la région*, 3: 11–62.

Koskela, M., K. Koskinen and N. Pilke (2017), 'Bilingual Formal Meeting as a Context of Translatoriality', *Target* 29 (3): 464–85.

Loi communale du 30 mars 1836. [s.d.], Gand: C. Annoot-Braeckman.

Meylaerts, R. (2011), 'Translational Justice in a Multilingual World: An Overview of Translational Regimes', *Meta*, 56 (4): 743–57.

Nouws, B. and Meylaerts R. (2018), 'La nécessité des Traductions: Translating Legislation in a Young Parliamentary Regime: The Case of Belgium (1830–1895)', *International Journal of the Sociology of Language*, 251: 111–30.

Pietikäinen, S. and Kelly-Holmes, H. (2013), 'Multilingualism and the Periphery', in S. Pietikäinen and H. Kelly-Holmes (eds), *Multilingualism and the Periphery*, 1–16, Oxford: Oxford University Press.

Ryckeboer, H. (1997), *Het Nederlands in Noord-Frankrijk. Sociolinguïstische, dialectologische en contactlinguïstische aspecten*, Gent: Vakgroep Nederlandse Taalkunde.

Soleil, S. (2017) 'L'emploi de la langue française et des néologismes dans les textes juridiques étrangers du XIXe siècle', *Parallèles*, 29 (1): 90–106.

Schreiber, M. (2016), 'Covert Multilingualism: The Case of the Translation Policy in France and Belgium during the French Revolution and the Napoleonic Era', *Across Languages and Cultures*, 17: 123–36.

Taillefer, J.-B.-L. (1868), *Commentaire de la loi du 5 mai 1855 [...] sur l'organisation municipale*, Paris: A. Durand et Pedone Lauriel.

Vandenbussche, W. (2004), 'Triglossia and Pragmatic Variety Choice in Nineteenth-Century Bruges: A Case Study in Historical Sociolinguistics', *Journal of Historical Pragmatics*, 5 (1): 27–47.

Van Gerwen, H., Bourguignon, M. and Nouws, B. (2017), 'Translating Law in 19th-Century Belgium: Criticisms of Official Translations of Laws and Decrees', *Tilburg Law Review* 22 (1–2): 99–137.

Van Ginderachter, M. (2018), 'How to Gauge Banal Nationalism and National Indifference in the Past: Proletarian Tweets in Belgium's Belle époque', *Nations and Nationalism* 24 (3): 579–93.

Van Goethem, H. (1990), *De taaltoestanden in het Vlaams-Belgisch gerecht, 1795–1935*, Brussel: Paleis der Academiën.

Vanhecke, E. (2004), 'Taalkeuze in Vlaamse stadskanselarijen in de negentiende eeuw', *Taal & Tongval*, 56: 48–64.

Vanhecke, E. and de Groof, J. (2007), 'New Data on Language Policy and Language Choice in 19th-Century Flemish City Administrations', in S. Elspaß et al. (eds), *Germanic Language Histories 'from Below' (1700–2000)*, 449–69, Berlin/New York: Walter de Gruyter.

Willemyns, R. and Daniëls, W. (2003), *Het verhaal van het Vlaams. De geschiedenis van het Nederlands in de Zuidelijke Nederlanden*, Antwerpen: Standaard Uitgeverij/Utrecht: Het Spectrum.

Wils, L. (2001), *Waarom Vlaanderen Nederlands spreekt*, Leuven: Davidsfonds.

Wils, L. (2008), 'Het officiële taalgebruik in Vlaanderen in de negentiende eeuw', *Wetenschappelijke tijdingen*, LXVII (2): 115–27.

Witte, E. and van Velthoven, H. (1998), *Strijden om taal. De Belgische taalkwestie in historisch perspectief*, Brussel: VUBpress.

6

Translating in an emerging language policy: Tampere city council 1875–1887

Kaisa Koskinen

1 Introduction

Research on multilingualism and language policies has established some basic tenets that this chapter builds on. First, the coexistence of more than one language always entails some translatorial movement between languages, creating a translation space (Cronin 2006: 68). This translatorial movement can take the form of institutionalized practices or operate through the micro-decisions made in everyday life (Wolf 2012). Second, whenever we make decisions about how to deal with the multiplicity of languages, we all engage in doing language policy (Spolsky 2004). That is, language policy need not be official or even spelled out; it can also emerge incrementally from practices. Third, language policies always have translational repercussions, whether or not they explicitly aim to ban, control or promote translating or interpreting (Grin 2010; Meylaerts 2013).

The object of this chapter is the gradual process of institutionalization, that is, the process towards an established language policy with its concomitant translation practices, in the context of local governance in nineteenth-century Finland. Following Spolsky (2004: 39), this chapter is based on the understanding that language policy is realized at three levels: in addition to language planning and regulations, it also plays out through language ideologies and language attitudes as well as through everyday micro-decisions over language choice. In a way, the most fundamental level, the *sine qua non* of language policy, is that of the everyday micro-level of actual practices: language policy that is not implemented in practice remains a dead letter. The next level is that of language planning, which is most explicitly realized through providing a legislative framework. The outer circle of attitudes and language ideologies forms the cultural and ideological context that frames the other two levels.

This chapter traces how these three levels of language policy and translation interact in one local context of municipal government, the late-nineteenth-century Tampere, Finland. More specifically, I focus on the formative years during and immediately after the new legislation of local governance issued in 1873 led to a reorganization of local institutions everywhere in the Grand-Duchy of Finland. The nexus of my analysis is the gradual development of the language policy of the newly established Tampere city council, starting from its first meeting in 1875 and continuing until 1886 when the language policy issue was settled. The longitudinal aspect has been selected to emphasize the incremental nature of governance practices. Michel Foucault (1978/2007: 108–9; see also Koskinen 2014a) discusses the gradual process of governmentalization, that is, the development of particular governmental apparatuses and the establishment of an ensemble of 'institutions, procedures, analyses and reflections, calculations and tactics' of governing. Here, my aim is to trace the procedures, tactics and calculations related to language and translation policies in the governmentalization of one municipal institution. This aim has been operationalized through a selection of four key moments during the time span in question. The analysis of these 'dense moments' provides a longitudinal case study of the three levels of language policy in action through a cross-examination of three data sets: the minutes of the city council, local media of the time and the relevant legislation.

As across Europe, the nineteenth century was a time of national revival in Finland, and the language issue – that is, advancing the case of Finnish – was a central element of this revival. Administration at both national and municipal level had been almost exclusively Swedish, but new language legislation began to gradually improve the status of Finnish during the latter half of the nineteenth century. This new legal framework and the evolving language attitudes set the background for new language practices in governing institutions. In this political and cultural climate, the new municipal councils in dominantly Finnish-speaking areas such as Tampere became instrumental in developing a more democratic language regime at the local level. For my purposes, the 'carte blanche' situation of the council, as a newly established institution only beginning to sort out its language practices, provides a microcosm in which to observe the emerging and developing relations between language planning, language ideology and translation practices.

The micro-level practices during the first year of the new Tampere council, and their effects on the language planning level, have been studied in close detail earlier (Koskinen 2017, 2019). This chapter takes a more longitudinal approach and also takes stock of media discussions, contrasting the prevailing language ideologies as expressed in local newspapers with the language planning efforts in the council. The chapter unfolds as follows: Section 2 illuminates the context of my data, looking into the characteristics of Tampere and in particular its language situation and the language battle between Finnish and Swedish fought not only at the national level but also in local newspapers which provided a platform for expressing and debating language attitudes at the time. Section 3 introduces the new city council and its linguistic set-up. Section 4 describes my data and methodology. The four dense moments are discussed in Section 5, and the results are then contemplated in Section 6.

2 The context of Tampere

In the 1870s, Tampere – the Manchester of Finland – was a dynamic and rapidly growing industrial centre, and the third biggest town in Finland, in the then autonomous Grand-Duchy of Russia (1809–1917).[1] Between 1870 and 1900 Tampere grew threefold in size and fivefold in terms of inhabitants (Vähäpesola 2009a). The Tammerkoski Rapids that run through the city centre powered the new factories that had been set up on both sides. The employment opportunities provided by these factories attracted masses of young Finnish-speaking workers from the surrounding countryside. Tampere had always been dominantly Finnish-speaking, but the industry-led urbanization process further increased the number of Finnish-speakers.[2] In 1880, 7.4 per cent of the inhabitants were Swedish-speaking, and the percentage went further down to 5.6 per cent in 1900 (Vähäpesola 2009b). The linguistic set-up in the demographics of Tampere included a handful of languages, but the numbers for any other languages, including Russian (twenty-four inhabitants in 1880; Koskinen 2014b), were tiny – approximately 1 per cent of the total population. In spite of its small size, foreigners were an economically and culturally important group, as many of the factory owners, top management and skilled engineers were of foreign origin (mainly German-speakers), and Russian merchants contributed to the bustling economy.

Under Russian rule, the dominance of the Swedish language, and the relative absence of Russian, may appear rather unexpected. But when Tampere (Tammerfors) was first founded in 1779, Finland was under Swedish rule, and Swedish was the language of administration. Finnish, in turn, was the language of the peasantry that had only begun to emerge as a written language, largely via translation activities (Paloposki 2007). When Sweden was forced to hand its easternmost regions over to Russia in 1809, the new rulers allowed the Swedish language to continue to dominate in governance. Russian was never widely spoken among the elite groups of Finland, and the Russian rulers originally had little faith in Finnish as a language of administration nor in the Finns' ability for independent governance and sophisticated cultural life. They feared that banning Swedish would have equalled banning legality and civilization. Still, the new rulers also saw supporting the rise of Finnish as a way of severing the ties with Sweden, and over the century a number of legislative steps to advance the use of Finnish were taken (Engman 2009: 230–3).

During the period under study, sovereign rule was gradually giving way to a more democratic form of governance, and the first forerunners of modern political parties were emerging. In this process, the language issue was a dividing factor. Since the 1840s, language attitudes had become an increasingly heated element in the Fennophile 'Fennoman' movement (in the 1890s this radicalization of attitudes led to a split between more radical/liberal and more conservative Fennomans, with repercussions to the political balance because of the loss of unity). It had an equally radicalized counterpart, the 'Svecomans', or suecophiles. In line with Romantic nationalist movements sweeping across Europe, the local Fennomans equated the use of Finnish with patriotism and labelled Swedish as a 'foreign' language. It is not too surprising that many Swedish-speakers felt that their entire identity was at risk. The language issue was, however, divisive also among the Swedish-speakers. Some of them were actually among the most ardent supporters of the case of *Finnish*, and their contributions were essential for the gradual progress of Finnish.

Tampere was recognized as a hotspot of this radicalization. One can identify various reasons for this development. As opposed to the cultural capitals of Turku (Åbo), Helsinki (Helsingfors) or Viipuri (Vyborg), with their old nobility, cultural and educational institutions and cosmopolitan flair, Tampere was a young, bustling city of Finnish-speaking workers. Its rapid growth, technologization and international contacts must have given the inhabitants a forward-looking sense of progress and modernization. The lack of any national or regional governance institutions in Tampere, and its growing cadre of businessmen, most of whom were Finnish-speaking, resulted in a fairly thin layer of Swedish-speaking higher bourgeoisie upper class in Tampere. The layer was also rapidly getting thinner: in the 1870s, at the beginning of the time span studied here, little less than 10 per cent of the Tampere inhabitants belonged to the upper class; in 1890, the figure was less than 1 per cent. At the same time, the bourgeoisie class expanded from 10 to 40 per cent because of the growth of merchants' and artisans' group. By far the biggest group was still the workers: 60 per cent of the inhabitants belonged to this group by 1890 (Vähäpesola 2009c).

Why the case of Finnish would have been felt particularly pressing in Tampere is easy to understand. It is less easy to understand why it led to such heated debates, especially as it is known that many of the few Swedish-speakers were bilingual and supportive of the case of Finnish. The numbers reported earlier indicate that the power balance was rapidly shifting, and the old elite was being challenged by both the growing entrepreneur class and the workers who were getting both more numerous and increasingly restless and empowered by the international workers' movement. This may have felt overwhelming for some, and the language question was both a concrete issue to take stand on and a symbolic battle of status between groups. At the same time, multilingualism, and the translatoriality it brought forth, was a fact of life in Tampere, and foreign languages were viewed favourably in the press. The local and national linguistic duel was fought between the two local languages only. In spite of compelling numbers, for historical reasons Swedish had the upper hand in Tampere: 'Swedish was the language of power, prestige, and upward social movement, while Finnish was the language of the uneducated masses' (Koskinen 2014b: 191).

Another explanatory factor behind the language conflict is the gradual development of party politics in Finland during the late nineteenth century. Before the birth of the first political parties in the modern sense (a short-lived Liberal party in 1880 and the Finnish Labour Party in 1899), the Finnish and Swedish parties were the first incarnation of representative party-like organizations, and this made linguistic and cultural orientation the most relevant division in the early political battles (Rasila 1984:544), probably leading to strategic aggravation of the expressed attitudes on both sides. Newspapers were the developing modern media of the time, and they provided the main forum for political debates, hence also for the language battle (Rasila 1984: 544–5). It follows that they also played an active role in translatorial and language policy action at the level of attitudes and ideologies. Although newspapers also travelled across Finland,[3] media was mainly produced and consumed locally. During the time span under study here, also the local newspaper scene of Tampere kept evolving. *Tampereen Sanomat* ('News form Tampere') had been founded in 1866, with Dr Otto Blåfield and F. E. Jernberg among founders. It was first the only local newspaper, and in spite of being published in Finnish it did not have significant active political leanings until after the other Finnish-language paper *Aamulehti* had been created. It rather operated in an enlightenment spirit and as an official channel for municipal announcements, which were published in both languages (Rasila 1984: 547–8). In the 1879 council elections when language issues were dividing the candidates into two groups for the first time, *Tampereen Sanomat* remained neutral (ibid.: 548).

Aamulehti ('Morning Paper') was founded at the end of 1881, after a year of turmoil both nationally and locally. It was an explicit mouthpiece for Fennophile ideals, and it promoted Christian morals and democratic values, which in practice meant promoting raising the status of Finnish to the same level with Swedish. Again, F. E. Jernberg was among the founders. The editor in chief F. W. Jalander, who was an ardent Fennoman, himself had no Finnish, and his editorials needed to be translated into Finnish by others. Jalander was replaced in 1884 by Kaarle Viljakainen, a young but already experienced editor with a moderate line in the language issue (Rasila 1984: 548–9). *Aamulehti* soon established itself as the main newspaper in the area, a position it still holds today. Its strong political stance in language and nationalist issues led to a counter reaction among Swedish-speakers, and *Tammerfors Aftonblad* ('Evening paper of Tampere') was established in 1882 to support the case of Swedish.

3 The city council

The decree on local government issued in 1873 had established an entirely new governance body, the municipal councils. A reform of the municipal institutions was a central phase in modernizing governance in Finland. As a new municipal actor, the councils sidelined the previous powerhouses of local governance, the magistrates, and also created a new division of labour between the church and the state (e.g. in education and welfare). This shift of power created a momentum for introducing new priorities and new practices of governance.

The city council of Tampere began its first operational year in January 1875. The council elections in 1874 were a step towards representative local democracy, but not a giant leap. Tampere had 6,700 registered inhabitants but only 67 votes were cast (Rasila 1984: 569). Most inhabitants did not even have the right to vote. Those in the service of a patron were not seen to be independent enough to cast their vote until after 1917 (Rasila 1984: 582–4). Of the twenty-one new councilmen (independent women were allowed to vote but not to run for office), Dr Otto Blåfield got the most votes and was elected the first chairman. He was to become instrumental in establishing bilingual practices in city government (Koskinen 2017: 47).

Through the linguistic set-up of the first council, the previously entirely Swedish-speaking local government now saw a rise in Finnish-speaking councilmen (Koskinen 2017: 47). The council thus needed to overcome linguistic and cultural barriers in its own meetings. As the council began its work, a further barrier was soon found to exist between the at least moderately pro-Finnish council and the adamantly Swedish-speaking magistrate run by the mayor. The most problematic linguistic barrier was still the one between the Swedish administration and the Finnish population. From the outset, the newly elected Finnish-speaking councilmen became operational in the gradual democratizing of local governance, and developing a more democratic language regime was an essential element of it.

4 Data and method

In this chapter, the interplay of the three levels of language policy will be charted through an analysis of four 'dense' points where the plot thickens, combining three main sets of data: council minutes, national legislation and debates in the local newspapers. The council as an institutional actor is the nexus of the analysis. Three of the dense points have been identified through looking into the moments when the new city council first debated and established its language policy (and its translation practices) in 1875, and later revised and reassessed this policy in 1878 and in 1886. The general climate of language attitudes will be charted through analysing the debates in three local newspapers, *Tampereen Sanomat* (TS; Finnish), *Aamulehti* (AL; Finnish) and *Tammerfors Aftonblad* (TA; Swedish) around the dense points identified through other data sets as described earlier. One dense point, year 1881, has been selected also because of its media relevance. During that council election year, heated debates over 'the language issue' raged. At the end of that year *Aamulehti* was established specifically to support the cause of Finnish, and this in turn led to the founding of *Tammerfors Aftonblad* in 1882 to support Swedish.

Since language policies are also governed by national legislation, and the council is therefore not entirely free in its language choices, the changing jurisdiction is another relevant factor, and two dense points were also brought on because of the changing legal context (1875, 1881). The full timeline of the

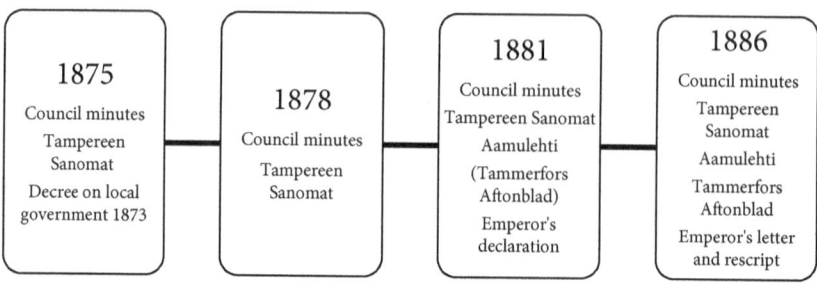

Figure 6.1 Timeline and data sets of the dense points.

dense points, and the data sets for each, is shown in Figure 6.1. All translations from any of these data sets are mine.

Data has been collected from three sources:

1. The minutes of the council have been stored in the Tampere City Archive where they are available on microfilm.
2. The relevant legislation has mainly been downloaded from an open source depository (https://fi.wikisource.org/wiki/Luokka:Kielilainsäädäntö).
3. Newspapers were searched in the national open-access digital archive (https://digi.kansalliskirjasto.fi/sanomalehti/).

In sourcing the minutes, I have relied on both historical research (Rasila 1984) and my own previous research on the emerging translation practice and translation policy (Koskinen 2017, 2019). This has allowed me to economize archive work to the minutes of particular years and also of particular meetings, but this targeted approach may of course have also led to overlooking other potential dense points. Legislation frames the project at both ends. The new degree on local government (*Kunnallisasetus* 1873) was the motor for the process as it set the scene for the development of the new institution, thus also creating an opening for reforming the municipal language practices. At the other end of the continuum, new regulations can be seen to close this window of local opportunities as an imperial letter of 1886 decreed Finnish to have an equal status with Swedish, and an additional notice given in 1887 set new ground rules for choosing between different language options by ordering that municipal authorities must use the language of the council minutes – in the case of Tampere, Finnish. Legal data has not been sourced in any open-ended manner; the relevant acts and degrees have been hand-picked from the database according to prior knowledge and previous historical research.

Newspaper material is brought in to investigate how the council decisions and practices were rendered and commented on in the press and how the attitudes towards language issues and translation evolved. Searching the database was executed in two steps: first, in an open-ended and data-driven manner, with a keyword combination (in Finnish) of 'Tampere', 'languages' and 'council' to identify potential dense points (this led to selecting year 1881 as a dense point) and then with more direct searches to the issues of the three above-mentioned newspapers published before and after relevant dates identified from other data sets. Notably, the first search was executed in Finnish only, which introduces a bias into the research design, giving primacy to the Finnish newspapers, but it needs to be borne in mind that the first Swedish paper in Tampere was only established in 1882 and there is no local Swedish newspaper data prior to that. For 1886 a separate search with a keyword in Swedish ('språk', language) was conducted.

5 Dense points

5.1 Establishing the policy (1875)

In January 1875, the new council met for the first time. The minutes of the first meeting and from the entire first year of operation have been analyzed before from the perspective of translatorial action (Koskinen 2017). I summarize these findings here. Since the councils were a new institution, and prior administration had been Swedish-only, there was no routine and no practices in place to maintain bilingual procedures. Language and translation issues were thus among the first items on the list. In the first meeting on 20 January (§ 4) it was at Chairman Blåfield's suggestion decided that all councilmen can use either Swedish or Finnish, but that if they are not able to express themselves in both languages (i.e. to self-interpret), interpreting will be provided by volunteer members of the council. This practice clearly supported bilingual delivery.

It was further decided that the minutes be kept in Swedish only but that decisions will be written in both Swedish and Finnish (i.e. translated into Finnish by Secretary Jernberg who was also responsible for drafting the minutes in Swedish). This limited translation was considered the best combination of 'economy and justice'. The reference to justice is noteworthy as it signals a language ideological move away from (German) Romantic nationalism and towards the rising (Anglo-Saxon) social radicalism and consequently towards seeing language less as a cultural question than as a pressing social issue (Engman 1995: 187). In other words, the argument for translation is not based on using Finnish because of being in Finland in the spirit of a one nation, one language ideology, but on using Finnish so that the Finnish-speaking lower-class majority can understand and participate. To summarize, the first policy was supportive of bilingual practices, relying on self-translation and volunteer interpreting. In a combination of pragmatism and idealism, the councilmen accepted the existing difficulty of pushing Finnish to a prominent position, but many of them were willing to take personal initiative to support its entry into this domain of use by volunteering to translator and interpreter roles (Koskinen 2017).

Tampereen Sanomat reported the decisions without comment (e.g. TS 26.1.1875). This pragmatic ideology of rehearsing the language to increase its expressive force and repertoire was, however, clearly shared by the paper. For example, in a lengthy commentary titled 'On Finnish protocols in district courts?' the readers were encouraged to exercise their right to demand documents in Finnish in accordance to the language act of 1863:

> Luulemme jokaisen järki-ihmisen ymmärtävän, että tärkeän kielimuutoksen menestys riippuu tykkänään siitä, että jokainen oikeutta käyvä asetuksen määräämäin rajain sisällä vaatii suomenkielisiä protokollia – sillä ainoastaan sen kautta suomenkielisiä protokollia todellakin ilmestyy, ainoastaan sen kautta tuomarit harjaantuvat kielemme käyttämiseen ja ainoastaan sen kautta vihdoin itse kielikin taipuu ja muodostuu mukavaksi välikappaleeksi. (TS 23.2.1875)[4]

This issue of language use in juridical processes comes up repeatedly in *Tampereen Sanomat*. The language decree issued in 1863 had allowed for a twenty years' transition period to set up a system of also producing official documentation in Finnish. The transition period was needed, as in the mid-nineteenth-century Finnish was still quite underdeveloped, and the 1870s is often considered as a watershed period in the path to modern Finnish (Engman 1995: 188). In 1875 the end of this period was drawing closer, and institutional pressure to conform to the new requirements was increasing. Media attention contributed to mounting expectations. In an opinion piece, author L–ko points to the translatorial nature of the *Swedish* protocols in an ironic style and with three exclamation marks:

> Asian oudon mielestä, luulisi olevan päivää selvemmän, näet kuin on suomalainen lautakunta, suomenkielellä tutkitaan todistajat samaa kieltä – enimmästi – puhuvat riita kumpanit [sic] j.e.p., niis oudon mielestä on vaikeaa että kääntää pöytäkirjalle asian toiselle kielelle. Vaan itse hyvät herrat asian parhaiten tietävät!!! (TS 6.10. 1874)[5]

Announcements are an interesting subgenre of newspapers, and official announcements are one window to daily language practices. Since *Tampereen*

Sanomat was in 1875 the only local newspaper, it was also the official channel for municipal institutional communications, and in this year these were published bilingually. Among these were invitations to council meetings, always in both Finnish and Swedish. This was nicely in line with the explicit language policy and translation decisions made in the council. The announcements of the public readings of the previous meeting's minutes at the court hall, in turn, were published only in Finnish which indicates that the reading may also have taken place only in Finnish, in sight translation mode as the minutes were written in Swedish.

A more unexpected finding from the point of view of established language policy was the micro-cracks in the image of the magistrate, which has been pictured as the bastion of Swedish language in the municipal scene both by contemporaries and in history books. I was therefore surprised to find in the issue of 20 April 1875, for example, four announcements officially signed by Mayor Procopé (known as an ardent defender of Swedish) and published only in Finnish, whereas only one announcement was published in Swedish. One of the announcements in Finnish only was furthermore directed at the councilmen, who themselves had agreed on a bilingual policy that foregrounded Swedish over Finnish, and who published their own announcements bilingually.

5.2 Institutionalization of Finnish (1878)

The council had started its operations in 1875 in a consensus-seeking atmosphere, but tensions soon began to rise both nationally and locally. On 9 January 1878 the council reopened its decision from 1875 at the initiative of Gustav Selin, a local businessman and a fierce Fennoman (Koskinen 2019). The new decision (§ 12) overturned the balance of the two languages 'until otherwise perhaps ordered': Finnish now became the language of the minutes, and only decisions were to be translated into Swedish. The minutes of 9 January follow this new policy, being kept in Finnish. *Tampereen Sanomat* duly reports this as all other decisions in the meeting (TS 22.1.1878), but the matter is stated briefly and without commentary.

From some other content in the paper one can see that its language policy was changing in pace with the council. In 1875, *Tampereen Sanomat* had adopted the policy of bilingual announcements. Now it has shifted its policy back towards Finnish only, and issued an editorial statement (signed U.T.) that went in line with the new council policy and was probably affected by it:

> Kumpika kieli, suomi vai ruotsi on Tampereella yleisempi? Suomi, sillä umpiruotsalaisia on vaan kymmenkunta. Kummalla kielellä olisivat kuulutukset

ja ilmoitukset julkaistavat Tamp- S:issa? Tietysti ainoastaan suomeksi; yksityiset tehkööt kuitenkin niin kuin tahtovat, mutta kaupungin yleiset kuulutukset ainoastaan suomeksi.[6]

It is noteworthy that the difference between public and private announcements, that is, institutional and non-institutional communication, was clearly demarcated, and a different policy line was proposed for each. To facilitate the favoured policy, the paper also adopted practical measures: in the previous issue the paper offered translation services for those who needed help in providing their announcements in Finnish.

The final sentence of the piece is explicitly conciliatory: '*Tätä ei ole kirjoitettu kielikiistan halusta*' (This has not been written to provoke the language strife). The paper, still the only one in town and also tied to its role as the official information channel, may have wanted to emphasize its peacefulness, but it also seems clear that the language attitudes had become more radical. The following provocative opinion piece was published with an innocent-looking title 'Proposal':

> Yksinkertaisin ja helpoin tapa maalin saavuttamisessa olisi kieltää kaikkia, jotka oleksivat kaupungissa ja sen lähistöllä puhumasta ruotsia ja lukemasta mitään tällä kielellä, vaan se olisi kohtuutonta suurta ihmispaljoutta vastaan ...] Mutta kun seurakunnalla on vapaus kieltää vähemmän tunnettujen henkilöiden kuntaan tulemasta, ehdottaisimme että seurakunta tästälähin kieltäisi ottamasta sellaisia henkilöitä, jotka ainoastaan puhuvat ruotsia. Useita vuosia kuluisi ... vaan sen kautta loppuisi kielikiista ja suomalainen asia edistyisi; eikä myöskään sellaisesta päätöksestä muitaakaan vieraita kieliä puhuvain henkilöiden harrastukset tulisi loukatuiksi. (TS 2.4.1878, no 13)[7]

The tone of the text is reminiscent of today's social media discussions on migration, with one significant difference: the writers of this text wanted to make explicitly clear that they did not object to any other foreign languages and they had no issue with other people coming in. It was only Swedish that was seen as threatening. In Section 5.1, I mentioned the changing ideology from nationalistic to social argumentation in the council a few years earlier. This kind of discourse is a reminder that different ideologies can coexist, and the same language attitude – and language policy – may be a result of different paths of reasoning.

5.3 Turmoil (1881)

In 1878 the pressure was already mounting in the language issue. Three years later the tensions were even higher, both at national level and in Tampere. In early 1881, one nexus of the language debates was the municipal chamber of finance, a new institution created in 1873 in the same degree as city councils but placed under the auspices of the magistrate's office. Officially, it had minimal independent powers; in practice, it became the executive committee of the council (Rasila 1984: 443). In Tampere, its position between the increasingly Finnish-speaking council and the Swedish-speaking magistrate put the chamber of finance's language policy to the spotlight. On 5 February 1881, *Tampereen Sanomat* took an active language political role in pushing its desired solution in advance to it being taken up in the next council meeting. The close connections between the paper and some of the councilmen were always known, but the council issues and language decisions had earlier been reported neutrally and only after meetings, whereas the more fervent language attitudes were expressed in other texts. This time the paper anticipated the upcoming council meeting of 9 February, when the item of the chamber of finance's language of communication with the council was to be on the agenda. The paper provided background and rationale, seeing the development as a logical continuation from the council decision made in 1878 and evoked the idea of officials gaining practice in writing in Finnish as the transition period set in the 1863 language act was coming to an end (TS 5.2.1881).

The council meeting was not, in spite of the moral support from *Tampereen Sanomat*, smooth sailing. Gustaf Selin once again acted as the initiator, proposing that Finnish should be made the official language of the chamber of finance. The case was debated, but after the vote (11–18), the council cautiously decided that it was not clear whether it had jurisdiction over the matter, and that it would only express a recommendation. After the meeting (TS 12.2.1881) the paper published a clearly upset report on the 'lengthy quarrel', painting Reverend Tallqvist as the villain of the story, both for raising dubious legal aspects to begin with and for doing this 'naturally only in Swedish'. Jernberg, in turn, was pictured as an avid advocate of the cause of Finnish.

Attitudes became increasingly divided in May 1881, when the seventy-fifth birthday of Johan Vilhelm Snellman was celebrated across the country (Rasila 1984: 548). Snellman was a Swedish-speaking statesman, professor, publisher and language activist, who had been influential in the language strife. In his numerous publications (in Swedish) he had laid the ground for the Finnish nation and forwarded the case of Finnish. In 1881, his birthday offered a perfect opportunity for Fennomans to push their agenda forward. *Tampereen Sanomat* published a long text that not only reported the festivities but also participated in building social tension against the ruling class, pitching it against the Finnish-speaking '7/8 of the population' (TS. 25.5.1881). It started by commenting how for the first thirty-five years of the Grand-Duchy the officials had 'been able to sleep soundly after dinner, to sit their evenings playing cards and drinking up their hot toddies while the priests made sure that the jolly peasants were given an odd prayer book for consolation'. As teetotalism was high on the political agenda, and playing cards was considered sinful by many, the depiction clearly aimed to discredit the Swedish-speaking governors. The mention of the odd prayer book in the citation refers to a severe lack of books in Finnish in the first half of the nineteenth century, and the fact that the available reading material had mostly consisted of religious materials, whereas 'on natural sciences only one booklet' was available. To remind the readers of how bad the situation had been, the text then moved to the issue of official languages and to complaining how officials of all ranks used to be Swedish-speaking, and how they had required all paperwork to be in Swedish.

In May the legal context changed. On 9 May 1881 the new emperor Alexander III issued a declaration concerning the institutional language use in courts and in governance, supporting the case of Finnish. On 28 May 1881 (and later again in 7 January 1882) it was published in *Tampereen Sanomat* in full. The manifesto reinforced the 1863 decree and anticipated the end of the transition period by emphasizing that the courts and governing institutions have the power to issue documents in Finnish if that was the language first used by the person who first raised the issue even without explicitly being asked to do so. The practical difficulties potentially created by this policy of using a less than fully developed language of institutional communication were acknowledged by adding the proviso that when an ad hoc word was resorted to and the word in Finnish was not widely known, the intended meaning was to be given by a Swedish expression in brackets.

Rising awareness of linguistic rights among Finns created tensions and led to a de facto two party system also at the local level, as politically active men became organized around either the Finnish or the Swedish language (Rasila 1984: 570). It turned out, however, that voters were less polemical than the public debates might lead us to believe, and the two nominees elected with the highest number of votes in 1881 (senior councilmen Frans Sumelius and Otto Blåfield) were both listed as candidates on both sides. All in all, the election was a triumph for the Finnish side: from the ten seats that were filled (each year one-third of the seats was open for re-election), five were secured by the Fennoman side; two more went to Blåfield and Sumelius who were favourable to the cause, and the Swedish party only got three seats (ibid.).

Towards the end of the year increasingly heated discussions led to two new newspaper projects. In January 1882 the first issue of *Aamulehti* was published. Rasila (1984: 547) argues that it was founded because many Fennomans felt that *Tampereen Sanomat* lacked language political edge. *Aamulehti* was expected to be more radical in its approach. The first issue (AL 4.1.1882) reports that a complaint had already been filed against the new paper for Fennophile agitation. The paper denied the allegation, arguing that this could not be the case as half of the journalistic staff had previously worked in 'the patriotic *Tampereen Sanomat*'. A likely scenario is that these journalists were among those who felt the policy line adopted by *Tampereen Sanomat* was too moderate.

The aftermath of year 1881 in general, and the founding of *Aamulehti* in particular, also led to the establishment of a Swedish-speaking counterforce, *Tammerfors Aftonblad* later in 1882. It functioned as a symbol of the re-enforced Swedish identity of a small minority surrounded by a (locally) major language that was gaining prominence at a time when the situation where the minority made the decisions on behalf of the majority (Lönnroth 2009: 125) was becoming increasingly untenable. In the inaugural issue (TA 3.6.1882) the mission of the new paper was described as serving the needs of those who do not read Finnish fluently (implying the widespread bilinguality of the intended readership), and the language policy line was defined as 'impartial' and aiming to avoid 'the unfortunate newspaper polemics' of the Finnish-speaking press, 'which most of the reading public consider upsetting rather than constructive'. This self-proclaimed non-partisan voice of reason was repeated in numerous issues of the paper where Fennoman positions were reported in reproaching tones that reflected an assumed moral high ground. This attitude no doubt aggravated the conflict. Lönnroth's interpretation of the policy line is more positive; he sees it an indication of tolerant attitudes among Swedish-speakers (2009: 145–7; cf. 163). Indeed, apparently tolerant attitudes towards the Finnish language were also given space in the paper, but also paternalism is explicit. The lead article portrays the Finnish peasant as a noble savage, and identifies the Finns' poor skills in foreign languages as the root cause for language issues in governance (TA 30.6.1882).

5.4 Final Challenge (1886)

Year 1881 had been a watershed in the language strife, both in terms of sharpening attitudes and in terms of media visibility. The new outlets on both sides of the language barrier provided new opportunities for debates and public commentary. A further complication came from the increased efforts of

Russification towards the end of the 1880s, with intensified efforts in promoting the Russian language. Success was meagre. In practice the effort mainly led to favouring Finnish over Swedish. A new decree reinforcing the use of Finnish in courts and offices was issued. The transition period set in the 1860s had come to an end, and from the beginning of 1882 onwards, newly appointed officials had to master both Swedish and Finnish. One might have also expected to find the local language policy in Tampere settling for a harmonious coexistence of the two languages. In practice, things went in the opposite direction. In May 1882 the council non-ceremonially simply dropped the Swedish translations of decisions in the minutes.

Tensions that had developed in 1881 were also kindled in the media. It seems clear that the founding of two new newspapers, one on both sides of the strife, hardened attitudes and created media bubbles reminiscent of today's social media, allowing each side to develop a sense of right-mindedness and painting the other side in negative colours. An interesting detail is the label 'vikings' in the media data used to refer to Svecomans. A search with (*viikinki* OR *viking*) reveals that this label was first used in *Aamulehti* in 1882. In total, there are 101 hits in the three newspapers across the period under study (only a couple of times referring to the actual Viking times, and once to a ship named *Viking*). Throughout this time, the usage in Finnish papers has clear negative connotations. The hits in *Tammerfors Aftonblad*, however, reveal an interesting pattern: they first emerge in upset recounts of what has been said elsewhere but towards the end of the period begin to be used in a fairly neutral way to indicate identity. The label was not *Aamulehti*'s own innovation though, and its origin is on a racially motivated nationalistic and radical movement inside the Svecomans, centred around the journal *Vikingar* (1870–4). In other words, the original connotations were definitely meant to be positive. The Tampere use patterns seem to deviate from the capital-centred discourse in ways that would merit an analysis in itself. The main observation for our current purposes is in the ways in which also this label was used to promote antagonistic attitudes on both sides.

The community around *Tammerfors Aftonblad* and the founding of a 'conversation club' for Swedish-speakers in Tampere in 1885 (following the establishment of a similar club for Finns in 1882) seem to have given a new sense of momentum for the Tampere Svecomans, and in 1886 the issue of council languages was revisited. In March, councilman Mörtengren raised the issue of returning to translating decisions and voting proposals into Swedish. The item was tabled (minutes 3.3.1886, § 63), but the council returned to it in its next meeting in April. Referring back to the decision on 1878 that had never been explicitly overturned, Mörtengren then demanded a return to a legal state of affairs (minutes 7.4.1886, § 85). The council continued discussion in its meeting in May. *Tampereen Sanomat* reported the council debate in detail, foregrounding the role Mr Jernberg and citing his arguments of the changed legal situation (after the decree of 1883) at length. Of interest here is also Jernberg's interpretation that since the decree talks about 'language', and not 'languages', returning to bilingualism is out of the question (TS 22.5.1886).

I had earlier also gone through the council correspondence during 1875 and found that while the council wanted to actively promote Finnish, the inhabitants who wanted to advance their case in the municipal administration expected Swedish to help their case, and the great majority of the incoming correspondence was drafted in Swedish. In 1886, the language attitudes had changed, and the majority of the letters were now in Finnish, but approximately one-third was still in Swedish. An interesting detail is that when Otto Blåfield approached the council in his town doctor capacity, in 1886 he did so in Swedish, whereas in 1875 he had been instrumental in establishing Finnish as a language of governance, also through his own language choices. The ideology of bilingualism that he had consistently forwarded had helped push Finnish forward, but it was in 1886 a minority position, as local governance and language attitudes were moving towards monolingualism.

After discussion, debate and preparatory work, the council voted for legalizing the current practice, and so Swedish was voted out from the protocols, although it was still used orally. Throughout the lengthy decision process, *Tampereen Sanomat* and *Tammerfors Aftonblad* took an active part. *Tampereen Sanomat* argued for the Finnishness of Tampere and painted the suggestion of also adding Swedish as unreasonable (TS 17.4.1886). *Tammerfors Aftonblad*, in contrast, saw it as a sensible and pragmatic practice that is 'so economical and so just' that is should have been accepted without any further ado (TA 12.3.1886). *Tammerfors Aftonblad* also argued that the few monolingual Swedish-speakers in Tampere were 'surely the ones in whose pockets the council will mainly dig into' (TA 12.3.1886), an argument the Finnish-speaking side found offensive, emphasizing democratic language rights for the people. *Tammerfors Aftonblad* took a superficially moderate tone, but its paternalistic style must have been difficult to swallow on the Fennoman side. For example, on 26 March, the paper commented on national and local language efforts to put Finnish forward as follows:

> Men den bildade och politiskt mogna opinionen i landet – och lyckligtvis finnes ännu en sådan – har allt skäl att djupt beklaga den förhastade åtgjärden,

framkallad som den är af någre okloke skrikhalsar, hvilka, ställande ernåendet af föremålet för sitt barnsliga kältande högre än allt annat, med en politisk lättfärdighet som med sårighet söker sin like, spelat hazard om fosterlandets dyrbaraste intressen.[8]

The two papers also debated with each other, reporting on what the other had said and refuting the claims in varying degrees of moral outrage (see, for example, TS 20.2.1886 and 3.4.1886). On a couple of occasions (20.2.1886; 16.3.1886) *Tampereen Sanomat* complained about a clumsy and erroneous translation of its article in *Tammerfors Aftonblad*, but all in all there is a curious absence of any critique towards the Finnish translations in the media and also in council discussions. It seems as if the status of Finnish was too fragile to unsettle by translation criticism.

In 1886, the Fennophile movement was at its height in Tampere, but also new divisions were emerging, allowing the Svecoman side to regain power. In the election, the two Fennoman sects that were formed at the national level were now debating between themselves, and also the two local Finnish newspapers were divided (TU liberal, AL more conservative). As divisions emerged around new topics, language was no longer necessarily seen as a primary issue, although *Aamulehti* actively sought for compromises among Fennomans to block some Svecophile candidates (Rusila 1984: 571–2). Indeed, the election results were bad for Svecomans. The clear winner, then, was the cadre of businessmen, many of them Finnish by origin but fluently bilingual because of their professional background (Rasila 1984: 573). This, however, did not lead to a strengthening of bilingual practices. As if signalling the beginning of a new era for the council, Otto Blåfield was no longer running for office (and died later in the same year). He had systematically supported the use of *both* languages in the council, but attitudes among Finnish-speakers were no longer supportive of bilingualism. *Aamulehti* (26.9.1886; see also AL 11.3.1886) depicted the idea of forcing a representative body of an entirely Finnish (*'umpisuomalainen'*; emphatic) town to use 'mixed languages' (*'sekakielinen'*; a pejorative term) as ludicrous, and said that those 'ten or so' men who live in Tampere without bothering to learn the local language and 'bragging about their ignorance' are an exception not to be listened to. In the light of this it is interesting to note that the practice of 'oral translation' (by the secretary) is mentioned in passing as an ongoing practical solution (TS 3.4.1886; 16.3.1886; TA 12.3.1886). The debate only concerns the written official documentation of the meetings.

In the new elections for the 1887 council held at the end of 1886 voting numbers were higher than before. However, for a number of Finnish-speakers language had ceased being a primary concern and that the internal division of the Fennoman side had become increasingly pronounced. One day before the election, *Aamulehti* reminded Finnish-speaking voters that the Svecomans will surely 'vote as one man', and warned that a failure to do the same on the Finnish side will lead to a Svecoman victory, which in turn will allow them to 'change the council into Svecoman, both in spirit and in language' (AL 2.12.1886). In spite of *Aamulehti*'s campaign the voting results showed that some influential Finnish-speakers had indeed favoured Swedish-speaking candidates. *Tampereen Sanomat* (TS 31.12.1886) commented with shock, disappointment and worry, foreseeing an increasingly Swedish-speaking administration. This gloomy prognosis did not materialize. On the contrary. Although the local power balance was shifting towards Swedish, language planning efforts at national level had created a legal framework that gave Finnish strong support, and it was becoming evident that Swedish was fighting a losing battle. Indeed, also in Tampere the new normal (i.e. Finnish only) was gradually accepted, and in 1887 the debate began to die out. In the 1887 election language was no longer seen as a decisive dividing factor.

6 Conclusion

Between 1875 and 1886 the council language policy evolved, through numerous translatorial turns, from monolingual Swedish to monolingual Finnish. The three interrelated levels of language policy – planning, practices and attitudes – contributed to this development in multiple ways. Generally, it is easy to accept the idea that a language policy brings forward some translation practices. This chapter, however, examines the opposite direction of causal emplotment: how the use of particular translatorial strategies at the micro-level can be seen to actively push forward particular language policies, and how debates over language hierarchies and translation practices can be seen to both reflect and fuel the conflicting language attitudes of the time.

The dense points discussed in this chapter, and their three different data sets, allow us to zoom into the constantly evolving language planning at national level, the changing language and translation decisions at local level and the surrounding climate of language ideologies and attitudes. Of these three levels the nationwide language planning activities provide a legal framework that the local environment adapts to but has few possibilities to actively influence. In contrast, the council practices and media debates are intertwined, and the media has an active language policy role.

The case of the Tampere city council shows that translation is not only a reaction to an existing linguistic context but also a tool for actively shaping that context. Translation is often seen as a benevolent activity, in service of more participatory governance through multilingualism. This case unsettles that assumption by showing that translation can also be used as a scaffolding device, to help an underdog language move gradually into a dominant position. At first, introducing translation enabled bilingual practices; a few years later language rights for minorities were no longer seen as a valid argument, and those in favour of bilingualism fought a losing battle. Putting translation in the service of Finnish was not only a language choice but also tied to a number of other societal aims such as workers' rights, democratization and the gradual development of a civil society. Language issue was also a platform for training party politics, and as the political map developed, other kinds of divisions became more central.

Notes

1 On the gradual development of Finland as a nation see, for example, Engman (1995).
2 The Finlayson cotton mill was a major employer at the time, and the lucrative employment possibilities also drastically increased the number of young women in the population, tilting the demographics of Tampere towards an over-representation of (unmarried) women in all age groups between 15 and 40, and earning it the nickname of 'Cotton girls' town' (Rasila 1984: 244).
3 Railway network that was also being built at the time was also essential for the dissemination of news; Tampere was connected to Helsinki and Turku by rail in 1876.
4 'Any sensible person will surely understand that the success of a significant language change is entirely dependent on everyone who is engaged in juridical matters demanding, within the limits of the statute, protocols to be provided in Finnish – it is the only way to ensure that Finnish protocols will begin to be published, the only way to ensure judges will gain practice in using our language and the only way through which the language itself will bend and mould into a comfortable tool.'
5 'To the uninitiated it would appear to be clearer than day that when you have a Finnish jury, examination in Finnish, witnesses in Finnish and – mostly – Finnish-speaking adversaries and so on, so the uninitiated would think that it is difficult to translate the issue into another language in the protocol. But of course the good gentlemen themselves know best!!!'
6 'Which language, Finnish or Swedish, is more common in Tampere? Finnish, as there are only a dozen of monolingual Swedes. In which language should

announcements and notices be published in Tampereen Sanomat? Only in Finnish, of course; private businesses can still do as they see fit, but the official municipal announcements only in Finnish' (TS 12.3.1878).

7 'The simplest and easiest way to reach the goal would be to forbid anyone who resides in this town or in its vicinity from speaking Swedish or from reading anything in this language, but this would be unreasonable for many people ... But as the parish has the right to forbid any unknown person from entering the town, we propose that from now on it would refrain from accepting any persons who only speak Swedish from moving in. Many years would pass ... but this would end the language strait and the case of Finnish would make progress; and this decision would not hinder or hurt the endeavours of those speaking other foreign languages.'

8 'But an educated and politically mature opinion in this country – and luckily there still exists one – has every reason to deeply regret the hasty measures called forth by some not too clever bawlers who, putting their childish aims above anything else, have hazarded fatherland's most valuable interests with political flightiness an equal of which is hard to find.'

References

Primary sources

Kielireskripti [rescript on language]. Keisarillisen Majesteetin Armollinen Asetus Suomen kielen asettamisesta yhdenmoisiin oikeuksiin Ruotsin kielen kanssa kaikissa semmoisissa kohdissa, jotka välittömästi koskevat maan nimen-omaan suomalaista wäestöä. Suomen Suuriruhtinanmaan Asetus-Kokous 26/1863.

Kunnallisasetus [decree on local government]. Asetus kunnallishallituksesta kaupungissa. Suomen Suuriruhtinanmaan Asetus-Kokous, 40/1873.

Uusi Keisarillisen Majesteetin Armollinen Julistus, koskeva laajennettua oikeutta Suomen kielen käyttämiseen tuomio-istuimissa ja virastoissa Suomenmaassa. Annettu Helsingissä, 9 p:nä Toukokuuta 1881. [Emperor's declaration on the extended right to use Finnish in courts and offices in Finland. Helsinki, 9.5.1881]

Asetus Ruotsin ja suomen kielen käyttämisestä erinäisissä virastoissa ja tuomioistuimissa Suomen suuriruhtinaanmaassa. Annettu 29.12.1883.

Hänen Majesteettinsa Keisarin ja Suuriruhtinaan Armollinen Käskykirje Ruotsin ja Suomen kielten käyttämisestä asiain käsittelemisessä virakunnissa ja virallisessa kirjeenvaihdossa. Suomen Suuriruhtinanmaan Asetus-Kokous 18.3.1886/11. (Julkiluettava saarnastuolista).Annettu Hatsinassa, 18 (6) p:nä Maaliskuuta 1886. [Emperor's rescript on using Finnish and Swedish in offices and in official correspondence. To be read out from pulpit. Hatsina, 18.3.1886.]

Keisarillisen Majesteetin Armollinen kirje Turun Hovioikeudelle, sisältävä tarkempia määräyksiä Suomen ja Ruotsin kielten käyttämisestä asioita virakunnissa käsiteltäissä ja virallisessa kirjeenvaihdossa. Suomen Suuriruhtinanmaan Asetus-Kokous 4.4.1887/6. Annettu Helsingissä, 4 p:nä Huhtikuuta 1887. [Emperor's letter to the Turku court of appeal, containing further provisos on using Finnish and Swedish in offices and in official correspondence. Helsinki, 4.4.1887]

Minutes of the Tampere city council 1875, 1878, 1881, 1886. Tampere city archive.

Tampereen Uutiset, Aamulehti, Tammerfors Aftonblad: https://digi.kansalliskirjasto.fi/s anomalehti/ (accessed 27.9.2018)

Secondary sources

Cronin, M. (2006), *Translation and Identity*, London and New York: Routledge.

Engman, M. (1995), 'Finns and Swedes in Finland', in Sven Tägil (ed.), *Ethnicity and Nation Building in the Nordic World*, 179–216, Carbondale and Edwardsville: Southern Illinois UP.

Engman, M. (2009), *Pitkät jäähyväiset. Suomi Ruotsin ja Venäjän välissä vuoden 1809 jälkeen* [The Long Goodbye: Finland between Sweden and Russia after 1809]. Helsinki: WSOY.

Foucault, M. (1978/2007), *Security, Territory, Population. Lectures at the College de France 1977–1978*, ed. M. Senellart, trans. G. Burcell, New York: Palgrave Macmillan.

Grin, F. (2010), 'Translation and the Dynamics of Multilingualism', Cahier de recherche élf n°3. Université de Genève, Observatoire élf. Available online: http://www.unige.ch/traduction-interpretation/recherches/groupes/elf/documents/elfwp3.pdf

Koskinen, K. (2014a), 'Institutional Translation: The Art of Governing by Translation', ed. Ji-Hae Kang, *Translation in Institutions*. Special issue of *Perspectives*, 22 (4): 479–92.

Koskinen, K. (2014b), 'Tampere as a Translation Space', *Translation Studies* 7 (2): 186–202.

Koskinen, K. (2017), 'Translatorial Action in Non-professional Translation Communities: The Tampere City Council in 1875', in Kristiina Taivalkoski-Shilov, Liisa Tiittula and Maarit Koponen (eds), *Communities of Translation and Interpreting* (VitaTraductiva), 37–61, Montreal: Éditions québécoises de l'oeuvre.

Koskinen, K. (2019), 'Translatorisuus dynaamisen kielipolitiikan välineenä Tampereen kunnallishallinnossa 1870–1880-luvuilla [Translatoriality as a Tool for Dynamic Language Policy in 19th Century Local Government in Tampere]', in Arja Nurmi, Saija Isomaa and Päivi Pahta (eds), *Kielten ja kulttuurien mosaiikki: Valta, periferia ja arki*. Helsinki: SKS.

Lönnroth, H. (2009), *Svenskt i Tammerfors*, Tampere: Tampere University Press.

Meylaerts, R. (2013), 'Multilingualism as a Challenge for Translation Studies', in Teoksessa Carmen Millán and Francesca Bartrina (eds), *The Routledge Handbook of Translation Studies*, 519–33, Routledge: London and New York.

Paloposki, O. (2007), 'Suomentaminen ja suomennokset 1800-luvulla' [Translating and Translations into Finnish during the Nineteenth Century], in H. K. Riikonen, Urpo Kovala, Pekka Kujamäki and Outi Paloposki (eds), *Suomennoskirjallisuuden historia I* [History of Translated Literature in Finland], 102–26, Helsinki: SKS.

Rasila, V. (1984), *Tampereen historia II. 1840-luvulta vuoteen 1905* [History of Tampere II. 1840–1905], Tampere: The City of Tampere.

Spolsky, B. (2004), *Language Policy*, Cambridge: Cambridge University Press.

Vähäpesola, J. (2009a), 'Kaupunki 1870–1900', in *Koskesta voimaa*. Digital source of Tampere history. University of Tampere. Available online: http://www15.uta.fi/koskivoimaa/kaupunki/1870-00/index.htm (accessed 24 August 2018).

Vähäpesola, J. (2009b), Äidinkieli, kansallisuus ja uskonto. Available online: http://www15.uta.fi/koskivoimaa/kaupunki/1870-00/kielijauskonto.htm (accessed 24 August 2018).

Vähäpesola, J. (2009c), Tampereen väestö 1870–1900. Available online: http://www15.uta.fi/koskivoimaa/kaupunki/1870-00/vaesto.htm (accessed 24 August 2018).

Wolf, M. (2012), *Die vielsprachige Seele Kakaniens. Übersetzen und Dolmetschen in der Habsburgermonarchie 1848 bis 1918*, Wien & Köln & Weimar: Böhlau.

Part Three

Interpreting in harbour towns

Consuls and other interpreters in Cork Harbour, Ireland

Mary Phelan

1 Introduction

In 1801 the Act of Union brought about the United Kingdom of Great Britain and Ireland, putting an end to the Irish parliament and allowing Ireland to be governed from Westminster via officials based in Dublin Castle. The population of Ireland expanded rapidly at the start of the nineteenth century; from 4.5 million in 1801 to just under 7 million in 1821 and over 8 million in 1841. However, this expansion was rapidly followed by the great famine and extensive emigration, reducing the population to 4.4 million in 1901. Remarkably few foreigners were resident at the time. For example, in the 1871 census, out of a total population of 5.4 million, only 8,643 were foreign subjects, a figure corresponding to less than 0.2 per cent of the population. Of these, almost half were from Europe, mainly from France, Germany, Italy, Norway, Switzerland and Spain and they included a significant number, 1,321, of seamen who happened to be in Irish ports on the night of the census.

Julio César Santoyo has pointed to the history of interpreting as 'one of the most notorious empty spaces in our field' (2006: 13). Anthony Pym suggests that 'people of different backgrounds came together in urban centres, particularly big cities' (2009: 44) and goes on to call for the 'humanization' of translators (2009: 45). Pym recommends focusing on individual translators rather than their texts, suggesting that this approach will allow researchers 'to model intercultural decision-making as an ethical activity', something that will enable an understanding of the reasons behind translators' decisions. Unfortunately, what interpreters heard in one language and said in another is not recorded; there are no texts. For court interpreters, the first issue is to identify the interpreters –

who were they? Pym suggests that individual translators are engaged 'in many aspects of cross-cultural communication', and interpreters in the nineteenth century were certainly engaged in cross-cultural communication. In this chapter, we endeavour to humanize the foreign language interpreters based in Cork Harbour in the nineteenth century, to find out who they were and what their background was, but also to find out, if possible, how they approached the task of interpreting.

2 The legal system

Irish law is part of the common law system. In the nineteenth century, the investigation of crimes and the role of the interpreter were quite different from the time of writing. The usual process was that if a serious crime was discovered, a magistrate investigated and took depositions or statements from witnesses. Then the grand jury went through the indictment to decide if the case should go to trial, to begin with at the lowest courts, the petty sessions, and if sufficiently serious, the case would be referred to the quarter sessions or, in the case of murder, to the assizes. From 1836 the Prisoners' Counsel Act allowed defendants to see copies of depositions and counsel to make a speech their on behalf. However, prior to the Criminal Evidence Act 1898, defendants were not entitled to give evidence.

Interpreters had to take an oath to 'well and truly interpret and explain to the Court (and Jury) the evidence given in this case according to the best of your skill and understanding. So help you God' (Humphreys 1867: 376) and then had to swear in any witnesses who did not speak English. As suggested by the oath, the role of the interpreter was seen as being for the court and the jury rather than the defendant. The role of the interpreter was discussed in *R v Lee Kun*, an appeal against the conviction of a Chinese man in London who was not provided with interpreting during his trial for murder. According to the judgement, defendants who did not speak English were allocated an interpreter during magisterial investigations to ensure that they understood the evidence against them. Chief Justice Lord Reading noted that practice varied from court to court with some judges insisting on interpreting being provided in all cases while others allowed defence counsel or defendants to waive access to an interpreter. In addition, a distinction was made between cases where defendants had access to legal counsel and cases where they did not. For example, if a defendant had legal counsel 'the practice has been for the Court not to require the translation of the evidence unless the accused or his counsel applied for it' (*The King v Lee Kun* (1916: 343) 1 K.B. 337).

The Irish courts were familiar with interpreters who were made available for monolingual Irish speakers and for Deaf people. There was statutory provision from 1773 to 1774 for the grand juries to pay Irish language interpreters a salary of £10 a year to work at assizes level. Further legislation was introduced in 1837 whereby the grand juries could pay Irish interpreters at quarter sessions courts a salary of £30 a year. Irish interpreters were employed in Cork city until at least 1856 (*Southern Reporter & Cork Commercial Courier* 4 March 1856) and in the county of Cork until at least 1928 (*Southern Star* 8 December 1928). Interpreters, to begin with family members and later Deaf school teachers and chaplains, were made available for Deaf people (Leonard 2015: 10). Unlike the salaried Irish language interpreters, foreign language interpreters were selected on an ad hoc volunteer basis as the need arose. It was a case of accepting the best, or perhaps the only, person available on the day. No evidence of payments to foreign language court interpreters during the nineteenth century was located.

An unusual feature of the courts at the time was the jury *de medietate linguae*. Niamh Howlin details how from 1354 Jews in both criminal and civil cases in England could opt for a jury that included six members of their religion. However, around the start of the eighteenth century, the system changed and half of the jury could be made up of any six foreigners regardless of their native language (Howlin 2010: 65). The right was extended to all aliens and continued until 1870 (Howlin 2010: 56 and 80). The small number of foreigners resident in Ireland meant that some foreign language interpreters also took on the role of jurors.

Over the course of the nineteenth century, there was increasing regulation of merchant shipping, and local marine boards were set up to examine ships' masters and mates. The Cork mercantile marine board came into being in 1851 and held examinations in navigation and steamship early that year (*Cork Examiner*, 31 March 1851). Interpreters were required to interpret for witnesses who did not speak English at the board of trade, established in Ireland in 1840 thanks to subscriptions from the people of Dublin (Mooney 1845: 370) to hold enquiries into collisions between ships.

3 Cork Harbour

This chapter focuses on Cork Harbour during the nineteenth century and its three ports in Cork city, Cove and Passage West. (Cove was renamed Queenstown to mark Queen Victoria's visit in 1849 and the name was changed to Cobh after the establishment of the Irish Free State in 1922.) There were petty sessions in all three ports, and there was an assizes court in Cork city. Cork city's motto is *Statio bene fide carinis* or a safe harbour for ships, in recognition of its very large natural harbour, 6 kilometres long by 2 kilometres wide and reputedly large enough to shelter all of the nineteenth-century British navy. According to a local directory called *Guy's Almanac*, some two and a half million tons of shipping entered Cork Harbour each year (1875: 292). The harbour was used for exports of butter, meat, live animals and corn and for imports of sugar, tea, coffee, wine, tobacco, salt, herrings and corn (Marmion 1855: 539). However, there were ongoing problems due to the fact that the waters were shallow, and there was a need for infrastructure to meet the needs of visiting ships. In 1822 the Cork Harbour commissioners were charged with improving the port, harbour and the river Lee. They carried out works in 1848 as did the admiralty which organized the construction of a pier and two boat harbours. Dredging work continued in different sections of the port over many decades. In Figure 7.1, Queenstown is located south of Great Island while Passage West is west of Great Island.

Queenstown is best known in Ireland as the departure point for many Irish emigrants leaving for the United States of America. It is also linked with two very large ships: The first being the Titanic which anchored offshore in 1912 to take

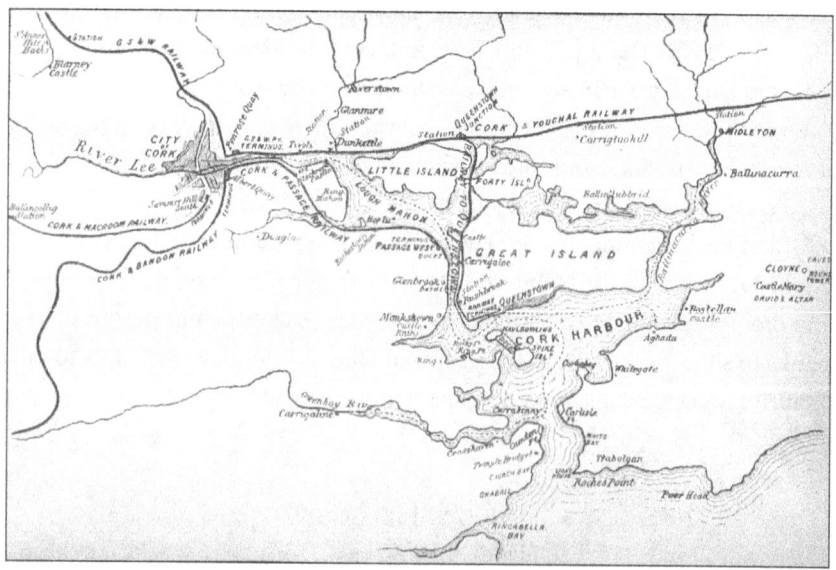

Figure 7.1 Cork Harbour *Guide to the most picturesque tour in Western Europe*. Cork: Guy & Co., 1891.

on passengers and mail before setting off on its final voyage. The second is the Lusitania which was torpedoed by a German submarine in 1915 while sailing from New York to Liverpool and sank off the town. According to Marmion, previous to the American War of Independence (1775–83), Queenstown consisted of just a few fishing huts. However, during that war, fleets destined for America, the West Indies and the Mediterranean docked in Queenstown to take on provisions and naval stores (Marmion 1855: 518–21). Large ships started anchoring in the harbour in 1859; mail and passengers were then carried by smaller vessels to the quayside. In 1877 an act of parliament was passed to allow for construction of a deep-water quay at Queenstown, and this work was completed in 1883 (Coakley 1919: 83–6). The new quay was mainly used by government ships and army transports, and was used extensively during the first Boer war (1880–1).

By 1835 Passage West, a trading and ship building port, located 8 kilometres from Cork city, had a large dry dock for the construction, maintenance and repair of ships. Prior to 1850, larger ships had to dock at Passage thus incurring extra costs as half their cargo had to be unloaded and taken on smaller boats to the city. As the ships were then lighter, they could enter the city. There was also a pier built by the St George's Steam Packet Company where passengers could disembark and cargo could be unloaded (Lewis 1837: 419). From 1862 a train linked Cork city to Queenstown, and in 1876 the mail trains from Dublin to Cork were extended to the town. There were also ferries between various towns.

According to the 1851 census, the population of Cork city was 86,485 while that of Queenstown was 10,906 and that of Passage West was 2,857. The large amount of trade in and out of Cork Harbour meant that there was a constant need for interpreters who could work with ships' captains, seamen and merchants and negotiate deals; help people in shops and taverns; and, the situation arising, act as interpreters for the board of trade, and indeed in court.

4 Method

As part of a larger study, digitized newspaper archives were searched using the keywords 'court' and 'interpreter'. For the purpose of this chapter, the author selected results relating to Cork Harbour and foreign languages. Very few results were found for the decades before the 1830s, mainly because at that time newspapers sourced their news from the London newspapers and there was little local coverage. Where found for the following decades, many court reports mention 'an interpreter' or that 'an interpreter was sworn' and provide no further information on the identity of the interpreter. However, some reports do identify the interpreters although this can be problematic if it is just 'Mr Barry' or 'Mr O'Mahony' because without any additional information it can be impossible to establish who exactly the person is, particularly in the case of common surnames. Where the identity of the interpreter could be established, searches of digitized newspaper archives, local directories and the websites ancestry.co.uk and findmypast.ie were carried out to obtain supplementary information.

5 Findings

Most interpreting situations that took place on ships, for example, or in ports are undocumented, but some of those that took place in public have been recorded in newspaper reports, and they indicate that some people, both Corkonians and foreigners, were bilingual or indeed multilingual. The newspaper reports show that many defendants, plaintiffs and witnesses were seamen from merchant ships whose crews could consist of men from different countries who did not necessarily share a language. The charges brought in court cases where interpreters were required include murder, manslaughter, smuggling of tobacco and alcohol, disputes between captains and seamen, stabbings by and of seamen, and cases where seamen found themselves in houses of ill fame and were robbed.

Foreign language court interpreters belonged to two groups: (a) consuls and vice consuls who spoke foreign languages and (b) bilingual or multilingual foreigners and locals. Ethical issues relating to accuracy and impartiality arise in some instances.

5.1 Consuls as interpreters

In relation to the role of consuls in a legal context, Tuson explains that when witnesses were examined, depositions could be taken in writing in their presence. The depositions then had to be read over and signed by the witness with the consul also signing to authenticate the document. The consul was also to provide a written statement outlining the details of the case. In criminal cases, depositions were made in the presence of the accused. Where witnesses did not speak English, depositions were to be made 'through a competent interpreter, sworn to interpret truly, and the name of the interpreter and the fact that he was so sworn should be stated on the deposition, and certified by the Consul' (1856: 79).

Consuls, vice consuls and consular agents were appointed to all the large ports around Ireland – Dublin, Belfast, Limerick, Londonderry, Waterford, Wexford – and to Cork and nearby Queenstown. They were nominated by their government, approved by the British government, and then a letter was sent from Dublin Castle to the local mayor to notify him of the new appointee. Local consuls reported to their consul general in Dublin who in turn reported to his consul general in London. Almanacs indicate that very few consuls, vice consuls and consular agents had foreign names. For example, in 1863 there were four in Cork: Francis Michelli for Austria, Paolo Stefano Minich for Honduras, George Miloro for Italy and Nicholas George Yourdi for Greece (*Laing's Cork Mercantile Directory* 1863: 168), while in 1875 there were only two: Michelli was still in place and the other person was Paolo Stefano Minich now representing Chili, Hayti and Honduras (*Guy's Cork Almanac* 1875: 293).

An early example of a consul acting as interpreter was the Portuguese consul Adeonato da Silva Lima (1826–88), who was born in London. In 1851 da Silva Lima married Sarah O'Donnell, youngest daughter of Herbert O'Donnell, a justice of the peace and large landowner. In 1854 he acted as interpreter for a Portuguese seaman who alleged that a local woman had robbed him and stripped him of his clothes which she pawned (*Cork Constitution*, 9 February 1845). By 1861, according to the *Post Office London Directory* (Ancestry.com), he was a wine merchant in London. The family later lived in Portugal.

Frenchman Claude Marcel (1793–1876) is particularly interesting because of his published works on the teaching of languages. To begin with he was a soldier and was shot in the shoulder at the siege of Antwerp during the Napoleonic Wars in 1814. The exact date of his arrival in Ireland is unclear, but he was chancellor in Cork from at least 1824 and consul from at least 1848 until his resignation in 1863 when he returned to France (Institut français de l'éducation website). While in Cork he gave private classes in French and Italian, gave lectures on education, and wrote two books on the topic: *Language as a Means of Mental Cultures* (1853) and *Premiers Principes d'Education* (1855) (see Smith 2009 for more information). Claude Marcel was a juror on a jury *de medietate linguae* on at least two occasions (*Cork Constitution* 18 March 1852, *Cork Examiner* 21 March 1853). No records were found of Marcel acting as interpreter, but on at least one occasion, he deputed his son Justin Marcel (1833–1920) to do so. The case involved a woman who was charged with robbing a Frenchman of a purse containing six sovereigns in a house of ill repute. Justin Marcel did not take an impartial role; he told the court that 'this poor man came to Cork from Waterford with the intention of going home, but he was then robbed of all the money in his possession' (*Cork Constitution*, 2 October 1855).

According to Agstner (2004: 41), as there was extensive corn trade with Ireland, the Austro-Hungarian Empire decided to appoint an honorary consul agent in 1845. Unusually, from 1854 to 1870, the consul was paid. In 1854, Francis M. Michelli (1808–76), originally from Trieste, who had previously worked as a translator and shipping agent in London, was appointed honorary consul agent at Queenstown on a large salary of £260. Michelli was also entitled to collect consular fees, which, according to Agnstner, averaged out at £1,536 a year. In 1864 Michelli was made provisional consul on a salary of 2,100 guilders plus an allowance of a similar amount and 1,500 guilders to run the office. In 1860 he was the interpreter for the master and two crew members of the Austrian brig the Picro which sank in Cork Harbour after a collision with the Cumberland steamer. The men were suing for damages for their clothes and effects (*Cork Examiner*, 30 March 1860). This case was heard at the court of admiralty which at the time sat in Dublin.

Nicholas George Yourdi (–1879) was consul for Greece and on his death was replaced by his brother Elefterios George Yourdi known as Ely or E. G. Yourdi (1835–1910) who was a consular agent until 1897 when he was officially appointed vice consul (*Cork Examiner*, 4 October 1897). Apparently, the Yourdi family was 'very distinguished and noble' and the Yourdi brothers had to emigrate after the Greek war of independence (1821–32) (*Cork Constitution*, 12 December 1895). In 1850 the house of Yourdi in Syra, Greece, had 'failed to the amount of five hundred thousand drachmas (18,000*l*)' (*Freeman's Journal* 1 November 1850). Nicholas Yourdi married Marianne Wilkinson and according to a naturalization certificate (Ancestry.com), at least one of their children, John Robert, was born in Greece in 1856. The Yourdis' exact date of arrival in Ireland is unknown, but by 1859, Nicholas was the consul for Greece based in Queenstown. He was also involved in bottomry, a high-risk system of insuring ships whereby, in order to raise enough money to finance a voyage, a ship would be used as security. If the money was not repaid, then the ship would be forfeited. The risk was that if the ship sank, the lender would lose his money. The Yourdis had a ship called the George & John Yourdi and regularly imported corn from Constantinople and Odessa and steam coal. The Yourdi brothers frequently acted as interpreters in the courts: Nicholas in the 1860s and Elefterios in the 1890s. In 1895, Elefterios was the interpreter in a manslaughter case heard at assizes. The defendant was unrepresented because the British government only allocated interpreters in murder cases. Yourdi did not assume an impartial role and commented that 'the unfortunate deceased man brought it all on himself'. Interestingly, the prisoner was found not guilty and discharged (*Cork Examiner* 12 December 1895).

Paolo Stefano Minich (1833–?) had commanded the revolutionists in Italy in 1848. The date of his arrival in Ireland is unknown, but he married Sarah Grant in 1857 and their son was born the following year (*Cork Examiner*, 22 February 1858). In 1860, he left Ireland to join General Garibaldi in his campaign to quell uprisings in Sicily. In 1863, Minich inserted a notice in a newspaper warning that he would not be liable for any debts incurred by his wife (*Cork Examiner*, 21 April 1863). That same year, he was appointed vice consul at Queenstown for the Republic of Haiti (*Dublin Evening Mail*, 7 January 1863). Minich was a ship agent and consul for a number of states – not only Haiti but also vice consul for the Ottoman Empire, Honduras and consul for Chile. In addition, he was the representative of a number of insurance underwriters from different countries (*Cork Constitution*, 8 November 1877) and developed 'a thriving and prosperous' business (*Cork Constitution*, 28 March 1878).

Minich acted as interpreter at Queenstown petty sessions on at least one occasion when two Italian sailors were charged with deserting a ship and threatening the life of the captain (*Southern Reporter & Cork Commercial Courier*, 7 October 1862). However, he found himself in court in 1878, charged with perjury and an attempt to defraud an insurance company of £1,200. The facts of the case were that an Italian ship called the *Unione S* was to travel from Philadelphia to Cork with a cargo of corn. However, the corn became saturated with seawater, supposedly because the vessel got stranded before leaving the Delaware River. The insurance policy stipulated that compensation would only be paid out if the vessel got stranded or was lost. The trial focused on Minich's role as interpreter for the owner of the ship. According to the *Freeman's Journal*, the captain, mate and a sailor had informed Minich in Italian that the ship was not stranded, but Minich had drawn up a protest or written declaration in which he stated that they had told him that the ship was stranded. Minich, the captain, mate and sailor went before a notary where the three members of the crew swore that the declaration was correct with Minich acting as interpreter. The declaration was then sworn by a notary public. Minich was defended in court by high profile lawyers Peter O'Brien and Isaac Butt and the latter pointed to the absence of a motive because Minich was unlikely to gain in any way. In fact, the only person who could benefit was the purchaser of the cargo, Charles Cantillon, a magistrate and former mayor of Cork, and it seemed very unlikely that he would be involved in an attempt to defraud the insurance company (*Freeman's Journal*, 28 March 1878).

It is very difficult to work out what happened in this case: Was it a genuine misunderstanding where Minich thought the crew members had said that the ship was stranded? Did Minich attempt to protect the crew? His familiarity with insurance matters should have meant that he would be exceedingly careful about such matters. Another possibility is that the crew changed their story and Minich was the scapegoat. Despite the absence of a motive, the jury found Minich guilty and he was sentenced to twelve months' imprisonment. However, according to the Irish Prison Registers (findmypast.ie), his sentence was commuted to six months on account of the poor state of his health.

Giorgio Miloro, known as Chevalier Miloro (1812–81), was the consul for Italy for about twenty years. He was also a shipowner, ship agent, a town commissioner and even a member of the Queenstown model yacht club. He married Anne McLaren in 1853, and they had one son Giorgio Vincent. According to newspaper reports, Miloro was a frequent interpreter in court. For example, in 1857 he acted as interpreter at Passage West in the investigation of a murder (*Cork Constitution*, 5 September 1857), and in the 1870s he was the interpreter at a stabbing case (*Cork Constitution*, 27 October 1871), followed by another stabbing case where, most unusually, Miloro gave £2 to the victim and also paid the fine of £1 and 10 shillings in costs, one-third of which was to go to the victim (*Cork Examiner*, 12 February 1874). In 1875, Miloro was the interpreter for an Italian witness in a case where five seamen from an English ship were charged with wilful and malicious injury to an Italian ship (*Cork Constitution*, 5 October 1875). In 1879, Miloro was asked to interpret for two Italian sailors, on drunk and disorderly charges (*Cork Examiner*, 29 July 1879).

Miloro interpreted at board of trade inquiries on at least two occasions. In 1876 he acted as interpreter for the board of trade at an inquiry in Queenstown about the brig Sussex which went down in the Wilmington River in Georgia, United States (*Cork Examiner*, 7 September 1876). Miloro also interpreted at an inquiry into a collision between a steamship belonging to the Cork Steamship Company and an Italian brig (*Cork Constitution*, 6 February 1878).

Another consul who acted as interpreter on a number of occasions but was a native English speaker was James Demery (1837–1903), who was originally a shopkeeper and then a ship's agent and consul for Spain. The exact origin of his connection with Spain could not be established. Demery ran a lodging house called the *Albergo Italiano* which eventually comprised several houses (*Cork Examiner*, 7 August 1880). In 1873, he was tried at Queenstown petty sessions for aiding in unshipping three gallons of rum. However, although he was convicted, the magistrates recommended that the damages be reduced and suggested that it was a bona fide transaction between Demery and Minich (*Cork Constitution*, 4 October 1873). Like Nicholas Yourdi, he was involved in bottomry insurance in the 1870s (*Cork Examiner*, 27 October 1873). In 1879 he raised funds for people affected by heavy flooding in Murcia, Spain (*Cork Examiner*, 21 November 1879). He interpreted for Portuguese, Spanish and Italian. Demery was upwardly mobile: he bought a house on Queen Street in Queenstown for £295 in 1863 (*Cork Examiner*, 13 May 1863). As consul, he advertised that he issued bills of health (*Cork Constitution*, 2 May 1873). His eight-bedroom mansion in Fort Lisle West, Queenstown, was put up for auction in 1885 along with furniture and 'a splendid Tricord cottage piano', rare old Indian china, 'a magnificent selection of oil paintings', foreign stuffed birds and several sets of oriental china (*Cork Constitution* 1 October 1885). Demery emigrated to Australia circa 1893 with his wife and four adult children and died in Sydney in 1903 (Ancestry.com).

5.2 Other foreign language interpreters

In 1876 there was a very unusual case, possibly the only occasion on which an interpreter travelled from England to Ireland specifically for a court case. The Caswell mutiny case involved the trial of a Greek man, Christos Baumbos, charged with murdering the captain, first mate, second mate and steward during a mutiny on a ship which was travelling from Buenos Aires to Cork. Baumbos did not speak English, and at Queenstown petty sessions, there was some discussion about how to proceed and the chairman recommended that they have 'a proper interpreter, one who had no interest in the matter'. Greek consul Nicholas Yourdi told the court that 'there's only myself and my brother here, who are Greeks'. However, magistrate Mr Beamish rejected his offer outright, saying, 'You have nothing to say to it at all. Your brother is a most respectable man, but still he is your brother' (*Cork Examiner*, 16 May 1876). It is not entirely clear why the courts were not willing to have the consul as interpreter on this occasion. It may have been because he had instructed the lawyer for the defence or because, like Baumbos, he was Greek, or perhaps because he was involved in shipping and might have found it difficult to be impartial when interpreting for an alleged mutineer.

Most unusually, Joseph Cartwright, the son of a collector of customs, born on the Ionian Islands (Breathnach 2003: 107) who had previously interpreted at the Lennie mutiny trial in London, was recruited to act as interpreter at petty sessions in May and at assizes in late July. At the first trial at assizes, it was decided that all questions and answers should be put down in writing and Cartwright would then translate 'the result of the examination' to Baumbos (*Irish Times*, 27 May 1876). This procedure may have been time-consuming and probably explains why the defendant's counsel agreed that, to save time, the interpreter would only interpret the important points of the evidence (*Irish Times*, 28 July 1876). As explained in section 2, this was acceptable practice at the time because Baumbos had legal counsel. However, a newspaper reporter commented that, with the exception of some 'ship's language', Baumbos 'seemed to be utterly ignorant of the evidence' (*Cork Constitution*, 28 July 1876). As the jury could not agree, with eleven in favour of conviction and one in favour of acquittal, Baumbos was put on trial for a second time. A question arose about two words – 'tutti mort' – reportedly said by one of the Greeks. Cartwright translated the phrase as 'all dead' adding (quite unnecessarily) that this was distinct from 'tutti mostri' which would mean 'all brutes' (*Cork Constitution*, 24 May 1876). Later he informed the court that he spoke Italian perfectly and that he knew 'even the distinction between the Venetian and Neapolitan dialects' (*Irish Times*, 29 July 1876). Baumbos was found guilty and sentenced to death. According to newspaper reports, Cartwright interpreted the sentence of death 'exhibiting great emotion' (*Irish Times*, 1 August 1876). Yourdi, who was present throughout the trials in his role as consul, told the court that he had communicated by letter with the prisoner's father who had been a captain in the Greek navy during the war of independence against Turkey (*Cork Constitution*, 28 July 1876).

A frequent interpreter for Italian was Reverend Gerald Brenan or Brennan (1810–63), a Catholic priest who had studied for the priesthood at the Capuchin convent of Frescati in Rome. After returning to Cork he was appointed chaplain in the Cork workhouse where he contracted famine fever (*Cork Examiner*, 7 July 1863). In 1852, he interpreted for an Italian who was charged with feloniously assaulting a woman and with stealing a small sum of money from her (*Southern Reporter*, 16 March 1852). He informed a judge that he was a part-time prison chaplain (*Cork Examiner*, 21 March 1853) where no doubt he got to know and counsel detainees and prisoners. Indeed, in 1852, he interpreted for a man who was charged with murder and had already spent five months in prison awaiting trial. This case is interesting because Brenan asked the court if he could make a remark. Apparently, he had been in communication with the defendant's parish priest from whom he had received a letter that very morning giving the defendant 'the very highest character'. Brenan disregarded any notion of impartiality and argued on behalf of the defendant that it would be 'a great hardship' to keep him in prison. He also told the court:

> He is a stranger, my lord, to the Consul, and though he has got a very good character of him, it is unlikely he would go bail for him. Besides a bail would be no advantage to him in a strange place without employment. He feared the man was so excited by the transaction that he would destroy himself.

The court agreed to await the advice of the attorney general (*Cork Examiner*, 19 March 1852). At Cork assizes in 1857 an Italian who was charged with assault opted for a jury *de medietate linguae* (*Southern Reporter*, 30 July 1857). Brenan was also a witness in the case and gave testimony as to the behaviour of the defendant, basically to the effect that he was insane (*Cork Examiner*, 31 July 1857). He also acted as interpreter in a manslaughter case in 1863 where the judge addressed the defendant saying, 'I have addressed you in as plain language as I could, so it might be interpreted easily to you' (*Southern Reporter*, 2 April 1863). Clearly, this particular judge was making an effort to allow for ease of interpreting.

Gabriele Goidanich (1833–85) was born in Lussingrande, Austria, the island of Veli Lošinj in present-day Croatia. His father, Pietro Goidanich, was a civil servant. His brother Giovanni, a shipbroker, was based in Waterford where he was consul for Waterford and New Ross. Gabriele Goidanich was charged with smuggling tobacco in 1861 (*Cork Examiner*, 8 October 1861) and eight years later appeared in court as an interpreter for a man facing similar charges (*Southern Reporter*, 11 December 1869). Goidanich was awarded a Board of Trade certificate of competency as Master in the Merchant Service in 1863 and married Arabella Eva O'Sullivan in 1866. He was a ship agent and involved in the Queenstown Ship Chandlery Company, and on his death in 1885, his estate was worth £886, a considerable sum for the time.

Interpreters could be asked to provide explanations to defendants. For example, in 1855, a Spanish speaker was accused of stealing a gold chain. A man called John Rawley was sworn in as interpreter and informed the court that the defendant said he had stolen the chain. The interpreter was asked to explain the effect of his confession to the defendant. Rawley then told the court, 'I have told him that he will be punished very severely, and that he may be a long time in prison, but he still says he stole it.' The judge then asked him to 'stand by, and try and learn from him who and what he is' (*Southern Reporter*, 22 March 1855). In effect, Rawley was being asked to take on the role of investigating magistrate. While this was unusual, the judge may have encouraged this approach in the hope that direct communication would help resolve issues.

Emmanuel Tedesco (1833–98), born in Valetta, Malta, was awarded Board of Trade certificates of competency in the Merchant Service as Only Mate in 1858, and as Master in 1861. He took both examinations in Cork. In 1866, he married Eliza Baggot. In 1881, he was a sailmaker (*Slater's Directory* 1881). However, some years later he was the hotel keeper at Kilmurray's Hotel in Queenstown (*Cork Constitution*, 30 August 1894). Tedesco acted as interpreter a number of times. In 1866 he was the interpreter in a case against two crew members of a Maltese vessel who were accused of fighting (*Cork Examiner*, 10 April 1866). In 1872, a man possibly erroneously referred to in the newspaper as Mr Fedesco, but who was most likely Mr Tedesco (handwritten 'T' and 'F' may have been confused), was present at Passage West petty sessions when local interpreter James Hanley alias 'Rucco' was interpreting in a case about a ship master's use of abusive and threatening language. Tedesco intervened and alleged that Hanley was 'completely manufacturing the answers of the witness'. He then agreed to take over the interpreting (*Cork Examiner*, 3 January 1872). Tedesco acted as interpreter on at least one occasion in 1873 (*Cork Constitution*, 28 August 1873). His name is not mentioned again until a murder case first heard at Queenstown petty sessions in 1882. In this case, Tedesco translated the depositions into Italian (*Cork Examiner*, 24 January 1882).

Nicholas Yourdi played an interesting role as consul at a trial where the interpreter was a local teenage boy. In 1855, the interpreter for a Greek sailor complaining of ill-treatment was a barefooted, 'most raggedly dressed' boy aged thirteen or fourteen called Patrick Callanan who 'astonished the court by his ability in making the complainant's statement intelligible to the court'. He informed the court that he also spoke Portuguese, Spanish and Italian – languages which he had acquired by virtue of talking to foreign seamen. The mayor, who was presiding, was impressed and promised to send for him whenever he needed an interpreter (*Nenagh Guardian*, 28 November 1855). However, the following year, a very different picture emerged when Yourdi was in attendance at the police office court in Passage West in a case involving two Greek crew members' complaints about food and wages. A local boy called Clenane, most likely Callanan again, was sworn in as a witness to testify as to the food on board. He was then sworn in as interpreter and told the court that he had been interpreting 'as long as I can remember'. Yourdi intervened saying, 'The translation that boy has given is very wrong'. Yourdi then challenged another interpreted question, saying, 'Oh, your worship, this boy is doing very wrong. He says to the witness, "I am putting now the case before you, you must answer me."' However, the boy swore that he did not say such a thing, he merely asked the question but the witness 'did not give me the right answer'. When the boy interpreted the original question again, he told the court that the witness had said 'he would not be satisfied with it', but Yourdi claimed he had said 'no such thing; he says he does not understand you' (*Cork Constitution*, 8 January 1856). The second case showed how important it was for the consul to attend the case; he was the only person present who was in a position to understand and signal inaccurate interpreting.

Pasquale Tomassini had lived in England for a number of years before moving to Ireland. He was the proprietor of two hotels, one in Queenstown which he put up for sale in 1857 and a second at Warren's Place in Cork city. He took out a small advertisement in the newspaper in 1867 to the effect that he had returned from Italy and had received a shipment of wine direct from his vineyard at Monte Dago (Ancona) in Italy (*Cork Examiner*, 25 February 1867). Tomassini sold the Cork hotel in 1868, and he seems to have returned to Ancona. From at least 1876, his son Albert P. Tomassini (1846–1902), who was born in England, was British consul there (*Thom's Directory*). The issue of payment to foreign language interpreters arose in 1851 at Cork city criminal court. Tomassini had just finished interpreting for the captain of a ship from whom four women had allegedly robbed the sum of £19. After the accused had been found guilty, the solicitor for the prosecution observed that Mr Tomassini was entitled to his expenses. However, the judge said that that could only be done by presentment, as happened in the case of the Irish interpreter who was paid by the grand jury. He suggested that Tomassini could perhaps be paid as a witness in the case (*Cork Constitution*, 22 March 1851). Expenses could be paid to witnesses in assizes cases as outlined in Table 7.1. Interpreters would most likely have been included in the second category along with commercial and law clerks. However, no record has been located of interpreters of foreign languages receiving witness expenses for their interpreting work.

Correspondence with the Chief Secretary's Office at Dublin Castle suggests that it was only in 1903 that a foreign language interpreter was paid for his work; John Burke from Belfast was paid 2 pounds and 2 shillings for interpreting for Italian at Belfast assizes (CSO LB 91: 488, National Archives of Ireland). No earlier records of payments to interpreters of foreign languages were located although it is possible that the courts were in a position to make payments perhaps out of petty cash or fines, for example. Joseph Cartwright who travelled from London to interpret in the Caswell mutiny case must have been paid, and his travel and accommodation and other expenses may have been covered centrally by

Table 7.1 Witness expenses (Annual Report of the Local Government Board for Ireland)

Personal Allowance	Minimum per day	Minimum per night	Maximum per day	Maximum per night
1. Labourers	2s	1s 6d	5s	2s 6d
2. Farmers, shopkeepers and their assistants, commercial and law clerks, artisans &c	5s	5s		
3. Warders and other gaol officials, except governors	5s	5s		
4. Governors of gaols and petty sessions clerks	7s 6d	7s 6d		
5. Merchants, bank officials &c	5s	5s	10s	10s
6. County surveyors' assistants, land surveyors &c	4s	4s	10s	5s
7. Resident magistrates, and other government officials not classed above	10s	10s		
8. Doctors, solicitors, engineers and handwriting experts	21s	10s	42s	10s
9. Clergymen, private gentlemen, officers of the Navy and Army &c	5s	5s	42s	10s

Note: 's' stands for shillings, and 'd' stands for pence.

Dublin Castle. It is also likely that in civil cases litigants paid interpreters out of their own pockets – even Irish speakers had to pay interpreters out of their own pocket or depend on a volunteer in civil cases.

Carl Rudolph Felton (1833–1906), known by his middle name 'Rudolph' and occasionally referred to as Randolph, was born in Germany. In 1863, he married Ellen O'Sullivan. Felton's main source of income seems to have been as a water clerk, a clerk from a ship owner's or agent's office, who boards an arriving ship (*Oxford English Dictionary*). However, he also worked as an interpreter and on the 1901 census his occupation is listed as 'retired interpreter'. In 1873 Mr Harvey, consul for the North German Confederation, applied to Queenstown petty sessions to have a man called Johann Muller extradited to London on foot of a warrant issued by a judge in Cologne. Fenton was sworn in as interpreter and deposed that the English translation of the warrant was correct. He went on to swear that the seal was the official seal and that one copy was issued for the constabulary in Germany while a duplicate was sent to Ireland (*Cork Examiner*, 30 September 1873).

There are mentions of other interpreters, although they may not have worked in the courts. For example, Mr Spiteri was a hotel keeper, Greek interpreter and ship agent who had arrived in Queenstown in 1850 (*Cork Constitution*, 22 June 1854). Similarly, Count Gerissimo Masino Valsamachi was a shipbroker and interpreter (*Cork Examiner*, 21 June 1854). Meanwhile, Maurizio Gabardini was known as the interpreter in Passage (*Cork Constitution*, 11 September 1852; *Southern Reporter*, 4 December 1860) while Marco Giovanni Cola from Queenstown was described as 'interpreter and ship agent' (*Cork Constitution*, 24 September 1866).

On some occasions it proved difficult to locate an interpreter. The Norwegian language presented a problem at Queenstown petty sessions in 1872 when the master of a Norwegian ship was charged with assaulting a crew member and with having fired a shot at him. The chief mate gave evidence, and it was proposed that a coasting pilot called Hansen act as interpreter. Captain Seymour, consul for Norway, raised the issue of impartiality, cautioning that the pilot depended on Norwegian captains for work, but did not actually object. However, the court had great difficulty understanding the answers as conveyed by the ad hoc interpreter (*Cork Examiner*, 22 October 1872). Similarly, in 1882 at the same court, no interpreter could be found for a Spanish seaman who was facing a murder charge. The victim being an Italian, consuls Demery and Minich for Spain and Italy respectively were present in court. Demery informed the court that 'a gentleman who he knew would be there at half-past eleven for the purpose of interpreting'. The magistrate questioned why an interpreter was not provided at once but was told that 'we could not get one in the town; it is very difficult to get people who speak Spanish here'. The magistrate then commented that 'it ought not to be so difficult in a town like this' (*Cork Examiner*, 24 January 1882).

6 Conclusion

In line with Pym's recommendation regarding 'humanizing' translators, we have identified and 'humanized' a number of interpreters who in fact were not in large urban centres but instead were based in quite small places – particularly Queenstown – where shipping and trade provided opportunities. The foreign consuls who acted as interpreters all appear to have been well educated and enterprising with a very good knowledge of English and a number married local Irishwomen. They also had an advantage in that they attended the courts frequently in their role as consuls and would have been familiar with court processes and legal terms. Consuls, vice consuls and consular agents played a central role in sourcing interpreters for the courts. Their presence in court was of value because they acted as safeguards in interpreted cases. However, as most consuls spoke only English, they were not in a position to comment on the accuracy of interpreting, something that put the citizens of the countries they represented at a disadvantage. Sometimes, possibly when nobody else was available, those consuls who spoke the relevant language took on the role themselves. However, this could be complicated because consuls knew a lot about the cases and most likely formed their own opinions. In some cases, as we have seen, they were not impartial.

Interpreters who were not consuls may also have found it difficult to be impartial. For example, Reverend Gerald Brenan was also a prison chaplain and got to know defendants quite well, so much so that on at least one occasion, as we have seen, he appealed to the court on behalf of a defendant charged with murder. There was some awareness of the importance of impartiality with an interpreter being sourced from London for the Caswell mutiny trial. Similarly, Captain Seymour, consul for Norway, counselled that a coasting pilot depended on Norwegian captains for work. Overall, the provision of interpreters was ad hoc, and while we have seen that accuracy was clearly an issue in the cases of the teenage boy and the Norwegian coasting pilot, we do not know what the level of accuracy was overall. Apart from court cases and board of trade inquiries, it is clear that there were many commercial opportunities for interpreters; clearly language skills were extremely useful in Cork Harbour at the time.

References

Primary sources

Ancestry www.Ancestry.com
Annual Report of the Local Government Board for Ireland, being the 11th Report under the Local Government Board (Ireland) Act 35 and 36 Vic c 69, with appendices (1883).
Censuses of Ireland 1801, 1821, 1841, 1871, 1901 http://histpop.org/ohpr/servlet/
Cork Constitution
Cork Examiner
CSO LB 91 Chief Secretary's Office Country Letter Book, National Archives of Ireland.
Dublin Evening Mail
Findmypast www.findmypast.ie & British Newspaper Archive
Freeman's Journal
Guy's Cork Almanac (1859), Francis Guy, Cork.

Guy's Cork Almanac (1875), Francis Guy, Cork.
Howlin, Niamh (2010), 'Fenians, Foreigners and Jury Trials in Ireland, 1865-1870', *Irish Jurist*, 45: 51–81.
HenryHumphreys (1867), *The Justice of the Peace for Ireland*, Dublin: Hodges Smith & Co.
Irish Newspaper Archive https://www.irishnewsarchive.com
Irish Prison Registers Findmypast.ie
Irish Times Digital Archive https://www.irishtimes.com/archive
The King v Lee Kun (1916) 1 K.B. 337.
Laing's Cork Mercantile Directory (1863), Henry & Coghlan, Cork. http://www.cork pastandpresent.ie/places/streetandtradedirectories/corkmercantiledirectory 1863.pdf.
Lewis, Samuel (1837), *A Topographical Dictionary of Ireland*, vol. II, London: S. Lewis and Co..
Marmion, Anthony (1855), *The Ancient and Modern History of the Maritime Ports of Ireland*, London: W. H. Cox.
Mooney, Thomas (1845), *A History of Ireland from Its First Settlement to the Present Time,* Published by the author, Boston.
Nenagh Guardian
Post Office London Directory (1861), Ancestry.com
Slater's Royal National Commercial Directory of Ireland (1881), Manchester.
Southern Reporter & Cork Commercial Courier
Southern Star
Thom's Irish Almanac and Official Directory of the United Kingdom (1876), Dublin: Alexander Thom & Sons.
Tuson, E. W. A. (1856), *The British Consul's Manual*, London: Longman.

Secondary sources

Agstner, R. (2004), 'Austro-Hungarian Consulates in Munster 1845–1914', *North Munster Antiquarian Journal*, 44: 39–51.
Breathnach, S. (2003), *The Riddle of the Caswell Mutiny*, Irvine, CA: Universal Publishers.
Coakley, D. J. (1919), *Cork: Its Trade and Commerce*, Cork: Guy & Co. Ltd.
Howlin, Niamh (2010), 'Fenians, Foreigners and Jury Trials in Ireland 1865–70', *Irish Jurist*, 45: 51–81.
Institut français de l'éducation. Available online: http://www.inrp.fr/edition-electron ique/lodel/dictionnaire-ferdinand-buisson/document.php?id=3126
Leonard, C. (2015), *Interpreters and Deaf People in Irish Courts 1815–1924.* Available online: academia.edu
Oxford English Dictionary

Pym, A. (2009), 'Humanizing Translation History', *Hermes – Journal of Language and Communication Studies*, 42: 23–48.

Santoyo, J. C. (2006), 'Blank Spaces in the History of Translation', in G. L. Bastin and P. F. Bandia (ed.), *Charting the Future of Translation History*, 11–43. Ottawa: University of Ottawa Press.

Smith, R. (2009), 'Claude Marcel (1793–1876): A Neglected Applied Linguist?' *Language & History* 52 (2): 171–81.

8

Maritime interpreters in nineteenth-century Barcelona: A failure story in translation policy

Albert Branchadell

1 Introduction

This chapter addresses translation policy in maritime trade in nineteenth-century Barcelona, when the capital city of Catalonia and its surrounding area became Spain's first industrializing region and its seaport – especially after its modernization in the 1870s – became the largest Spanish port on the Mediterranean (and the second largest in the whole Spain).[1] This turned Barcelona into a gateway to global trade, which exponentially increased the need for translation and interpreting services in town and set the context for the establishment of a specific corps of maritime interpreters.

In the nineteenth century, Spain was a heavily centralized state of the French type in which regional languages like Catalan were banished from public life. In this setting of imposed monolingualism – which was only interrupted during Catalonia's brief occupation by Napoleon (1808–14), who favoured Catalan to obtain loyalty of the local political elite – translation and interpreting services in the port of Barcelona were solely provided into Spanish, despite the fact that both maritime interpreters and port authorities were more often than not native Catalan speakers. The Catalan national revival – that supported the use of Catalan in all domains of public life – only took root by the end of the century, when maritime interpreters in Barcelona were about to vanish.

In 1829 Spain adopted her first Code of Commerce, modelled on the Napoleonic *Code de commerce* of 1807. The traditional French *courtier interprète et conducteur de navires* ('interpreter broker and ship driver') was copied and pasted into the 1829 Spanish Code of Commerce as *corredor intérprete de buques* ('vessel interpreter broker', or VIB, renamed in the 1930s as *intérprete marítimo*, 'maritime interpreter'). This state-employed professional type had already sprung up in the port city of Bilbao in the eighteenth century, a sui generis combination of the otherwise distinct roles of (a) stockbroker with notary public powers and (b) provider of translation and interpreting services into Spanish. The 1885 reform of the Code reasserted the 1829 regulation and further provisions on this profession extended into mid-twentieth century.

Despite its long existence, VIBs have not been treated in a serious way in scholarly literature, so that all that exists on this topic amounts to a couple of tentative papers (Santoyo 2003; del Pozo 2010). Against the backdrop of growing maritime trade in Barcelona, this chapter endeavours to outline the (slow) birth, (scant) achievements, and (quick) demise of VIBs in this city.

The structure of this chapter is as follows. Section 2 presents my theoretical framework, in which I try to pull two strings together: translation policy, on the one hand, and the sociology of professions, on the other. Section 3 reviews previous literature on the topic. Section 4 highlights the importance of the port of Barcelona as the setting where vessel interpreter brokers performed. Section 5 gives a historical outline of vessel interpreter brokers in Spain from the point of view of the state decisions made to create and empower them. Section 6 is specifically devoted to the short-lived experience of vessel interpreter brokers of Barcelona (1882–1903), a city which concentrated a quarter of all of Spain's vessel interpreter brokers. And the final concluding section summarizes the findings of this chapter.

2 Theoretical framework

In front of simplistic definitions of translation policy as 'a set of legal rules that regulate translation in the public domain' (Meylaerts 2011), my topic of research is one that demands a more complex approach to the matter. In his pioneering book on language policy, Spolsky (2004) distinguished between three components of the language policy of a speech community: 'its language practices …, its language beliefs or ideology … and any specific efforts to modify or influence that practice by any kind of language intervention, planning or management'. Following this suggestion, González Núñez (2016) developed a concept of translation policy that encompasses translation management, translation practice and translation beliefs. The main insight of González Núñez that I want to draw on is the idea that there may be 'tension' between management, practice and belief. I am especially interested in his concept of 'practice not mandated through legal rules', which can be easily upgraded to 'practice *opposed to* legal rules'.

The potential inconsistency between management and practice is at the heart of Spolsky's general approach to language policy. Spolsky (2004: 217) stressed that 'language practices, beliefs and management are not necessarily congruent'. According to him, 'Looking at the language policy of the established nations, one commonly finds major disparities between the language policy laid down in the constitution and the actual practices in the society' (2004: 217). This leads to the question of whether language policy can ever succeed. In the optimist–pessimist divide, Spolsky admitted that the records favour the pessimists: 'There are comparatively few cases where language management has produced its intended results' (2004: 223). No matter what the empirical plausibility of this statement is, I want to adopt Spolsky's insight on this particular condition for success: the implementation of language management 'depends in large measure on its congruity with the practices and ideology of the community' (2004: 218). (In this study I will leave translation beliefs aside.)

This study is about the failure of Spain's translation policy in the very specific domain of maritime trade in Barcelona in the nineteenth century. From the point of view of translation management, in this chapter I will look at the explicit decisions made by the Spanish government and Spanish legislators from outside the domain. These decisions are to be found in Spanish laws, royal decrees and royal orders. All these decisions point in the same direction: the establishment and empowerment of an official corps of 'vessel interpreter brokers' in all Spanish ports open to international maritime trade. From the point of view of translation practice, I will gather some evidence according to which things were not as they ought to be in view of the decisions made. This mismatch between management and practice has some points of contact with Wolf's (2012: 16) distinction between institutionalized and habitualized translation. In her approach, these two types of translation belong to two different domains: administration, on the one hand, and everyday language contacts, on the other. What is specific to my research topic is the competition between institutionalized and habitualized translation within the same domain of international maritime trade. In a way, what I am going to outline here is a failed process of institutionalization in the sense of Koskinen (2014). 'Institutional' vessel interpreter brokers in Barcelona did not manage to override habitualized translation. Given the brevity of their existence (1882–1903), it is next to impossible to view these vessel interpreter brokers as 'stable and fixed entities' (Kang 2014: 473): their very evanescence compels us to examine 'the processes and historical trajectories through which they emerged' (ibid) – and the processes through which they vanished.

The overt competition between vessel interpreter brokers and other professional groups is what enables me to vindicate the relevance of the sociology of professions for my research topic. I will rely on Abbott (1988), which was successfully reviewed by Monzó (2009) for the specific field of translation. From Abbott (1988) we can draw his overall insight on professionalization. With respect to other approaches to this phenomenon, Abbott moved the focus to 'a fundamental fact of professional life: interprofessional competition' (Abbott 1988: 2). In relation to this, he developed the notion of jurisdiction – a segment of the labour market – and jurisdictional boundaries, which are 'perpetually in dispute'. He went on to claim that 'it is the history of jurisdictional disputes that is the real, the determining history of the professions' (Abbott 1988: 2) and that 'interprofessional relations are the central feature of professional development' (Abbott 1988: 18). In this regard, two essential questions for my case study are as follows: What was the vessel interpreter brokers jurisdiction intended or supposed to be? And why did they not succeed in seizing control of it? The inconsistency between policy and practice that I will show reveals a clash between a policy-driven profession and other professions that kept control of their jurisdictions on the ground and opposed outsiders who, in their view, attacked that control. My story can be summarized as follows: in the nineteenth century, Spanish policy created a corps that was meant to seize control of a jurisdiction that – at least in Barcelona – was not really 'vacant' in practice. In sum, the case of vessel interpreter brokers is the case of a failed profession: if professions are 'exclusive occupational groups applying somewhat abstract knowledge to particular cases' (Abbott 1988: 8), vessel interpreter brokers clearly failed on the account of exclusivity. The decisive struggle that they lost was precisely that one. In the end, the demise of vessel interpreter brokers is just a token of the phenomenon that Abbott (1988) named 'professional death'.

As I said, Monzó applied the teachings of Abbott to the field of translation and interpreting professions. Monzó (2009) described two 'jurisdictional struggles' specific to this field: the struggle between sworn translators and interpreters (TIs) and notaries public and the struggle between certified TIs and court TIs. Both struggles have some inevitable points of contact with the struggle between vessel interpreter brokers and sworn interpreters of the nineteenth century. (Outside the world of Abbott's jurisdictional struggles, see also Koskinen and Dam 2016 for a discussion on the boundaries of the translation profession and Grbić 2010 for the boundary issue in the *interpreting* field.)

On top of the notions of jurisdiction and jurisdiction dispute or struggle, Abbott provides other valuable tools for my research topic. Most of the formal properties – or 'professional paraphernalia' – of established professions can be observed in vessel interpreter brokers: 'entry by examination and other formal prerequisites' (Abbott 1988: 4), a 'list of authorized practitioners' and 'professional discipline' (Abbott 1988: 24), and of course professional associations (the *colegios* in Spanish terminology) with their internal regulations, governing bodies and so on. (In Barcelona, as we shall see, vessel interpreter brokers – who already had a tariff of their own – were granted the right to wear a distinct uniform.) Secondly, the role of time and place that Abbott remarked is of great relevance for our case as well. An interesting question would be why vessel interpreter brokers faded so quickly in Barcelona (1882–1903) while they lasted for so long in Bilbao (1737–1940s). Thirdly, the relevance of state participation in professionalization is crucial to our case. Spanish vessel interpreter brokers were *state* officials; without state action, there would not have been vessel interpreter brokers outside Bilbao. This brings us back to the field of institutional translation and the tension between institutional or governmental and non-governmental translators. One possible reading here is that the demise of vessel interpreter brokers in Barcelona illustrates a typically capitalist victory of market forces over state regulations.

3 Previous research

The existence of VIB is mentioned in a good number of handbooks and dictionaries of the nineteenth century which contain a gloss of the relevant provisions of the Code of Commerce. *La bolsa, el comercio y las sociedades mercantiles* (1882, 1883^2, 1883^3, 1884^4) by José Montero y Vidal is somewhat exceptional in this context, inasmuch as it provided the number, names, and the day when they took office of appointed VIB of all Spanish ports, and so enables us to gauge how widespread the body of VIB was on the eve of the new, 1885 Code of Commerce. The number of appointed VIBs can be seen in Table 8.1.

Several twentieth-century handbooks and specialized encyclopaedias also dealt with VIB. All these works share a common feature: they focus on legislation and have little to say about practice. For this, one has to turn to the only book ever written by a VIB (Arriaga, 1913, 1923^2) and the two single contemporary academic papers that deal with VIBs, Santoyo (2003) and del Pozo (2010).

Table 8.1 Appointed VIBs in the 1880s

Port	N
Barcelona	10
Bilbao	22
Santander	2
San Sebastián and Pasajes	4
Alicante	1
Huelva	2
Gijón	2
Total	43

Arriaga (1913, 1923^2) is a sort of vade mecum for Bilbao's vessel interpreter brokers: it contains a short history of VIB in Bilbao (including a list of acting VIBs), a large section on relevant legislation, a number of reports issued by the *Colegio* of Bilbao (relevant to the jurisdictional struggles that VIB were involved in), a number of forms and templates (including a blank 'copiador de traducciones'), and even a glossary at the back with all the technical terms, a multilingual list of mercantile expressions, plus a funny section on 'marine proverbs'.

No matter how useful it is, Arriaga (1913, 1923^2) is everything except a standard academic text. In this specific genre only two papers seem to exist to this day. Santoyo (2003) is a pioneering approach to VIB in Bilbao and other Basque ports in Spain. He provided dozens of names, but he was not able to describe the real activity of VIB nor went on to describe any jurisdictional struggle between VIB and other professions. And he had nothing to say on other Spanish ports outside the Basque region. Del Pozo (2010) tried to be more comprehensive, with relative success. After sending many information requests to several bodies all over Spain, she was able to report very few findings, and none on the port of Barcelona.

Besides Santoyo (2003) and del Pozo (2010), a third contemporary paper is also worth mentioning. Although not focused on VIB, Peñarroja's (2000) history of sworn interpreters in Spain mentions VIB in passing on a nonetheless important account, which is the competition between sworn interpreters and VIB over the same translation and interpreting jurisdiction.

As it can be noticed, no book or paper has ever been written in English on Spanish VIB. The only mention to VIB in English (under the name of 'maritime interpreters') is a brief comment in Baigorri (2015): 'In the domain of legal interpreting, the sworn interpreters' corps, as a group distinct from the maritime interpreters or those who acted overseas, was established through legislation enacted at various points in time.'

4 On the port of Barcelona

In the late nineteenth century the harbour city of Barcelona was an urban agglomeration with a densely populated industrializing hinterland (her population more than doubled between 1857 and 1910: from 230,607 to 587,284 inhabitants).

One of the main features of the nineteenth-century Spanish port system – which continues to this day – was the high concentration of port activity in a short number of central ports. A good indicator of this concentration is the share of the first five Spanish ports in the all-Spain maritime trade. According to Castillo and Valdaliso (2017), in 1880 the ports of Bilbao, Barcelona, Cádiz, Cartagena and Huelva had a share of 61.35 per cent. In 1900 Bilbao, Barcelona, Huelva, Santander and Valencia reached 66.27 of total trade.

If one classifies these Spanish ports by throughput (measured in tons), Barcelona ranked first in mid-century (Figuerola 1849), and second (after Bilbao) in the last two decades of the century (Castillo and Valdaliso 2017). Although Barcelona ranked second in terms of weight of traded goods, according to Castejón (1974: 130) it was the first commercial port as far as the value of traded goods is concerned. In a nineteenth-century source we find data on the value of imported and exported goods that support this statement. According to Rafo (1861), in 1857 the port of Barcelona ranked first in the value of imports with 608,482,039 *reales de vellón* (rs.vn.; the Spanish monetary unity prior to the *peseta*), far ahead of Valencia with 424,270,144 rs. vn. In the case of exports it ranked first as well with 391,712,167 rs. vn. followed by Cádiz with 320,551,034. The total value of 1,000,194,206 rs. vn. was almost a quarter of the added value of the main 15 Spanish ports. According to Carreras and Yáñez (1992: 104), maritime trade in Barcelona was a sensible proportion of overall Catalan GDP, ranging from 23.8 per cent in 1870 to 48.6 per cent in 1890 and 27.6 in 1900.

Another feature of the Spanish port system in the late nineteenth century was port specialization. Bilbao stood out as an export-minded port – iron being the most important good (Puerta 1996) – whereas Barcelona was more focused on import (coal and other raw materials which were demanded by fast-growing Catalan industry). In this import-oriented context, there is no doubt that coal was the top product (Carreras and Yáñez 1992). At the turn of the century around 50 per cent of all port traffic involved coal. (See also Servicio de Estudios en Barcelona, 1968: 277 and 281f.)

Table 8.2 Movement of ships in 1889–1890

	Incoming	Outgoing
Domestic	2,277	2,046
Foreign	1,011	998
English	429	427
Italian	256	236
French	137	131
Norwegian	78	78
German	43	43
Danish	24	23
Swedish	22	20
Greek	16	16
Austro-Hungarian	12	12
Russian	10	10
Dutch	1	1
Portuguese	1	1

In Ricart (1894: 121) we find the number of incoming and outgoing ships according to their flag from 1 October 1889 to 30 September 1890, which gives a clue on the languages that VIB had to translate (Table 8.2).

5 Setting up a corps of vessel interpreter brokers

The first Spanish legislative text to regulate VIBs was the Ordinances of Bilbao enacted in 1737, which probably found their inspiration in French seventeenth-century legislation. According to them, VIBs had to be proficient in at least one foreign language. (French, English, Dutch and 'Flemish' were singled out as examples.) In addition to their role as interpreters and translators for foreign captains, VIB were meant to 'help' local merchants and ship captains in the trading of their goods. One interesting point is that of optionality. As set out by the Ordinances, Bilbao merchants and ship captains who preferred to act 'by themselves' could not be forced to use VIB.

The Ordinances of Bilbao, together with the French Code of Commerce of 1807, underlie the first Spanish Code of Commerce, which was enacted in 1829. The Code established that in every port licensed for international trade there should be a number of interpreter brokers proportional 'to the extent of its trade relations'. A novelty with respect to the Ordinances is that interpreters were supposed to be proficient in *two* foreign languages. The Code regulated the appointment of VIB in the same lines as that of standard brokers, with the only differences that the deposit they had to pay was half of what was established for standard brokers.

The *atribuciones privativas* ('exclusive responsibilities') of VIB were set in Article 731:

1. To intervene in charter contracts that captains or consignees of ships do not sign directly with charterers.
2. To assist the captains and supercargos of foreign ships, and to serve as interpreters in the declarations, protests and other proceedings that may occur to them in the courts and public offices, on the understanding that captains and supercargos are free not to use brokers when they can clear these proceedings by themselves or are assisted by their consignees.
3. To translate the documents that the said foreign captains and supercargos have to present in the same offices, certifying that the translations are done correctly and faithfully, without which they will not be admitted.
4. To represent captains and supercargos in court, when they do not appear personally, or by means of the ship owner or the consignee of the ship.

With the help of the French Code of Commerce, the 1829 Spanish Code of Commerce exported the French-inspired Bilbao institution of VIB to all Spanish ports. The factual implementation of VIB outside Bilbao is quite another story. In a throughout search of *Gaceta de Madrid* (Spain's official journal of that time) I did not find any disposition on the appointment of VIB to specific ports outside Bilbao until 1875.

After 1875 there is an array of royal orders that create positions of VIB in different ports. In 1877 a royal order decreed the creation of two jobs of VIB for the port of Sevilla, and a second order did the same for the port of Gijón, that so far 'lacked' such professionals. A royal order of 1878 noticed that 'contrary to what is stated in article 729 of the Code of Commerce' the port of Málaga also lacked VIB and created six such positions for this port. Barcelona was somewhat late in this process. It was only in 1881 that a royal order (26 August) created ten positions of VIB in the port of Barcelona. The wording of this royal order is extremely useful to understand what was going on in Spanish ports some fifty years after the first Code of Commerce was enacted. The essential thing is that the port was not operating without interpreting services: in the absence of licensed VIB, these services were provided by 'plain' brokers, by sworn interpreters and by the consuls of agreed nations. A last remark is also insightful: the *atribuciones privativas* ('exclusive responsibilities') of VIB as set in Article 731 of the Code of Commerce could not be performed by sworn interpreters nor by standard brokers that were not also licensed as VIB.

As I said, ten jobs of VIB were created for the port of Barcelona. The royal order says that ten will be enough to meet the needs of the port of Barcelona, 'according to a report of its city council'. I searched for this report with no success, but I did find another document which is relevant to this story: the minutes of the meeting where the necessary number of VIB for the port of Barcelona was discussed (22 March 1881). The report that was initially presented to the city councillors set the number of required VIB at four. When he heard this, city councillor Juan Coll took the floor to argue that four was insufficient 'given the importance and trading relationships of this capital city'. In a deliberate bluff, he pretended to know that other city councils were betting on *ten* jobs of VIB, and he proposed to amend the report in order to set the number of requested VIB at ten. With no apparent debate, the city council accepted his amendment and that is why the royal order mentions ten not four VIB.

In any case, granting abstract jobs was one thing, and appointing specific people to these jobs and the creation of *colegios* was a different thing. In the case of Barcelona one year elapsed between the royal decree of 1881 and the appointment of Barcelona's first VIB in 1882. And four more years went by until the *Colegio* of Barcelona had its first regulations in 1886.

After the 1882 appointments, a major normative change occurred. In 1885 the old Code of Commerce was replaced by a new one. Article 88 established three mediating actors: 'agentes de cambio y bolsa' (*exchange and stock market agents*), 'corredores de comercio' (*stock brokers*) and 'corredores intérpretes de buques' (VIB). Article 90 introduced the possibility of creating specific *colegios* for each type of agent. Article 93 further stated that licensed brokers shall act as notaries public. To perform as a VIB, the Code of Commerce established the same requirements as the other agents plus the obligation to accredit, either by examination or by public establishment certificate, 'knowledge of two foreign modern languages'. A royal order of 1891 ruled that VIB were restricted to authorize translations from the languages they mastered; as for other languages, Customs Authorities were allowed to resort to 'other interpreters'.

Article 113 of the new Code of Commerce established the obligations of VIB (I am quoting the official translation of the Code here):

1. To intervene in charter contracts, maritime insurance and bottomry loans, when required to do so;

2. To aid the masters and officers of foreign ships and to act as interpreters for them in the statements, protests and other actions they are required to provide before the Courts and Public Offices;
3. To translate the documents that the said masters and officers may have to lodge before those same offices, whenever a doubt arises with regard to their meaning, certifying the translations are truly and faithfully performed;
4. To represent them on trial when neither they nor the ship owner or consignor are present.

As can be seen, paragraphs 2 and 3 of this Article 113 pointed in abstract terms to the interpreting and translation duties of VIB. Although no explicit mention was made to languages, it is clear that the target language was Spanish and that the source languages were all the possible modern foreign languages alluded to in Article 93. (In the tariff, English, French, German, Italian and Portuguese are mentioned along with 'any other language'.) A significant difference between the 1885 and the 1829 Code is to be found in paragraph 2. Whereas the 1829 Code explicitly stated that captains were 'free' not to use brokers, the 1885 one remained silent on this point.

The 1885 Code of Commerce did not specify the royalties that corresponded to VIB for their functions. This issue was dealt with in the Interim regulations for the organization and regime of Stock Exchanges (31 December 1885), whose Article 71 reads as follows:

Tariff of Vessel Interpreters Brokers

1. In maritime insurance 8% on the amount of the prize, charged from the insurer.
2. In the chartering of ships, 4% on the amount of freight, charged by the captain or charterer.
3. In the bottomry loans 1 per 1,000 on the amount of the capital loaned to be paid fifty-fifty by the giver and borrower of the loan.
4. For the proceedings referred to in par. 2 of article 113 [of the Code of Commerce] they will charge, if the time devoted by the VIB does not exceed one hour, 10 *pesetas*. For every 15 minutes that exceed that time, 2 *pesetas* 50 cents.
5. For the translation of document referred to in par. 3 of article 113 they will charge 5 *pesetas* for each sheet of 24 lines if the translation is made from French, Italian or Portuguese; 10 *pesetas* if it is from English or German, and 12 *pesetas* if it is from any other language.

As far as I know, this is the first time in history that a tariff for translation and interpreting services has been published in Spain's official journal. (It is worth noticing that this tariff remained intact for a long period. According to a royal decree of 1910 they were just the same; the only change was the addition of a double tariff for *inverse* translations.)

6 Barcelona's vessel interpreter brokers and their official professional association

6.1 The individual interpreters

The appointment of Barcelona's first ten VIB took place in 1882. This is the complete list of VIB that started to be officially operative on 25 September of that year (in alphabetical order):

1. Guillermo Ahman y Nottbert [or Nottbech]
2. Francisco Bech y Morera
3. Juan Cardona y Robert
4. Federico Condeminas y Torres
5. Felipe Eixarch y Arberola
6. Francisco Mascaró y Gaurán
7. Luis Oliver y Riera
8. Salvador Talavera y Barceló
9. Luis Toribio Sogorb
10. Antonio Torrents y Monner

I have found no information on the living languages they accredited to become VIB, although I have some clues on this account for some of them to which I shall return as we proceed.

What did these VIB do before the Barcelona *Colegio* was created? As VIB, most likely they did little. Their very visibilization was a slow process to begin with. In the first Bally-Ballière directory – a sort of yearbook of 'commerce, industry, judiciary, and administration' – published in 1882 Guillermo Ahaman (*sic*) appeared as 'interpreter' and Salvador Talavera as 'interpreter and maritime broker'. Thanks to this directory we know that at least two of the appointed VIB were active in the interpreting business prior to their appointment as VIB. The same information appeared in the 1883 and 1884 directories. The VIB surfaced for the first time in the 1885 directory: out of ten appointed VIB nine were mentioned in the directory, all except Guillermo Ahaman (*sic*), who was listed as 'customs agent'. The *Colegio de corredores intérpretes reales de navíos del puerto de Barcelona* also surfaced for the first time in the 1885 directory. Its headquarters were located on 1 Muntaner street, the home address of Antonio Torrents. (A look at successive editions of this directory reveals that the *Colegio* never had a headquarters of its own. In the 1886 and 1887 editions the *Colegio* had two mailing addresses: the home addresses of Luis de Oliver and Antonio Torrents. In the 1888 edition it had just one, Luis de Oliver's. From 1894 onwards, the directory did not mention any address at all.)

We don't know exactly when the *Colegio* was created. We do know that Antonio Torrents was unanimously elected president-trustee of the *Colegio* on 31 January 1883. And we know that its first regulations were passed through a royal order of 25 November 1886, and printed in 1888.

Directories like Bally-Ballière and Riera and other contemporary sources provide information on additional VIB to these ones. In 1892 the newspaper *La Vanguardia* informed that Manuel Condominas (*sic*) y Torres had been appointed as VIB of the port of Barcelona (19 June). Later that year the same newspaper informed that a certain Luis Mandado has resigned from his position as VIB (27 September). (Two days later the same source informed that his resignation had not been accepted.) In the Bally-Ballière directory of 1897 a certain Emilio Aguilar turned up under the heading 'Colegio de corredores intérpretes reales de navío'. In the Riera directory of the same year someone named José Oller made his appearance.

The same sources also reveal that some former VIB were or ended up performing neighbouring jobs.

In the Riera directories from 1896 onwards Guillermo Ahman (written Ahernán or Ahmann) and Felipe Eixarch were listed as sworn court interpreters. I spotted a token of Ahman's work as such. According to an affidavit dated 14 April 1883, an Italian citizen, Pietro Roselen, appeared before a notary public 'assisté de l'interprète-juré, don Guillermo Ahman'. As for Felipe Eixarch (b. 1851), he was listed as interpreter of French, English, German and Italian. His colleague Ramón Arabia Solanas was interpreter of Latin, Catalan (surprisingly), Portuguese, French, English and German. In 1897 Arabia added Italian to his languages, and in 1901 a new interpreter appeared, Martin Kraemer, who had French, English, German, Italian, Portuguese, Dutch, Danish and 'the Scandinavian languages'. In this edition Eixarch was listed as interpreter of French, English, Italian *and Catalan*, so that there were two sworn court interpreters with Catalan – and intriguing fact that I must leave for further research. Eixarch was also involved in education. We know that in 1887 he was in a contest for tenure in Italian at the Barcelona High School. He did not seem to get this contract, for in 1893 and 1894 he was advertising the so-called Escuela Práctica Comercial in Barcelona, of which he was director, where he taught Spanish, French, English, German and Italian (*La Publicidad*, 25 December 1893; 3 January, 30 March, 5 August and 16 August 1894). In 1912 he became lecturer of French, and in 1921 he retired from this position at the Figueres High School (a small city some 140 kilometres north of Barcelona).

As for Manuel Condeminas, in the 1899, 1901, 1902 and 1903 Riera directories he was listed as interpreter for the port's military government. In 1904, 1905 and 1908 he was listed both as military interpreter *and* VIB, although VIBs had seemingly ceased to exist.

What about the other VIBs of the list? Antonio Torrents (b. 1852) was the first and only president of the *Colegio* of Barcelona. There is plenty of information about Torrents: a whole dossier on him rests in the library of the Royal Academy of Arts and Sciences of Barcelona. Thanks to this dossier we know that Torrents was elected president of the *Colegio* on 31 January 1883. Among many other things, we also know that when he was accepted as member of the Royal Academy in 1889, he delivered a speech on administrative accounting. For our purposes, the most relevant piece of information on Torrents is contained in the welcome speech given by his patron: after mentioning his appointment as VIB, the patron remarked that 'even if he does not perform the aforementioned profession, he has been conferred the position of president-trustee of the *Colegio* since 1883'. A revealing circumstance indeed: Torrents did not earn his living as a VIB but rather as an accountant at Barcelona's *Diputación* (provincial government) and as a professor. For this reason there is no evidence in this dossier of his life as a VIB. In a long publication list containing eighty-three items there is just one work related to the activity of VIB, which was printed in 1888: *Compilación de disposiciones y formularios para los Corredores Intérpretes de Buques*.

One remarkable thing is that Torrents seems to have been alien to the pro-Catalan cultural milieu of his time. (The Catalan national revival is contemporary to the establishment of VIB in Barcelona.) Quite on the contrary, he was a great defender of Spanish. One of his publications is entitled 'La lengua española como lengua universal' (1900). The only text in Catalan in the whole Torrents dossier is a note written in 1913 by Eugeni d'Ors, a well-known Catalan writer then secretary of the Institut d'Estudis Catalans (Institute of Catalan Studies), to thank Torrents for the donation of his complete works to the Institute's library.

Francisco Mascaró (b. 1844), Torrents's first assistant, doesn't seem to have performed as VIB either. Mascaró was a wealthy man and a big landowner. According to Cañelles & Toran (2013), he worked as an agent for Veritas Helénico of Piraeus (1887) and for the Compañía de Seguros Marítimos, Fluviales y Terrestres 'La Italia' of Buenos Aires (1889). In Ricart (1894) the 'chartered interpreter' Franscisco Mascaró is mentioned as consignee of 'Italian, Austrian, and Greek vessels'. Well beyond the maritime affairs, Mascaró promoted a company to build a tramway line between Barcelona and the neighbouring town of Sant Joan d'Horta (1894). In Sant Joan d'Horta (now a district of Barcelona) he became famous as the owner of a castle. Mascaró had a political career as well, in the ranks of the Conservative party. He was councilman in the council city of Barcelona. Mascaró is the only VIB that deserved to name a street in Barcelona. According to Barcelona's catalogue of street names, Mascaró street took originally its name from our VIB, who in 1887 had bought the land where this street was opened.

Like Francisco Mascaró, his namesake Francisco Bech (b. ?) seems to have been involved in more lucrative affairs than interpreting. According to Moreno (2011), Bech was one of the prominent members of Catalan capitalism that created the Sociedad Anónima Naviera Española in 1916. While Mascaró had a castle, Bech owned a mansion. According to a municipal website, this building 'is an example of summer house of well-off people in the hill area of Barcelona'.

As I said earlier, in the 1899–1908 Riera directories, Manuel Condeminas Torres appears as interpreter of the port's military government. But he was involved in other kinds of maritime business as well. It seems that back in 1864 a shipping company named 'Sons of M. Condeminas' was created in Barcelona (*ABC*, 28 May 1926) by his father. Thanks to the newspapers, in the early twentieth century we can keep track of the movements of at least one steamship ('Carlos') owned by him.

As for Salvador Talavera (died 1899 or 1900), in Ricart (1894) he is linked to the dispatch of Norwegian, Swedish, Russian and Danish vessels. (In *La Vanguardia* of 14 October 1884 he was mentioned as consignee of Russian corvette 'Alma'.) Like his colleagues, he was also a businessman. He owned at least one ship (schooner 'Virgen del Carmen' is mentioned in *La Vanguardia*, 7 November 1882).

The only piece of news we have on Juan Cardona is that he died on 23 November 1908. And the only thing we know about Luis Toribio is that he was appointed president of the Academia Científico-Mercantil on 29 December

1882. I spotted no information on the three remaining VIBs (José Carreras, Federico Condeminas and Luis de Oliver). Other than biographical data, the most relevant point is that I found no evidence of the activity of Barcelona's VIB as VIB – at least in their translation and interpreting dimension. To be more specific, I have not spotted a single token of the translation book that VIB were supposed to keep according to Article 114 of the Code of Commerce.

6.2 The *Colegio* of Barcelona

As a group, the *Colegio* does not seem to have led a bright existence. On 7 May 1888 Barcelona's newspaper *La Vanguardia* reported that the Spanish government had authorized the VIB of Barcelona to wear in official ceremonies the uniform they had asked for. The next day *La Vanguardia* described this uniform: 'black dress coat with silver braid, set of buttons of the same metal, wearing the Catalan eagle in the cuffs, black pants, white tie and vest, hat, wearing the colors of the register of this city, and dress sword with silver hilt'. Unfortunately, I have spotted no picture of a VIB wearing such a uniform.

The most detailed piece of information on the Barcelona's *Colegio* is related to the organization of its library. In a letter addressed to the president of Barcelona's *Diputación* dated 21 December 1889, the *Colegio* requested a copy of the duplicate works in the corporation's archive to be able to start the library provided for in Article 32 of the *Colegio*'s regulations. On 3 January 1890, the Development Section of the *Diputación* agreed to accept this request, an agreement that was ratified by the plenary session of the *Diputación* on 7 January. On 21 January a list of the works and number of leftover copies of them that were in the Library of the *Diputación* was drawn up, and finally the *Diputación* decided to invite the *Colegio* to pick up a copy of each work contained in the said list. The truth is that the books thus obtained were not especially close either to the world of languages or to that of maritime trade. The list includes a self-help book like *Lo camí de la fortuna. Consells breus pera esser rich* ('The road to fortune. Brief tips for becoming rich'), the minutes of a conference on penitentiary affairs held in Stockholm, several treaties on phylloxera (a grapevine-destroying insect), and a good deal of poetry books. The only book related to maritime issues was called *Estudios sobre socorros y auxilios á náufragos* ('Studies on Relief and Assistance to Shipwreck Survivors').

This reference to wrecks comes in handy, because the *Colegio*'s failure was not far away in time. When did the *Colegio* collapse? According to Ricart (1894), in

1894 the *Colegio* was still operating with the 1886 composition. On 10 May 1903 Ricart wrote this on the *Colegio* in the journal *La Vida Marítima*:

> No pudiendo resistir la competencia de los agentes no colegiados, y teniendo que pagar una contribución anual, cada uno de ellos, de 1.500 PTA que les impuso la Hacienda, se cerró el Colegio. Así se cerrarán todos, si el Gobierno no apoya á esta clase tan necesaria para el comercio marítimo.[2]

The *Colegio* disappeared and so did the VIB of Barcelona. Arriaga (1913: 21, 1923[2]: 23) quotes a 1909 report from the *Colegio* of Bilbao, according to which in the port of Barcelona not a single VIB was in exercise. According to Arriaga (1923: 307), in the 1920s there was a single VIB in Barcelona, who was nonetheless attached to the *Colegio* of Bilbao. This Valentín González Bárcena, who was appointed by a royal order of 5 June 1922, is the last known VIB of Barcelona ever.

7 Conclusion

In this chapter I outlined the history of vessel interpreter brokers in Spain from the point of view of top-down translation management decisions. I focused on the Spanish laws, royal decrees and royal orders that formally introduced and regulated the functions of these professionals in the Spanish port system. After this all-Spain presentation, I moved the focus to the VIBs of the harbour city of Barcelona and the *Colegio* (official professional association) in which they were engaged. Two main findings stand out: (1) Beginning with the president-trustee of the Barcelona *Colegio* himself, there seems to be no evidence of the activity of VIBs of translation and interpreting services, and (2) in any case VIBs of Barcelona emerged and vanished rather quickly (1882–1903). Both findings uncover a veiled reality: at least in the port of Barcelona, agents other than VIBs were delivering translation and interpreting services to foreign vessels prior to the emergence of VIBs, during their existence and naturally after their demise. A huge gap existed between translation management decisions and translation practice on the ground.

Where Monzó (2009: 135) said that 'the jurisdiction formerly occupied by certified TIs, has been progressively claimed by notaries public and court TIs', we could say that VIBs were created to seize the jurisdiction formerly occupied by certified TIs (and other agents involved in maritime trade). But the truth is that VIBs did not succeed in taking root in Barcelona's port activity. Despite being an 'official' corps, they had trouble in establishing and defending their jurisdiction as a profession against both other brokers and sworn interpreters. To sum up: the profession of VIB collapsed in the midst of a double clash, a clash between VIBs and competing practitioners, and a clash between Spain's top-down policy – which extended a Bilbao, French-inspired institution to all Spanish ports – and the dynamics of maritime trade on the ground. Whereas the translation policy dictated from outside the domain required the intervention of VIBs in a number of circumstances, the translation practice relied on other agents.

In this volume a set of local viewpoints are used to gain insight into the historical knowledge of nineteenth-century translation. Kang (2014: 477) encouraged translator researchers working in diverse cultural contexts 'to tell the specific, local stories of their institutions that have thus far remained untold in translation studies'. If not an institution, Barcelona's VIBs were a true translation 'infrastructure' (Hlavac et al 2018). I would like to understand the present study as a 'specific, local' story regarding nineteenth-century translation that might contribute to various larger research topics that come under the umbrella of 'translation policy': (1) the 'success and failure' of translational regimes, parallel to the one that already exists in the mother discipline of language policy (e.g. Moormann-Kimáková 2016); (2) the processes of institutionalization and deinstitutionalization of translation (as suggested in Koskinen 2014); and of course (3) the world of jurisdictional struggles and boundary work, where some interesting inroads have already been made for translation and interpreting (Monzó 2009, Koskinen and Dam 2016).

Notes

1   This chapter would not have been possible without the help of many people that it is imperative to mention here: Marta Arumí, Carmen Bestué, Maria Jesús Espuny and Daniel Vallès (Universitat Autònoma de Barcelona), Jordi Baulies (Ministerio de Asuntos Exteriores y de Cooperación), Ingrid Cáceres (Universidad de Alcalá), Lluïsa Cases, Montse Gómez and Vicenç Ruiz (Col·legi de Notaris de Catalunya), Montserrat Comas (Biblioteca Museu Víctor Balaguer), Xavier Cortés (Arxiu Històric de la Cambra de Comerç de Barcelona), Josefina Fortuny (Reial Acadèmia de Ciències i Arts de Barcelona), Enric García (Museu Marítim de Barcelona), Virginia García de Paredes (Banco de España), Sílvia Hernández (Diputació de Barcelona), Jordi Ibarz (Universitat de Barcelona), Isabel Juncosa (Il·lustre Col·legi de l'Advocacia de Barcelona), Charo Martínez (Fundación Sancho el Sabio), Juan Carlos Pérez (Universidad del País Vasco / Euskal Herriko Unibertsitatea), Maribel

del Pozo (Universidade de Vigo), Eva Rodríguez (Real Academia de Ciencias Económicas y Financieras), Antonio Sáez (Senado de España), Julio César Santoyo (Universidad de León), Mariele Violano (Acadèmia de Jurisprudència i Legislació de Catalunya), and unidentified officials (Arxiu Municipal Contemporani de Barcelona).

2 'Not being able to resist the competition of unchartered agents, and [each of the VIB] having to pay a yearly contribution of 1,500 PTA imposed by the Treasury, the *Colegio* was closed. And so all will be closed, if the Government does not support this class so necessary for maritime trade.'

References

Abbott, Andrew (1988), *The System of Professions: An Essay on the Division of Expert Labor*, Chicago: University of Chicago Press.

Arriaga, Emiliano de (1913), *El libro de la correduría marítima*, Bilbao: Imp. y Enc. de José A. de Lerchundi.

Arriaga, Emiliano de (1923²), *El libro de la correduría marítima*, Bilbao: Bilbaína de Artes Gráficas, J. A. de Lerchundi.

Baigorri, Jesús (2015), 'Spain', in Franz Pöchhacker (ed.), *Routledge Encyclopedia of Interpreting Studies*, Routledge: Abingdon and New York.

Cañelles, Cèlia and Rosa Toran (2013), *Els governs de la ciutat de Barcelona (1875-1930): Eleccions, partits i regidors. Diccionari biogràfic*, Barcelona: Ajuntament de Barcelona.

Carreras, Albert and César Yáñez (1992), 'El puerto en la era industrial: una síntesis histórica', in Joan Clavera et al. (eds), *Economía e historia del puerto de Barcelona. Tres estudios*, Madrid: Editorial Civitas.

Castejón, Rosa María (1974), 'El movimiento comercial del puerto de Barcelona', *Revista de Geografía*, 8 (1–2): 129–57.

Castillo, Daniel and Jesús M. Valdaliso (2017), 'Path Dependence and Change in the Spanish Port System in the Long Run (1880–2014): An Historical Perspective', *The International Journal of Maritime History*, 29 (3): 569–96.

Figuerola, Laureano (1849), *Estadística de Barcelona en 1849*, Barcelona: Imprenta y Librería Politécnica de Tomás Gorchs.

Grbić, Nadja (2010), '"Boundary work" as a concept for studying professionalization processes in the interpreting field', *Translation and Interpreting Studies*, 5 (1): 109–23.

González Núñez, Gabriel (2016), 'On Translation Policy', *Target*, 28: 87–109.

Hlavac, Jim Adolfo Gentile, Marc Orlando, Emiliano Zucchi and Ari Pappas (2018), 'Translation as a Sub-Set of Public and Social Policy and a Consequence of Multiculturalism: The Provision of Translation and Interpreting Services in Australia', *International Journal of the Sociology of Language*, 251: 55–88.

Kang, Ji-Hae (2014), 'Institutions Translated: Discourse, Identity and Power in Institutional Mediation', *Perspectives*, 22 (4): 469–78.

Koskinen, Kaisa (2014), 'Institutional Translation: The Art of Government by Translation', *Perspectives*, 22 (4): 479–92.

Koskinen, Kaisa and Helle V. Dam (2016), 'Academic Boundary Work and the Translation Profession: Insiders, Outsiders and (Assumed) Boundaries', *The Journal of Specialised Translation*, 25: 254–67.

Meylaerts, Reine (2011), 'Translational Justice in a Multilingual World: An Overview of Translational Regimes', *Meta: Journal des traducteurs / Meta: Translators' Journal*, 56 (4): 743–57.

Montero, José (1882, 1883[2], 1883[3], 1884[4]), *La bolsa, el comercio y las sociedades mercantiles*, Madrid: Tip. del Asilo de Huérfanos del Sagrado Corazón de Jesús.

Monzó, Esther (2009), 'Legal and Translational Occupations in Spain Regulation and Specialization in Jurisdictional Struggles', *Translation and Interpreting Studies*, 4 (2): 135–54.

Moormann-Kimáková, Barbora (2016), *Language-Related Conflicts in Multinational and Multiethnic Settings: Success and Failure of Language Regimes*, Wiesbaden: Springer.

Moreno, Francisco Javier (2011), *El capitán de la marina mercante José Ricart y Giralt (1847-1930). Una aproximación a la historia martítima contemporánea de Barcelona*, Ph Dissertation, Universitat Politènica de Catalunya.

Peñarroja, Josep (2000), 'Historia de los intérpretes jurados en España', in *La Traduction juridique. Histoire, théorie(s) et pratique/ Legal Translation. History, Theory/ies and Practice*, ed. GREJUT, Geneve: Ecole de Traduction et d'Interpretation, Université de Genève.

Pozo, M. Isabel del (2010), 'Corredores intérpretes de buques', in José L. Cifuentes et al. (coord.), *Los caminos de la lengua: Estudios en homenaje a Enrique Alcaraz Varó*, Alicante: Universidad de Alicante / Universitat d'Alacant.

Puerta Rueda, Natividad de la (1996), 'El puerto de Bilbao: empresa de hierro y mar', in Agustín Guimerá and Dolores Romero (eds), *Puertos y Sistema Portuarios: Actas del Coloquio Internacional El sistema portuario español, Madrid, 19–21 octubre 1995*, Madrid: Ministerio de Fomento.

Rafo, José (1861), *Proyecto para la mejora y ensanche del puerto de Barcelona*, Madrid: Imp. de D. José C. de la Peña.

Ricart Giralt, José (1894), *Guía marítimo comercial de los puertos de la Península Ibérica. Volumen primero. Cataluña*, Madrid: Revista de Navegación y Comercio.

Ricart Giralt, José (1903), 'Los corredores intérpretes de buques', *La vida marítima*, 49: 248–9.

Santoyo, Julio C. (2003), 'Un quehacer olvidado: los intépretes-traductores de navíos', *Quaderns de Filologia. Estudis Lingüístics*, 8: 1–21.

Servicio de Estudios en Barcelona. Banco Urquijo (1968), *Análisis Económico del Puerto de Barcelona*, Madrid: Editorial Moneda y Crédito.

Spolsky, Bernard (2004), *Language Policy*, Cambridge: Cambridge University Press.

Wolf, Michaela (2012), *Die vielsprachige Seele Kakaniens. Übersetzen und Dolmetschen in der Habsburgermonarchie 1848 bis 1918*, Kiel and Wien: Böhlau. English version: Wolf, Michaela (2015), *The Habsburg Monarchy's Many-Languaged Soul*, Amsterdam/Philadelphia: John Benjamins.

Part Four

Translating for the public space

Translations in *Ljubljanski zvon*: The window into the cultural life of the late-nineteenth-century Ljubljana

Nike K. Pokorn[1]

1 Introduction

The aim of this chapter is to outline the role of translation in the cultural life of Ljubljana in the late nineteenth century as it was reported about and manifested in the most important Slovene literary journal of the period *Ljubljanski zvon* (Ljubljana Bell), published in the city of Ljubljana from 1881 to 1941. This chapter focuses only on the nineteenth century, that is, on the period from 1881 to 1900, thus covering 240 issues of *Ljubljanski zvon*. It is argued in this chapter that translation activity in this period did not primarily serve as a tool of intercultural communication (see, for example, House 2009), but as one of the means through which linguistic borders were imposed on a community that was to a large extent bilingual.

In order to provide some background information on the translational activity from and into the Slovene language, first, the most exhaustive Slovene electronic online bibliographic source (Co-operative Online Bibliographic System and Services (COBISS), www.cobiss.si) will be checked for all translations into or from Slovene published as books in the period 1800 to 1900; the bibliographical data will be compared according to different source and target languages of translations. Second, all nineteenth-century issues of *Ljubljanski zvon* will be analysed in order to identify any possible translations published in the journal, any theoretical and normative positions taken regarding translations, and the role that translation played in the life of the late-nineteenth-century Ljubljana.

The chapter is divided into five sections. In Section 1 some historical background is provided: an outline of a short history of the changing status of the Slovene language is followed by a brief presentation of the bilingual community living in the city of Ljubljana in the late nineteenth century and of previous research on the role of translation in the nineteenth-century Habsburg towns and cities. Methodological approach and the corpus are described in Section 2. In Section 3 the results of the research outlining the translation flows from and into Slovene in the nineteenth century are presented, and the presence of translations and normative statements regarding translation in the nineteenth-century issues of *Ljubljanski zvon* are provided, which are followed by a discussion and a conclusion in Sections 4 and 5.

2 Historical background

2.1 Slovenes and the Slovene language

The Slovenes are the western-most Slavic nation in Europe surrounded by four cultures using different languages: German to the north, Italian to the West, Hungarian to the East and Croatian to the south. The land traditionally inhabited by the Slovenes became part of the Carolingian Empire in the ninth century, but was then ruled almost continuously from the late thirteenth century until 1918 by the Habsburg dynasty. The Habsburg rule was interrupted for four years (1809–13) when these lands were occupied by Napoleon. After the withdrawal of the French forces, the territory was again incorporated into the Austrian (and later into Austro-Hungarian) Empire and remained its constituent part until 1918. The Slovene-speaking population of the Habsburg Empire could be found in four historic provinces, with the majority of Slovene speakers living in the province of Carniola (94 per cent of Slovene population, Wolf 2015: 39) with Ljubljana (Laibach) as its capital city (see, for example, Gow and Carmichael 2000: 13 and Figure 9.1).

The development of Slovene national character has always been closely linked to the use of the Slovene language. The first written record of the Slovene language is found in the Freising Manuscripts, a collection of confessions and sermons dating from around 1000 AD. However, despite these early literary attempts, the Slovene language was not generally written until the Reformation, when Protestants translated the Bible (1584), wrote tracts in Slovene, and published the first Slovene grammar and dictionary (see, for example, Ahačič 2007). The next revival of Slovene happened at the end of the eighteenth century, and reached its peak in the nineteenth century. Towards the end of the eighteenth

Figure 9.1 The ethnic groups of Austria-Hungary in 1910. (Shepherd 1912).

century, the first important poetry collections were published (1779–81), the first non-religious play in the Slovene language was staged in Ljubljana (1789), a Roman Catholic translation of the Bible into Slovene was created (1784–1802), the first newspaper in Slovene appeared in Ljubljana (published from 1797 until 1800), and the first scholarly grammar of Slovene was created (1808), which standardized and codified the language.

The French occupation proved particularly beneficial for Slovene aspirations for a greater language recognition: during the short period of French rule (1809–13), the reorganization of education was planned in the Illyrian provinces which provisioned also the use of Slovene as the local language in the primary school and lower grades of high school (Štih et al. 2008: 254). After the return of Habsburg rule, the Slovene language was relegated to its former position; however, the national revival was not thwarted: the first two chairs of Slovene language were established at the University of Graz (1812) and at the Ljubljana lyceum (1815), poetry collections were published (*Kranjska čbelica* 1830–4, *Poezije* 1847), the first novel in Slovene was created (*Deseti brat* 1866) and Slovene newspapers reappeared in 1840s (*Kmetijske in rokodelske novice* 1843, *Drobtinice* 1846) that were soon followed by others of various political orientation and specializations in 1860s (e.g. *Slovenski narod*), 1870s (e.g. *Zvon, Slovenec*) and 1880s (*Ljubljanski zvon*). In the middle of the century (1851) also the first Slovene publishing house, the Society of St Hermagoras, was founded by the Catholic priest Martin Slomšek in Klagenfurt (today Austria).

The revolutionary movement in 1848 touched upon the Slovenes as well – the first Slovene national programme was formulated by important prominent Slovene figures (e.g. the linguist and the future rector of Vienna University, Fran Miklošič) demanding a unified Slovene province within the Austrian Empire. Although this idea was not adopted by Vienna, the nationalistic political agenda gained in importance, so that from 1849 the *Austrian Civil Code, Imperial Law Gazette*, all the laws and ordinances were translated also into Slovene as one of the languages of common use in the Empire's Land (Wolf 2015: 89). The Slovene language, which gained the status of one of the ten languages of the common use of the Monarchy (*Landesübliche Sprache*) (Wolf 2015: 83), also became widespread in different cultural, scholarly and political organizations. The increasing importance of the Slovene language, however, did not change the fact that until 1919 when Ljubljana University was established, the Slovene intelligentsia was bilingual. For example, although the constitution of 1867 prohibited the imposition of any obligation to speak a second language at school (Wolf 2015: 58), by 1900 only the first four years of high-school education in Carniola were held in Slovene, while the final four grades were held in German, mainly due to the lack of Slovene textbooks (see Gabrič 2009: 13–21, *LZ*² 1900: 647).

2.2 The city of Ljubljana

The nineteenth century was for Ljubljana, the capital city of the province of Carniola, the century of change. First, the population dramatically increased in the second half of the century: if at the end of the eighteenth century Ljubljana had around 11,000 inhabitants, and in the middle of the nineteenth century 17,250, its population almost quadrupled towards the end of the nineteenth century when the Austrian census of 1900 recorded in Ljubljana more than 41,000 citizens (Pipp 1935). Second, its political importance grew: between 1809 and 1813 it became the capital city of Napoleon's Illyrian provinces, and then the capital of Carniola with its own Imperial-Royal Government (*k. k. Landesregierung*, since 1861). Third, the city's transport infrastructure and services saw some radical transformations: in 1849 the city got the railway connection with Vienna, and eight years later also with Trieste, in 1861 gas lighting, in 1890 water supply and in 1898 (after a devastating earthquake in 1898) electric streetlights were introduced.

During the nineteenth century in Carniola and in Ljubljana, German and Slovene both shared the status of the regional languages (*Landessprache*) and the languages of the common use (*Landesübliche Sprache*) (Wolf 2015: 63); however, Ljubljana was more bilingual[3] than the rest of the province: for example, while in the census of 1880 in the entire province of Carniola around 6 per cent of population declared that their language of common use was German (out of 481,000 inhabitants) (Rahten 2011: 237), 23 per cent of inhabitants of Ljubljana (out of 26,000) indicated German as their language of common use (although many of these were not German by origin – shifting from Slovene to a more prestigious German was considered by some citizens of Ljubljana as a sign of their improved position in the society)[4] (cf. Wolf 2015: 50). Although this percentage declined throughout the years, reaching 14.8 per cent (out of 36,500 inhabitants) in 1900 (Valenčič 1974), the German presence in Ljubljana was far from marginal, in particular in the cultural sphere.

In fact, during the nineteenth century Ljubljana continuously witnessed a competition of two cultures: the German and the emerging Slovene one. For example, although towards the end of the nineteenth century one could buy a number of Slovene newspapers published in Ljubljana, the oldest and the official newspaper of Carniola was *Laibacher Zeitung* (1778–1914), published in German (cf. Amon and Erjavec 2011). And, while in the middle of the nineteenth century Slovene theatre was still in its infancy, the German theatre had already been well established and had owned a special-purpose building for theatrical performances, in which the Slovene performances were allowed only a few times a month. The situation, however, changed towards the end of the century: when the provincial theatre was destroyed by fire in 1887, and a new building was erected, the performances in the Slovene language were more frequent and eventually became dominant. This linguistic cohabitation became so intolerable that it resulted in the complete separation of the two language groups. In 1911 Ljubljana thus had two separate theatres built: one for the performances in Slovene and the other for those in German (Lah 2010). This separation of two linguistic communities was advanced also by translational activities, since the vast majority of the plays staged in Slovene were, in fact, translations of foreign theatrical works into Slovene (see, for example, LZ 1884, 4/7: 444; 1885, 5/12: 761; 1886, 6/7: 446; 1887, 7/4: 255).

2.3 Research on the role of translation in Habsburg towns and cities

The ambiguous role of translation in the city has been the topic of some intense research in translation studies recently. The role of translation in the creation of urban space of the so-called 'dual cities', that is, the cities that are claimed by two historically rooted language communities (Simon 2012), has been outlined. Cities have been identified as the typical topoi of 'translation zones', that is, the areas of a particularly intensive interaction across languages, the intrinsically translational nature of cities was studied, and the historical periods when translation was crucial to political and cultural changes were identified (Cronin and Simon 2014).

In addition to that, TS scholarship started revealing an important role of translation in the nineteenth century (see, for example, Dizdar, Gipper and Schreiber 2015), marked with the pursuit of nation states when academics such as Wilhelm von Humboldt (1767–1835) explicitly defined the nation's language as the unattainable spirit of that nation and as the very feature that distinguishes one community from another (von Humboldt 1836: 37). TS scholars who focused on multilingual and multicultural milieus and their transformations through translation practice in that time when a single language was believed to be the most intrinsic characteristic of a nation, found Habsburg Monarchy to be of particular interest. Michaela Wolf (2015), for example, in her thorough study of translation policy in the Habsburg Monarchy and the Habsburg's polyphonic and interactional translation practice outlined the important and decisive role of translation in the construction of the Habsburg culture. Other scholars focused on pluricultural communicative spaces as they developed in Habsburg cities: Sherry Simon (2012) and Katia Pizzi (2016) thus investigated different forms taken by translation in the Habsburg Trieste; Matteo Colombi (2016) focused on the nineteenth-century Prague; and Laimonas Briedis on Vilnius (2016). The provincial Habsburg town of Laibach/Ljubljana, however, has not yet been the subject of TS investigation.[5]

The present study joins the research efforts of these TS scholars focusing on the translational nature of Habsburg cities and aims to outline the role of translation in the cultural life of Ljubljana in the late nineteenth century. The research will align with the study of translation policy in the Habsburg Monarchy by Michaela Wolf (2015) and with the conceptualizations of Naoki Sakai (2010), who defines translation not only as an act of border crossing but also as an act of drawing a border. It will be argued that translation as it was practised in that period in Ljubljana attempted to reduce the bilingual (if not plurilingual) communicative situations in the provincial city of Ljubljana, to create two distinct language communities and thus to establish national entities with clear national boundaries.

3 Methodological approach and corpus selection

3.1 Bibliographic research

Since the aim of this chapter is to describe the role of translation in the cultural life of Ljubljana in the late nineteenth century, first the translation flows from and into the Slovene language in that period will be outlined. The data on translations from other languages into Slovene and from Slovene into other languages were obtained from the most exhaustive Slovene electronic bibliographic source COBIB.SI provided by COBISS (www.cobiss.si). COBIB.SI database enables access to more than 5,000,000 records and provides data from the shared catalogue of Slovenian libraries. The bibliographic and catalogue databases were researched by using the so-called Expert search mode, which allows the use of Boolean and proximity operators, while the search was limited to translations that appeared as individual books only. The search results were then sorted according to the source language of the translation and to the genre of the source text.

3.2 Research on the presence of translation in *Ljubljanski zvon*

The role of translation in the cultural life of Ljubljana is outlined by focusing on the presence of translations in *Ljubljanski zvon*, the most important nineteenth-century Slovene literary monthly published in Ljubljana from 1881 to 1941 (see Figure 9.2). The chapter only focuses on the nineteenth century, that is, from 1881 to 1900, thus covering twenty volumes, that is, 240 issues. In the research reported in this chapter first, all issues of *Ljubljanski zvon* were checked in order to see if any translations were published in the literary monthly between 1881 and 1900; second, all theoretical positions taken regarding translations published in *Ljubljanski zvon* in this period were identified and their consequences on the politics of the journal were outlined; third, Feuilletons, which provide an insight into the cultural life in Ljubljana in the late nineteenth century, were analysed focusing on the role of translation in Ljubljana of the day.

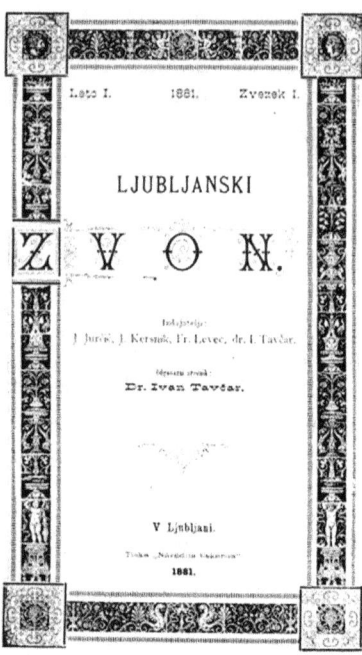

Figure 9.2 The cover of the First Issue of *Ljubljanski Zvon*.

Ljubljanski zvon, subtitled as a Literary and Scientific Journal, was predominantly a literary monthly that was published in Ljubljana since 1881 as a continuation of the first Slovene literary magazine *Zvon* published in Vienna (1870, 1876–80⁶). The emergence of *Ljubljanski zvon* was connected with a 'translation scandal' in the Viennese *Zvon*. Viennese *Zvon* was edited by one of the most prominent Slovene Romantic authors and literary critics Josip Stritar (1836–1923), who worked as a governmental translator for the Slovene language of the Imperial legal gazette (*Reichsgesetzblatt*) in Vienna. Stritar published in 1876 in his Viennese *Zvon* a novel *Gospod Mirodolski* (Mister Mirodolski) in instalments. Although the novel was largely based on Oliver Goldsmith's novel *The Vicar of Wakefield*, Stritar did not openly acknowledge its influence. When the first Slovene translation of *The Vicar of Wakefield* appeared in this same year, some readers, who were now able to compare the two works, accused Stritar of plagiarism. Stritar defended himself saying that he was only inspired by *The Vicar* and that his work was original. Despite his protestations, the public discussion of this issue led to a considerable drop of subscribers to Viennese *Zvon* which resulted in the fact that Stritar's monthly was discontinued, and *Ljubljanski zvon* appeared (V. B. 1891; Kopitar 1959/60; Bogataj-Gradišnik 1986).

Ljubljanski zvon was edited by the most prominent Slovene writers of the so-called liberal orientation (in its second year of publication, that is, in 1882, also the above-mentioned Josip Stritar joined the editorial group). The monthly was typically sixty-five pages long, and published mainly literary and scholarly works in Slovene: every issue started with a poetry section in which several poems originally written in Slovene were published, which was followed by the section containing short prose works or novels in instalments. The third section included scholarly works: for example, literary (biographies and literary criticism), historical or philological essays, and, rarely, also articles on the latest advances in natural sciences. Each issue of the journal typically ended with the so-called Slovene Herald (Slovenski glasnik, vol. 1–5) or Feuilleton (Listek, vol. 6–20) which was published in smaller font than the rest of the journal and was from four to fifteen pages long. Herald and Feuilleton (hereafter Feuilleton) provided information on different current issues: One section was devoted to announcements of newly published books (including translations into Slovene) – some of these books and translations were also briefly critically appraised. The second section focused on theatrical events in Ljubljana, informing the readers also on whether the work staged or whether the libretto of the opera was translated or not. The third section was devoted to art exhibitions. In the fourth the editors informed their readers of the death of important members of the community. Some pages were also dedicated to new publications in Czech and Croatian literary journals; occasionally this was supplemented by the information on literary developments and newest publications in Russia, Bulgaria, Serbia, Poland and Slovakia. And finally, these appendices also occasionally provided information on Slovene literary works published in different foreign literary journals (mainly from Czechia, Slovakia, Croatia and Serbia).

4 Results

4.1 Translation flows

According to COBIB.SI database, between 1800 and 1900, 379 literary works were translated into Slovene. The source languages of these texts are shown in Figure 9.3.

Almost half (n=175 or 46 per cent) of all literary translations into Slovene in the nineteenth century were translations from German. Other source texts were written either in one of the Slavonic languages (n=5) or in French, Italian,

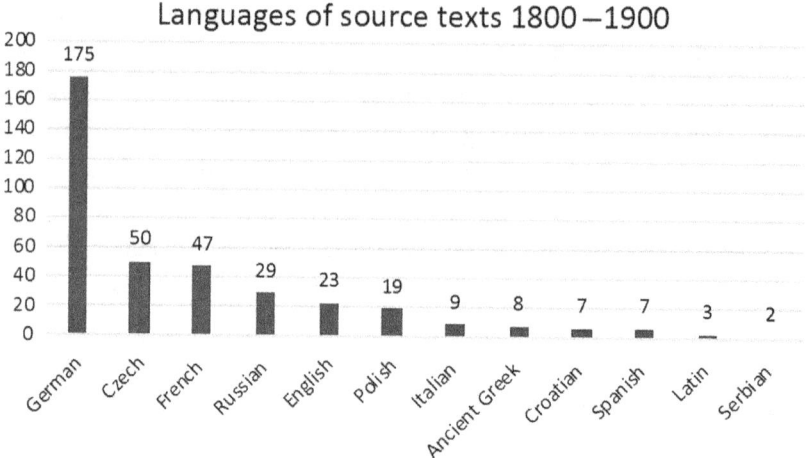

Figure 9.3 Number of literary translations into Slovene published as books according to the language of the original.

Ancient Greek and Latin. Since the translations of the works by the UK or US authors (such as William Shakespeare, Harriet Beecher Stowe and Benjamin Franklin) and those by Spanish authors (e.g. works by Cervantes) did not reveal whether the translators worked from the original or indirectly via German or Italian translations, I assumed that they were done directly from the original version. However, one might assume (as did the critics who reviewed these translations at the time of their publication) that quite a few of the translations from these two languages were in fact done via German translations.[7]

Most Slovene translations from that period fall into the category of prose (n=263); however, drama was also quite popular (n=105), while translations of poetry collections were scarce (n=10). The majority of the nineteenth-century translations into Slovene (n=280, 74 per cent) were intended for the adult readership; however, considerable attention was paid to young readers as well (n=72, 19 per cent). Particularly popular (n=54) was Christoph von Schmid (1768–1854), a Bavarian Catholic priest and educator, whose works were regarded as specifically well-suited for children (see, for example, LZ 1885, 5/4: 245). The rest were the works that were intended for both young readers and adults, like, for example, *Uncle Tom's Cabin* by Harriet Beecher Stowe (n=27, 7 per cent).

Translations of Slovene literary texts into other languages were quite rare in that period. In total only nineteen literary works were translated into foreign languages and published as individual books abroad. Surprisingly, in that period Czech (n=7) shared with German (n=7) the position of the most popular target language for translations of Slovene literary works. Other book translations (single book translations were made into Croatian, Serbian, Ukrainian, Russian and Slovak) clearly indicate that Slovene literary production targeted Slavonic literary market. As far as genre distribution is concerned, the most important export genres were poetry (n=9) and prose (n=9), while only one play was translated from Slovene in that period.

The authors whose works were most often translated into foreign languages were the most important Romantic poet, France Prešeren (1800–49) (n=6), and the author of the first novel in Slovene, Josip Jurčič (1844–81) (n=6).

4.2 Translations and theoretical or normative statements on translation in *Ljubljanski zvon*

4.2.1 *Translations in* Ljubljanski zvon

The survey of twenty volumes (i.e. of 240 issues) of *Ljubljanski zvon* that were published between 1881 and 1900 showed that the literary journal published no translations in the main sections of each issue. The only exception was volume 20 (published in 1900) when in the section, traditionally devoted to Slovene prose works, two short stories by Antonio Fogazzaro (1842–1911) translated from Italian were published (397–404; 558–562). In addition to that, translations were also included in issue 12 (vol. 20) of *Ljubljanski zvon* (1900) that was entirely devoted to the 100th anniversary of the birth of France Prešeren. France Prešeren (1800–1849) was the most praised Slovene Romantic sonneteer, the author of the first ballad and the first epic poem written in Slovene, who acquired the canonical status in Slovene literature and culture towards the end of the nineteenth century. Issue 20 of *Ljubljanski zvon* included six essays on Serbian, German, Swedish, Italian and Czech translations of Prešeren's poetry, one reprint of an already published translation of one of Prešeren's poems into Swedish, four new translations into Russian, and nine new translations into Italian.

Translations, however, were much more present in the final section of *Ljubljanski zvon*, called Feuilletons, which provided an insight into the cultural life in Ljubljana in the late nineteenth century and where special attention was paid to translations of Slovene literary works into other languages. In all 240 Feuilletons, the editors reported seventy-seven times on different translations of Slovene literary works (mainly poems) into foreign languages. Some of these reports (n=21) also contained translations of Slovene poems in different languages, and in a few of them (n=12) critical appraisals of the translated works were also provided.

The vast majority of all these translations were published in different periodicals in languages of the Austro-Hungarian Empire, that is, in German, Czech, Italian and Serbian (see Figure 9.4). The authors who were translated in that period belonged to the nascent Slovene literary canon (see Figure 9.5). The most praised Romantic poet, France Prešeren, was by far the most popular author: twenty different announcements in Feuilleton mention that either one or more of his poems were translated into some foreign language.

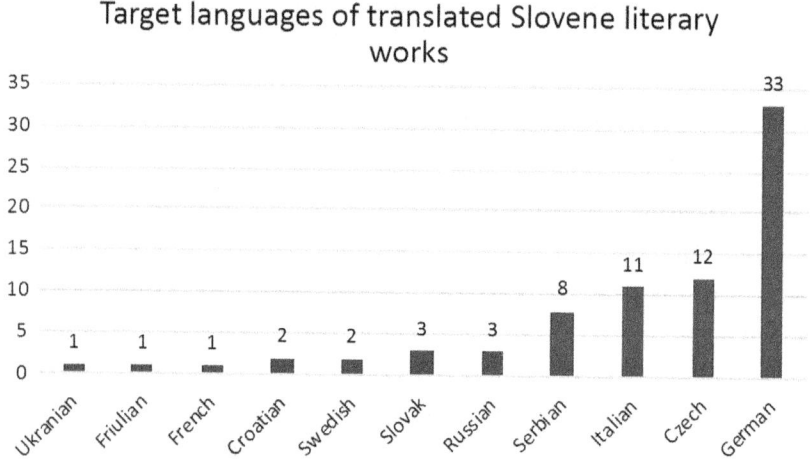

Figure 9.4 The number of different translations of Slovene literary works according to the target languages of translations.

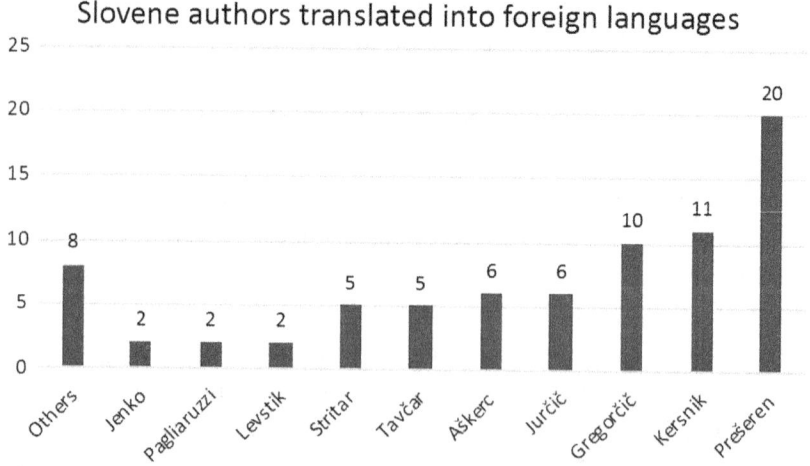

Figure 9.5 Most frequently mentioned authors whose work was translated into foreign languages.

In Figure 9.5 all authors who were mentioned at least twice as being translated into other languages are indicated (the category 'others' includes authors who were mentioned only once in the Feuilleton). Out of these ten authors (who were all men), five of them are poets (Fance Prešeren (1800–1849), Simon Gregorčič (1844–1906), Anton Aškerc (1856–1912), Josip Pagliaruzzi (1859–85) and Simon Jenko (1835–69)), while others also wrote prose and drama (e.g. Fran Levstik (1831–87), Josip Jurčič (1844–81), Ivan Tavčar (1851–1923) Janko Kersnik (1852–97)); however, poetry was the genre that was most often translated.

4.2.2 Theoretical and normative statements on translation in Ljubljanski zvon

The issue of translation was rarely discussed in the main sections of *Ljubljanski zvon*. Only twice, translation was given a more prominent position. The first one to address this issue was Josip Stritar, the author who was accused of plagiarizing Oliver Goldsmith's novel *The Vicar of Wakefield*, which caused a public outcry and hastened the demise of Viennese *Zvon*, the precursor of *Ljubljanski zvon*. In his essays, entitled 'Dunajska pisma' (Viennese letters), published in 1895 and 1896, Stritar discussed several issues: he praised the activities of the oldest Slovene publishing house (LZ 15/8: 496–500), wrote on social issues (LZ 15/9: 553–8), gave guidance on proper language use (LZ 15/10: 687–92), critically discussed naturalism in literature (LZ 16/1: 15–20), and also briefly expressed his views on literary translations. Faithful to his life-long mantra that only originality matters, he wrote:

> Kar se tiče prevodov, je moja misel ta: prevode samo za silo. Prevod je vedno le tuje blago; kdor more, naj spiše kaj izvirnega. Samo kar je izvirno, domače, to je naše. (Stritar 1896, LZ 16/1: 20)[8]

A year later, in 1897, the journal published an essay on plagiarism (LZ 1897 17/5: 291–95; 17/6: 349–57) by three anonymous authors, using pseudonyms alpha + beta + gamma, who responded to the fact that on 26 December 1885 a law on intellectual property was passed in Austria. The authors informed the readers that the law penalized the use of the same title or the form of some previous work of art, in particular if such a use could trick the audience (Article 22). In addition to that, a penalty was imposed on those authors who would not name the author or the source of their creation (Article 52) (LZ 1897, 17/6: 357). Although the authors welcomed the new legislation, they also argued that not all borrowings were plagiarism. They claimed that borrowings from the folklore, common myths and other literary works had always been done (they referred to

Goethe's *Faust* and Shakespeare's works) and should be regarded as an acceptable literary practice. They argued:

> Celo prevodi, katerih prevodilni jezik je tako samorašč, da čitatelja prav nič ne spominja na izvirnik – taki prevodi se po pravici v vseh slovstvih smatrajo kot pristna domača slovstva. /.../ Umetnik pač svoje samotvornosti ne kaže samo v izumitvi nove snovi, v tako imenovani umetniški 'invenciji', temveč njegova ustvarjajoča sila se nič manj ne utegne pojaviti v obdelavi stare snovi, v utelesitvi stare ideje; izviren je torej način izvršitve ali utelesitve. (LZ 1897, 17/5: 292)[9]

However, they warned that one should be careful with such borrowings: 'treba [je] pripoznati neke meje, katerih pošten umetnik nikdar ne prekorači, in o katerih se je omikani svet zedinil, ustanovivši mednarodna odločila v obrambo duševne lastnine'[10] (LZ 1897, 17/5: 292). They concluded that we should make a distinction between the plagiarists who slavishly borrow whole works of arts or their forms, and the artists who use borrowed materials as a foundation, a skeleton of a new work of art (LZ 1897, 17/6: 357).

As mentioned earlier, translations were more prominent in Feuilletons. All Feuilletons contained announcements of new translations into Slovene; however, only few of these translations were also critically assessed. These appendices also contained various normative statements regarding translations. The editors and different critics who rarely signed their names approached different topics connected to translation and translational activity. Among these topics are

a) the proper use of the Slovene language
   In the vast majority of these assessments, the editors criticized the language used in translation and pointed out meticulously all deviations from the developing language norm. The editors paid particular attention to the use of Germanisms (e.g. LZ 1884, 4/7: 441–443) and called for 'pravilen jezik' ('the proper language use', LZ 1883, 3/6: 203). When theatre critics, who mainly focused on performative aspects of theatre and opera performances, occasionally commented on the quality of translated librettos, they also pressed for the purity of language, for example, 'Libreto je sicer vselej le podrejena stvar, vender bi bilo skrbeti za to, da se nam podaja v <u>čistejšem</u> pismenem jeziku'.[11] (LZ 1891, 11/11: 702)

b) the ethics of translation, in particular the question of plagiarism
   The editors checked all new publications in Slovene to see whether these works were originals or translations. They explicitly urged all translators to explicitly mention the original author and the source language of the

source text on the title page (LZ 1883, 3/6: 203). In the period between 1881 and 1900 they exposed two translators who had claimed to have written original works, but have, in fact, translated them: the first case was the case of a translation of a play from Croatian (LZ 1882, 2/8: 508), the second case was a translation of a prose work also from Croatian (LZ 1882, 2/12: 768–69). In both cases the translators signed themselves as the authors of the works. The editors clearly rejected this practice of appropriation and concluded: 'Tako ne smemo delati!'[12] (LZ 1882, 2/12: 768).

c) the selection of the source text

Ljubljanski zvon pursued a particular cultural policy that was aimed against German cultural influence and supported establishing closer links with the cultures of other Slavonic nations. That policy was visible also in their translation policy. For example, when reviewing a translation of a certain Serbian play, the anonymous critic adds: 'Sploh bi želeli, da bi se naši prelagatelji nekoliko bolj ozirali na priznano dobre slovanske, osobito poljske vesel igre in ako prelagajo iz neslovanskih slovstev, da bi rajši po Mandelčevem vzgledu slovenili nam krasne francoske, nego okorne nemške igre'[13] (LZ 1882, 2/4: 251). The editors also advised Mr Markič, the translator of brothers Grimm fairy tales into Slovene, to choose next time a Slavonic original: 'Svetovali bi gospodu Markiču, ki ima, kakor se vidi, spretnost za take stvari, da bi nam poslovenil tudi nekoliko prelepih srbskih pripovedk'[14] (LZ 1887, 7/7: 447). The aim of this translation policy was to steer the readers from the German and Italian cultures:

> G. Podravski in z njim vred vsi prevodilci umotvorov iz drugih slovanskih jezikov naj pomislijo, da njih prevodov ne čitajo zgolj temeljiti poznavalci odnošajev drugih slovanskih plemen – ti so med nami silno redko sejani – nego da imajo njih prevodi šele namen, da odvrnejo naše ljudi, zlasti naš ženski spol, od čitanja nemških in laških knjig ter jih napotijo do prebiranja slovanskih umotvorov in do spoznavanja slovanskih reči'.[15] (LZ 1896, 16/3: 189)

d) the need to master the source language

As a result of their encouragement to translate works from other Slavonic nations, some translators started working with the languages they did not know well, which resulted in badly translated works (LZ 1897, 17/9: 574). The editors then started urging translators to work only with the languages they master: 'Toda neizogiben postulat za dobro prelaganje

– o tem smo že nekje drugje govorili – je ta, da bodi prelagatelj jeziku, iz katerega prevaja, prav tako vešč, kakor materinščini, poznajoč vse njegove finosti, podrobnosti in nianse.'[16] (LZ 1895, 15/8: 515)

e) Source- versus target-orientedness

There was no clear policy regarding the preferable translation strategy in Feuilletons. Some of the editors were partisans of the source-oriented translation strategy (e.g. 'Kdor se loti prelaganja, strogo se drži izvirnika in nikar nam ne pači tujega pisatelja s svojimi dodatki!'[17] (LZ 1884, 4/1: 57)). Others were more in favour of target-oriented translation strategies: 'Često smo že opozarjali, da je treba prevajati v duhu jezika našega, da ima naš jezik prav tako svoje posebnosti, kakor jih imajo drugi jeziki, in danes poudarjamo znova, da se nikakor ni smeti pretesno držati izvirnika'[18] (LZ 1890, 10/12: 766). The question of acculturation was particularly pertinent in theatre translation where the critic (he signed himself with Z., most probably Mr. Fran Zbašnik) advised against too radical localization: 'Ako vse dobro premislimo, moramo reči, da bi se drame sploh ne smele lokalizovati. /.../ Pravzaprav je torej lokalizovanje iger nekaj nenaravnega. Kakor n. pr. ne lokalizujemo iz tujih jezikov preloženih romanov, tako bi tudi dramatičnih proizvodov ne smeli lokalizovati. /.../ [K]ajti vsak pravi umotvor ima na sebi znake lokalnosti in individualnosti, in mika nas na njem morda baš to, kar ima za nas tujega, nenavadnega. Tudi je umetnost kolikor toliko sredstvo, s katerim širimo svoje duševno obzorje, in če gremo v gledališče k francoski igri, hočemo pač videti francosko življenje, a ne kakega drugega.'[19] The critic then admits that some localization is acceptable, but only for a particular kind of plays: 'Da se Shakespearjeve, Schillerjeve ali Goethejeve drame ne morejo lokalizovati, je pač vsakomu jasno. Sploh je videti, da prija lokalizovanje samo dramam nižje vrste, in še tem le z gotovimi pogoji'[20] (LZ 1899, 19/11: 704).

f) against indirect translations

The editors were also critical towards those translations that were not made directly from the original. They rejected indirect translations of all genres: for example, they were not happy with the translation of libretto from German, since it was originally written in French by George Ohnet: 'Ali si ni bilo moči preskrbeti prevoda po izvirniku?'[21] (LZ 1892, 12/4: 258). Similarly, they regretted that a Slovene translation of *Gulliver's Travels* by Jonathan Swift for children was made from a German adaptation (LZ 1894, 14/6: 378). And finally, they were also very critical of the first Slovene translation of Shakespeare's *Hamlet* where they detected traces of German translation in the Slovene version (LZ 1900, 20/1: 53–4). On the other hand, they complimented a translation of Ivan Turgenev's work into Slovene precisely because it was made from the Russian original: 'Vsaj pozna se mu, da prelaga res po ruskem izvirniku, a ne po nemških in hrvatskih prevodih'[22] (LZ 1884, 4/3: 186).

g) translations as signs of a success of a particular work of art
The commentaries in Feuilletons also revealed why all foreign translations of Slovene literary works were so meticulously followed: these translations represented to the editors and their readers a visible sign of a high quality of Slovene literature. When commenting on the German translation of Prešeren's poems, the editors add: 'To vedno zatekanje tujcev, zlasti Nemcev, k neusahljivemu viru Prešernove poezije nas po pravici navdaja z iskrenim ponosom in veseljem; kajti vprav ta pojav nam je nov dokaz, da je Prešeren – kar je prvi trdil in dokazal Stritar, slava mu zategadelj – svetovne cene pesnik in svetovni klasik, in baš mnogoteri njega prevodi v tuje jezike nam ga gotovo in za stalno uvrste v <u>svetovno literaturo</u> kot prvega slovenskega zastopnika'[23] (LZ 1897, 17/9: 580).

5 Discussion

During the nineteenth century, 379 literary works were translated into Slovene and published as individual books, and almost half of them (47 per cent) were translations from German. Since the reference to the original work or the indication whether the translator worked from the original work or via German translation was often missing in the publications, we might assume that the percentage of translations from German was, in fact, much higher. The majority of these translations were prose works (66 per cent) and intended for the adult readership (74 per cent). The peripheral status of Slovene literature is manifested in the fact that translations of Slovene literature to other languages were much less numerous than translations into Slovene: only nineteen Slovene literary works were translated into foreign languages and published as individual books, and almost half of them (47 per cent) were poetry collections. The authors whose work were most often translated into foreign languages (63 per cent of all publications) were the Slovene Romantic poet France Prešeren (1800–1849) the 'national' poet of Slovenia, and Josip Jurčič (1844–81), the author of the first novel in Slovene. These results show that during the nineteenth century the Slovene budding literary and translational field established most intensive cultural exchange with the German culture and that this exchange was not on equal footing. While the translations into Slovene were all created by Slovene speakers and published in the areas inhabited by Slovenes, some of the translations of Slovene literature into foreign languages were done again by Slovene native speakers and published in the areas inhabited by Slovenes. For example, all four German translations of Prešeren's poetry were published in Ljubljana and are a clear example of the practice of 'extraduction', that is, of the attempt to distribute important national language texts abroad through translation (D'hulst 2015). The fact that Slovene literature was translated into the Czech language as often as into the German language in that period also reveals a specific translation policy that attempted to redirect the cultural focus from the German onto Slavonic cultural areas.

Although *Ljubljanski zvon* was not an important vehicle for translation publication as it was the case with many other literary magazines in the Habsburg Monarchy (Wolf 2015: 232), translations were nevertheless present in every issue of the magazine in its appendix called 'Feuilleton'. The fact that translations were not given a more prominent position in *Ljubljanski zvon* was the result of the cultural policy of the day that promoted original works as the main building blocks of nascent literary field. Consequently, no translations were published in the main sections of the magazine (the first exceptions to this rule happened in 1900), and translations were relegated to the appendices, called Slovene Herald or Feuilleton, where new literary translations into and from Slovene, and translated theatrical and musical-dramatic productions were announced and occasionally assessed. The analysis of the assessments of translations into Slovene showed that the critics mainly focused on the proper language use and attempted to define and strengthen the language norm through translation criticism, while the announcements of translations of Slovene literary works into foreign languages revealed that the Slovene literary scene saw in these translations a proof that Slovene literature was of high quality and comparable to that of other national literatures.

The theoretical and normative statements connected to translation practice were rare in *Ljubljanski zvon*, and were not uniform. The magazine, on the one hand, published a letter by Josip Stritar in which he argued for a complete marginalization of translations ('Translations should be our last resort,' LZ 1896, 16/1:20)), and defended the position that all creative national forces should be devoted to original writings. On the other hand, a year later, an anonymous group of three authors defended a more open position, accepting translations as a part of national literary works and even allowing a certain degree of inspiration and borrowing from foreign sources in the original literary works (LZ 1897, 17/5: 292).

The majority of critical assessments of translations into Slovene published in Feuilletons focused mainly on proper language use, and used translation criticism as a medium for the definition of the language norm. Translation norms were also defined in these sections: for example, the editors insisted that the author and the language of the original should be mentioned in every translation and urged the translators to translate only from the languages they mastered well and rejected indirect translations. There was no uniform support of the target- or source-oriented translation strategy: some critics defended more source-oriented translations, others encouraged translation strategies that attempted to adapt the text to the target language culture. In general, however, the tendency not to acculturate too radically was defended by the magazine.

A particular cultural policy whose aim was to separate the Slovene culture from the German one was visible in the instructions by the editors regarding the selection of source texts. The editors encouraged the translators to avoid German originals that were described as 'cumbersome' and rather choose for their source texts Slavonic (e.g. Serbian or Polish) originals (LZ 1882, 2/4: 251; LZ 1887, 7/7: 447) and thus 'avert our people, in particular our women, from reading German and Italian books and lead them to read Slavonic works of art and to learn Slavonic things' (LZ 1896, 16/3: 189). Translation was seen as a force that could help tear the Slovene readers from the world where women could read German, Italian and Slovene and push them towards a more monolingual, Slovene environment.

Ljubljana in the nineteenth century was a dual city (Simon 2012), a city claimed by the German and the Slovene language communities. Both of them were historically rooted in this area and were engaged in numerous and unequal nationalist disputes with Slovene community painstakingly battling for cultural acknowledgement by the dominant and privileged German-speaking community (see Wolf 2015: 152). The cultural equality of the Slovene-speaking community was even harder to attain because some of the main vehicles of cultural life in Ljubljana were controlled by the German-speaking community: the theatre was dominated by the German community until the end of the century, the most important newspaper in the city *Laibacher Zeitung* was published in German, by the end of the century only the first four years of high school were offered in Slovene, and since there was no Slovene university higher education was available only in German. Consequently, all Slovene intelligentsia was bilingual, as were the majority of those who read literature. In addition to that, German also retained its privileged position in administration and legal environment, which it will lose only after the collapse of the Austro-Hungarian Empire, that is, after 31 October 1918. For example, a renown Slovene judge Fran Milčinski reported in his diary that even a month and a half after the collapse of the Empire, the hearings at Ljubljana court are still held in part in German (Milčinski 2000: 420).[24]

The insistence of editors of *Ljubljanski zvon* on the necessity of translations, expressed in *Feuilletons*, and the predominance of translational exchange with German thus reveal a particular translation and cultural policy: the editors of *Ljubljanski zvon* urged the Slovene public to attend Slovene musical and dramatic performances in Ljubljana, and to read Slovene books, even if these librettos, plays and books were originally written in the languages that the reading public of the day could fully understand and read. By promoting translations into Slovene and underlying their necessity they wanted to show that there was a need to establish communication between two 'fully circumscribed language communities' (Sakai 2009), two distinct ethno-linguistic unities. In their battle for national, political and cultural recognition and in their wish to improve the status of Slovene language, culture and community, they imposed a linguistic border on a community that was not linguistically separate and had managed to maintain bilingual (if not plurilingual) character for centuries. Translation was thus seen not only as a border crossing activity but also as an act of bordering, that is, an act or drawing a border (Sakai 2010). The main literary figures of that time thus wanted translation to draw and strengthen the border in the bilingual or polylingual society, delimit language entities and contribute to the building of national boundaries.

6 Conclusion

The analysis of literary magazine *Ljubljanski zvon* has thus shown that the discussion of translations into Slovene have mainly been used to impose the language norm, while the focus on translations of Slovene literature into other languages served to strengthen self-confidence of the budding national literature. *Ljubljanski zvon*, the most prominent Slovene literary magazine published in the nineteenth-century Ljubljana, was read by bilingual readers who were all educated in predominantly German schools. In the century when it was believed that nationhood depended on an exclusive language, the editors of *Ljubljanski zvon* promoted the creation of literature in the Slovene language and considered translations as one of the means through which polycultural communication could be reduced (cf. Wolf 2015: 112), and bilingual society could be transformed into two linguistically separate cultures. Translation became an act of co-figurative schematism (Sakai 2009), figuring out two distinct ethnolinguistic unities, a Slovene and a German one, and thus contributed to the end of the centuries long bicultural and bilingual life of the dual city of Ljubljana.

Notes

1 Nike K. Pokorn acknowledges the financial support from the Seventh Framework Programme for research, technological development and demonstration, grant agreement 609412 (Project DIFeREns2).
2 In references *Ljubljanski zvon* is abbreviated to LZ.
3 In fact, Ljubljana was more than bilingual at that time. The results of the census held in 1880 showed that 24,200 citizens of Ljubljana declared that their language of common use was Slovene, 5,058 declared it was German, 179 spoke Czech, 169 Italian, 27 Serbo-Croat, 13 Polish and 3 Rusyn (LZ 1891 11/3:186).
4 The historians estimate that 16.4 per cent of all citizens of Ljubljana were Germans (Valenčič 1974).
5 Ljubljana has only briefly been referred to in the article by Pizzi (2016), when she describes competing expressions of modernism in literature in in the early twentieth-century Trieste and Ljubljana.
6 Viennese *Zvon* was first published only for a year in 1870, it then reappeared in 1876 and was discontinued in 1880.
7 See, for example, Gangl's criticism of Cankar's translation of *Hamlet* where the critic claims that the translator must have taken for his source text a German translation of this Shakespeare's play. (LZ 1900: 53–4).
8 As far as translations are concerned, this is what I think: translations should be our last resort. A translation is always foreign goods; those who can, should write original works. Only what is original, domestic, is really ours. (All translations from Slovene into English are by the author of the article.)
9 Even translations, whose target language is so specific that it does not remind the reader of the original, are justly regarded in all literatures as original national literary works. /…/ The artist does not manifest his originality only in the invention of a new subject matter, in the so-called artistic 'invention', his creative force might also emerge in the transformation of an old subject matter, in the incorporation of the old idea; what is original is the manner of execution or incorporation.
10 An honest artist never crosses the boundaries that were defined by the civilized world in international laws on intellectual property.

11 Librettos are always a subordinate thing; however, we should insist that they are delivered to us in the <u>purest</u> literary language.
12 We should not do this!
13 In general, we would prefer if our translators searched among Slavonic, in particular Polish comedies, and if they nevertheless decided to translate from non-Slavonic literatures, it would be preferable if they translated, like Madelc, marvelous French and not cumbersome German plays.
14 We would advise Mr Markič, who is obviously skilled for such things, to translate into Slovene also some beautiful Serbian fairy tales.
15 Mr Podravski and all literary translators from other Slavonic languages should keep in mind that their translations are not read only by those who know well the manners of other Slavonic nations – such readers are very rare among us – but that the aim of their translations is to avert our people, in particular our women, from reading German and Italian books and lead them to read Slavonic works of art and to learn Slavonic things.
16 The inevitable postulate for good translation – we have mentioned that already – is that the translator should master the language he translates from as thoroughly as his mother tongue, knowing all its fineries, details and shades.
17 Whoever starts translating should stick closely to the original and should not distort the foreign writer with his own additions!
18 We have often warned the translators to translate according to the spirit of our language and have stressed that our language also has its own specifics like other languages, and today we stress again that one should not stick too close to the original.
19 If we give this subject a proper thought, we have to say that plays should not be localized at all. /.../ In fact, localization of plays is unnatural. As we do not localize translated novels, we should not have localized theatrical works as well. /.../ Every work of art has its own local and individual features, and these foreign, unusual features are its most attractive side. And besides, the art is one of the means through which we expand our spiritual horizon, and if we go to theatre to see a French play, we then want to see a French way of living, and not some other way!
20 It is clear to everyone that Shakespeare's, Schiller's and Goethe's plays should not be localized. It seems that localization is suitable only for plays of a lower status, and even in these cases under certain circumstances.
21 Was it really impossible to get a translation from the original?
22 It is clear that he translates from the Russian original and not from the German and Croatian translations.
23 This constant return of foreigners, in particular Germans, to the inexhaustible source of Prešeren's poetry justly swells us with pride and joy, since this

phenomenon is a proof that Prešeren – as it was claimed and proven by Stritar, and he should be praised for that – is a poet of global repute, a world classic, and the numerous translations into foreign languages will make him the first Slovene representative in <u>the world literature</u>.

24 Diary entry, 18 December 1918: 'Te dni sem prisostoval neki Hauffnovi razpravi; dr. Ambrositsch je govoril nemški; Hauffen pa ga je ogovarjal slovenski. (I have participated at one of Hauffen's hearings: Dr Ambrositsch spoke German; Hauffen addressed him in Slovene.) (Milčinski 2000: 420).

References

Primary sources

Ljubljanski zvon: mesečna revija za leposlovje, književnost in kritiko. 1881-1900. Edited by Fran Levec (1881–1891), Anton Funtek (1891–1895), Viktor Bežek (1896–1899), Anton Aškerc (1899–1903). Ljubljana: Tiskovna zadruga. ISSN 1408-5909, http://www.dlib.si/details/URN:NBN:SI:spr-OD47VJ7T

Secondary sources

Ahačič, Kozma (2007), *Zgodovina misli o jeziku in književnosti na Slovenskem : protestantizem*, Ljubljana: Založba ZRC, ZRC SAZU. (Linguistica et philologica, 18).

Amon, Smilja and Karmen Erjavec (2011), *Slovensko časopisno izročilo 1: od začetka do 1918*, Ljubljana: Fakulteta za družbene vede, Založba FDV.

Bogataj-Gradišnik, Katarina (1986), 'Stritarjev Gospod Mirodolski: Mladoslovenski roman na ozadju evropskega izročila', *Jezik in slovstvo*, 31/6: 181–91. Available online: http://www.dlib.si/?URN=URN:NBN:SI:DOC-A0SRV0Q7.

Briedis, Laimonas (2016), 'Locating Vilnius on the Map of Translation', in Sherry Simon (ed.), *Speaking Memory: How Translation Shapes City Life*, 23–44, Montreal & Kingston: McGill-Queen's University Press.

Colombi, Matteo (2016), '(Ethni)city under Scrutiny: Or, Tell Me Which Prague You Like and I'll Tell You Which Nation You Are (not)!' in Sherry Simon (ed.), *Speaking Memory: How Translation Shapes City Life*, 58–86, Montreal & Kingston: McGill-Queen's University Press.

Cronin, Michael and Sherry Simon (2014), 'Introduction: The City as Translation Zone', *Translation Studies*, 7 (2): 119–32.

D'hulst, Lieven (2015), '"Localiser" des traductions nationales: le Bulletin des lois en version flamande et hollandaise sous la période française (1797–1813)', in Dilek Dizdar, Andreas Gipper and Michael Schreiber, *Nationenbildung und Übersetzung*, 93–108, Berlin: Frank & Timme.

Dizdar, Dilek, Andreas Gipper and Michael Schreiber, eds. (2015), *Nationenbildung und Übersetzung*, Berlin: Frank & Timme.

Gabrič, Aleš (2009), *Šolanje in znanje na Slovenskem v izzivu 20. stoletja*, Ljubljana: Pedagoški inštitut.

Gow, James and Cathie Carmicheal (2000), *Slovenia and the Slovenes: A Small State and the New Europe*, London: Hurst & Company.

House, Juliane (2009), 'Moving across Languages and Cultures in Translation as Intercultural Communication', in Kristin Bührig, Juliane House and Jan D. ten Thije (eds), *Translational Action and Intercultural Communication*, Manchester: St. Jerome.

Kopitar, Tatjana (1959/60), 'Olivera Goldsmitha *The Vikar of Wakefield* pri Slovencih do leta 1876', *Slavistična revija*, 12 (1–4): 194–223. Available online: http://www.dlib.si/?URN=URN:NBN:SI:DOC-RX4JGNOO

Lah, Špela (2010), 'Slovensko-nemška dihotomija v Deželnem gledališču v Ljubljani med letoma 1892 in 1914: Slovene-German Dichotomy in Provincial Theatre in Ljubljana between 1892 and 1914', *Muzikološki zbornik* (Musicological Annual) 46/2: 95–108. Available online: https://www.dlib.si/stream/URN:NBN:SI:DOC-LALOSKAU/4b105504-47e3-4289-870c-ca1d774d2127/PDF (accessed 1 October 2018).

Milčinski, Fran (2000), *Dnevnik 1914–1920*, ed. Goran Schmidt, Ljubljana: Slovenska matica.

Pipp, Lojze (1935), 'Razvoj števila prevajalstva Ljubljane in bivše vojvodine Kranjske', *Kronika slovenskih mest*, 2 (1): 66–72. Available online: www.dlib.si/stream/URN:NBN:SI:DOC-0GBMI71V/7473cdee-a0c0-405b-aed2-39786b347805/PDF

Pizzi, Katia (2016), 'A Modernist City Resisting Translation? Trieste between Slovenia and Italy', in Sherry Simon (ed.), *Speaking Memory: How Translation Shapes City Life*, 45–57, Montreal & Kingston: McGill-Queen's University Press.

Rahten, Andrej (2011), 'Joseph Schwegel', in Igor Gerdina (ed.), *Med domom in svetom*, 233–42, Ljubljana: Založba ZRC.

Sakai, Naoki (2009), 'Dislocation in Translation', *TTR traduction, terminologie, redaction*, 22 (1): 167–87. Available online: https://www.erudit.org/en/journals/ttr/2009-v22-n1-ttr3935/044786ar/

Sakai, Naoki (2010) 'Translation and the Figure of Border: Toward the Apprehension of Translation as a Social Action', *Profession*, 10: 25–34.

Simon, Sherry (2012), *Cities in Translation: Intersections of Language and Memory*, London and New York: Routledge.

Štih, Peter, Vasko Simoniti and Peter Vodopivec (2008), *Slovenska zgodovina: družba - politika - kultura*, Ljubljana: Inštitut za novejšo zgodovino: Sistory. Available online: http://www.sistory.si/publikacije/pdf/zgodovina/Slovenska-zgodovina-SLO.pdf

V. B. (1891), 'Ruska biblioteka in naši prevodi slovanskih izvirnikov', *Dom in svet*, 4 (7): 330–2.

Valenčič, Vlado (1974), 'Etnična struktura ljubljanskega prebivalstva po ljudskem štetju 1880', *Zgodovinski časopis*, 3–4: 287–319.

von Humboldt, Wilhelm (1836), *Über die Verschiedenheit des menschlichen Sprachbaues und ihren Einfluss auf die geistige Entwicklung des Menschengeschlechts (1827–1829)*, Berlin: Königliche Akademie der Wissenschaften. Available online: https://archive.org/details/berdieverschied00humbgoog/page/n57 (accessed 1 October 2018).

Wolf, Michaela (2015), *The Habsburg Monarchy's Many-Languaged Soul*, Amsterdam/Philadelphia: John Benjamins.

10

Translating in the 'expanded' town: Translation practices in nineteenth-century Nicosia and Cyprus

Georgios Floros

1 Introduction

For Simon (2012: 3), a 'dual city' is one where 'the presence of two historically rooted language communities … feel a sense of entitlement to the same territory'. Dual cities are not really bilingual, but 'translational', in the sense that their languages do not necessarily participate 'in a peaceful and egalitarian conversation' (2012), but reflect 'relations that include indifference and negation as well as engagement and creative interference' (2012). Modern, partitioned and UN-monitored Lefkosia (Nicosia) is such a dual city, albeit neither bilingual nor really translational any longer. But nineteenth-century Nicosia was both truly multilingual – even if more through the peaceful coexistence of many languages than through their egalitarian conversation – and translational, through its controversial cohabitation by locals and rulers.

Nicosia, inhabited for more than 4,500 years, became the capital of Cyprus during the late tenth century, when Cyprus became part of the Byzantine Empire (cf. Christodoulou 1977). Ever since, the island underwent Frankish, Venetian, Ottoman (1571–1878) and British (1878–1960) rule before it became independent in 1960. At the outer rim of Europe and at the crossroads between East and West, Cyprus has traditionally played a significant role in the political and economic life of Greece, Turkey and Europe. Interestingly though, it took longer for Cyprus to follow the nineteenth-century trend of other European states regarding the emergence of national ideology and, by consequence, of national language ideology (and ideologies).

Nevertheless, cultural exchange in nineteenth-century Cyprus was all the more significant precisely because of the continuing parallel use of dominant and local languages, of language varieties and of minority languages. Everyday translation practice, albeit not exactly the result of strict and systematic language and translation policies or a creator thereof, as one would logically expect, did occupy a central role in the political life of the island, which, however, did not exclusively take place in the capital and seat of the governors. The city of Nicosia, surrounded by walls and located in the middle of the island, so as to be better protected against invaders, was always sort of complemented in its function as the centre of governance by the politically more peripheral, but economically equally – if not more – important port cities of Larnaca, Limassol and Famagusta. It was in these port cities where much of the international trade, a very prominent activity especially for Ottoman Cyprus, was conducted and where even foreign consulates were seated during the nineteenth century, since they played an important role in commercial activities. Therefore, it might be more accurate to talk about the 'expanded' Nicosia, an 'expanded' city, when it comes to the geographical occurrence and application of explicitly stated or unstated language/translation policies and practices. In other words, the language relations occurring in Nicosia were substantially diffused across other spaces as well, which need to be seen as complementary to those of Nicosia in order for these relations to form a coherent, and thus meaningful, model (cf. Cronin and Simon 2014). As a result, the political life took place in Nicosia, but much of the economic life and international relations was to be found in port cities, mainly in Larnaca.

This chapter will attempt to give an overview and evaluation of a period extending from 1785 to 1914. It is very difficult to define the precise duration of what we call the European *long* nineteenth century. Therefore, the above dates have been chosen only as rough boundaries, as they coincide with important historical events (cf. Hill 1972 and Stavrides 2012): 1785 is the year in which Cyprus was placed under the direct administration of the Imperial Council (the ministers' cabinet) of the Ottoman Empire after a series of changes in its administrative status within the Empire, which meant that the island was again directly controlled and influenced by the decisions of the *Porte* (*Supreme* or *Sublime Porte*, the central government of the Ottoman Empire). The year 1914 was when Cyprus was officially annexed to the British Empire as a protectorate. The British had already acquired control of Cyprus in 1878 (through the Cyprus Convention), but the island remained de jure under Ottoman rule until it eventually became a Crown Colony in 1925. Thus, the period under study encompasses two very important sub-periods of the history of Cyprus: the late Ottoman rule and about the first half of British rule.

Albeit very different in their overall administrative approach, the common trait of both the Ottoman and the British rule was their laissez-faire attitude towards educational and language policies (cf. Hadjioannou, Tsiplakou and Kappler 2011). In a nutshell, neither the Ottoman nor the British rulers showed substantial willingness to intervene in the educational life of the communities, thus education matters were largely left to the principal communities of the island. By consequence, the same held for language use and translation. As a result, Cyprus emerged as a multilingual space rich in translation practice, but rather poor in official translation policies, despite the remarkable central translation policy established especially by the late Ottoman Empire in Istanbul. A very indicative example of the somewhat lenient translation policy on the island was the way in which the prominent figure of the *Dragoman*, the official interpreter of the Ottoman governor representing the Porte in Cyprus, was chosen and appointed. Although the Dragoman ultimately needed to be approved by the Porte through a *berat* (license), he was chosen among the educated Greek or Armenian elite residing in Cyprus, usually at the suggestion of the Christian Orthodox Church (cf. Myrianthopoulos 1934).

The main reasons for the lack of a substantial language and translation policy across the Ottoman Empire until the late eighteenth century are to be found in the central administration of the empire. Language education in modern Turkish emerged rather late, mainly because of the preference of the Ottoman elites for the 'bureaucratic' Ottoman language at the expense of the everyday Turkish language, and the limited importance that the Porte gave to educational policies in general. As a result, the Ottoman state entrusted language services, such as translation or interpretation, to minorities or foreigners, both centrally and across the various provinces. For example, Meral states that '[b]y the end of the eighteenth and the beginning of the nineteenth century almost all the foreign affairs posts of the Ottoman state, from the Dîvân and embassy translator-ships to the hospodar-ship of the Danubian principalities, were held by Greeks' (2013: 115). These Greeks were usually members of the aristocratic families of the Phanar (today Fener) quarter in Istanbul. This is the tradition that also defined Cyprus in the first half of the period under study. As for the second half, Hadjioannou, Tsiplakou and Kappler 2011, who provide an extensive account of educational policies in Cyprus, argue that the British favoured an almost philhellenic discourse as regards education in Cyprus, at least in the first decades of their presence on the island. Philhellenism, the love for Greek culture, was an intellectual fashion that flourished especially during the nineteenth century in Europe, when the ancient Greek world was being rediscovered. To support their view, they quote Persianis (cf. 2003: 356), who reports that in 1880 the Earl of Kimberley, secretary of state for the colonies, rejected English as the language of education in Cyprus, thinking that Greek afforded ample means for an ordinary education. The British – at least in the period under study – did not interrupt the Ottoman translation 'regime' either, and the overwhelming bulk of translation practice between Turkish and English and between English and Greek focused on so-called pragmatic genres (non-literary translation).

What emerges as particularly important through this very limited intervention in education, language and translation policies during the long nineteenth century is that this laissez-faire attitude seems to have laid the foundations of more nationalist developments in the twentieth century, which are perpetuated to date. As will be shown below, the lack of intervention fuelled the continuous attachment of the two main communities of Cyprus, the Greek Cypriot and the Turkish Cypriot, to their respective 'motherlands' (cf. 2003), which culminated in the de facto monolingual and non-translational spaces of today, as strikingly represented by modern Nicosia. A historical approach with research in Venetian, Ottoman and British archives in Cyprus (the *Cyprus State Archives*, the *Holy Monastery of Kykkos Archives* and the *Archives of the Venetian Consulate in Cyprus*) and a mainly sociolinguistic approach to discussing them[1] are adopted in order to support the image of nineteenth-century Nicosia as a *dual* city.

2 The late Ottoman rule in Cyprus (1785–1878)

2.1 Population groups and languages

After more than 200 years of Ottoman rule, by 1785, the year in which Cyprus passed out of the jurisdiction of the Grand Vizier (cf. Luke [1921] 1989: 79) to be directly governed by the Porte, the island was inhabited by a multilingual society. Two main population groups, the Greek-speaking Christian majority and the Turkish-speaking Muslims, formed the largest part of the population. They were followed by Armenians (members of the Armenian Church speaking Armenian), Maronites (a Christian minority adhering to the Syriac Maronite Church, speaking the so-called Cypriot Arabic variety) and Latins (Catholic minority, speaking mainly French and Italian) as the main three of the other minority population groups in the island's cities. Although the two largest population groups were speaking a local variety of Greek (Cypriot Greek) and plain Turkish (which gradually developed to a Cypriot Turkish variety) respectively, the official language of the island used for all administrative purposes was *Osmanlıca* (Ottoman Turkish), a high variety consisting of Turkish, Persian and Arabic words, using Arabic script. At the same time, the Cypriot Christian Orthodox Church and the Greek-speaking educated elite were using a more 'intellectual' variety of Greek, the *katharevousa*, a 'pure' form of modern Greek hypothetically evolved from ancient Greek. Therefore, the situation on the island was both multilingual and *diglossic* (Ferguson 1959), with various different languages as well as language varieties being used simultaneously. This was the result of the adoption of the *İstimâlet* (appeasement, accommodation) and *Millet* (referring to a non-Muslim religious community) systems in Ottoman administration. These systems favoured a very flexible official policy within the Ottoman Empire for all conquered territories, that is, to allow ethnic groups within the Empire to retain their language, culture and religion under the Ottoman citizenship (cf. Johanson 2011, Dolgunsöz 2014).

Nevertheless, it seems that despite multilingualism, or perhaps because of it, Greek (especially the local dialectal variety) was also spoken – or, at least, understood – by members of all other small minorities (Armenians, Jews, Maronites) as well as by the Muslim Turkish population group for everyday communication purposes. It was not unusual, on the other hand, for the educated Greek and Armenian elite to learn Turkish, at least its high Ottoman variety, since the interpreters in Cyprus came mainly from these population groups. Kitromilides (1992) refers to a series of written documents from the archives of the Venetian consulate in Cyprus, which suggest that Greek was widely understood and used in Ottoman Cyprus. One of them was written in 1749 by Makarios, the Greek Orthodox Metropolitan of Kition (Larnaca) in Greek and indicates a Muslim among the witnesses to its signing, suggesting that this person must have been a competent user of Greek in order to assume such a role. Many other documents (1992) also suggest that Greek was widely used by the Muslim and other minorities for everyday communication, thus the need for translation or interpretation activities must have been very limited for everyday purposes.

2.2 Official translation policies

Contrary to what was happening in everyday life, at the more 'formal' levels of administration and litigation, translation and interpretation were practiced to a larger extent. From the very early years of the Ottoman Empire, *dragomans* (interpreters) were appointed both at central institutions of the Empire and in the conquered territories, that is, in the provinces of the Empire, for the communication between the Ottoman governors and the locals. In most Turkish bibliography, a dragoman is referred to as *tercümân*; however, the two words do not differ in their origin, as they derive from the Arabic *tarjuman* (cf. Salonen 1952). Meral (2013) provides a very detailed account of the different areas for which dragomans were appointed. Briefly, there were four such areas: The dragomans at the Imperial *Dîvân* (the central government, responsible for translation activities in diplomatic relations), the dragomans for the Imperial Fleet, the dragomans in the provinces and the dragomans in foreign embassies and consulates. For the Cypriot context, the most relevant categories are the third and the fourth ones. According to Meral (2013: 118) the third category is in turn divided into two kinds of translators: '[T]he ones employed in the provincial *Dîvân* were called in Ottoman official documents *translators of the Dîvân* (*Dîvân tercümanı*) or *translators of the Palace* (*Saray tercümanı*). Those employed in the courts were called *translators of the court* (*mahkeme tercümanları*).' These four areas are indicative of the importance the Ottoman Empire gave both to diplomatic and commercial relations with foreign countries, and to efficiently governing a vast variety of non-Muslim ethnic groups within the Empire.

In Cyprus, dragomans of the Divan came from the multilingual, educated elite and were usually of Greek or Armenian origin. Dolgunsöz (2014: 105) provides a plausible reason for this, informing us that '[f]or centuries, foreign language learning was seen as an unnecessary and even a sinful activity for Ottoman Muslims'. There is a vast bibliography on the role dragomans played within the governing system of the Ottoman provinces. As regards the Cypriot context in particular, dragomans are recorded to have been appointed ever since the early days of Ottoman occupation (1571). *Hadjigeorgakis Kornesios* was the most prominent among them, mainly because of the political role he assumed during his service (1779–1808), as he was actively involved in the 1804 revolt of the Muslim community in Nicosia and was executed in Istanbul because of this involvement. For extensive accounts of the provenance and role of dragomans in Cyprus and, in particular, of the life of Kornesios see, for example, Luke ([1921] 1989), Myrianthopoulos (1934), Hill (1972), and Theocharides (1986). Apparently, Kornesios came to such prominence in Cypriot history that there is even a folk song narrating his involvement in the revolt as well as his tragic end (see Papadopoullos 1981). This folk song has been the source for many historical accounts on the figure of Kornesios itself and his role during his service and in the 1804 revolt (cf., for example, Michael 2011 and Hadjikyriacou 2016). When Kornesios fled to Istanbul after 1804, he left his assistant *Nikolaos Nikolaides* to represent him. Just before Kornesios was beheaded in Istanbul in 1809, the central government appointed *Lambros* as his successor in 1808 (cf. Hill 1972: 118). Lambros was the last dragoman of Cyprus, since the office disappeared altogether in the aftermath of 1821, the year of the Greek revolt against the Ottomans in mainland Greece, which resulted in sweeping changes in the status of Greeks within the Empire. Kornesios' mansion in Nicosia was acquired by the Cyprus Department of Antiquities in 1979 and houses today the Cyprus Ethnological Museum.

Various documents from the archives of the Venetian consulate in Cyprus (cf. Stavrides 2016) and from the Cyprus State Archives prove that dragomans of the Divan were very wealthy and important figures in the administrative system, because – besides providing translation services – they also served as tax collectors for the Ottoman governor. Albeit dragomans were Ottoman state functionaries officially appointed by a *berat* specifying their privileges and were protected by the state and exempted from taxes, it was usually the high Christian clergy who proposed them for the specific post and dragomans could inherit their position to their descendants. This offered dragomans themselves a unique sense of power within the conquered multinational and multilingual society of Cyprus. The folk song mentioned above aptly presents the dragoman Kornesios as an over-confident figure in the political life of Cyprus. Therefore, it is not surprising that the Christian population on the island habitually saw dragomans as their representatives before the Muslim authorities, despite the fact that such a role was not foreseen by the Ottoman administrative system for the provincial dragomans. As Theocharides asserts (cf. 1986: 17), the real function of the dragomans needs to be sought in financial matters. Being second in order after the Ottoman governor in Cyprus, dragomans seem to have acquired prestige and importance not simply as a result of their education or because translation activities as such were considered particularly prestigious. They acquired such prestige because of the influence they could exert on the local population and because their skills allowed them to have immediate contact to other dragomans, as well as to the consulates and ambassadors of foreign powers. Their translation services – be they written or oral – were thus seen more as *mediation* services. The same held for dragomans in foreign embassies and consulates, as asserted by Meral (2013: 120). Moreover, they were not supervised by any other authority and Ottoman governors had to rely on the assumed credibility of dragomans in negotiations, a credibility won solely on the grounds of provenance, educational level and wealth, since they had not received any targeted training to become dragomans.

A rather different picture is formed regarding the translators of the court (*mahkeme tercümanları*). Unfortunately, there is generally very little information available on court translators. What we know is that court translators were appointed by the Muslim judge (*kadı*) according to the needs arising and that very rarely have they been recorded in documents of the court registers. Çiçek (2002) offers perhaps the most comprehensive account on court interpreters in Nicosia, having researched the sharia court registers of Nicosia. According to the data examined by Çiçek, the judges appointed court interpreters for a period of a year if they were deemed honest and just, and always after approval of the central government, that is, by a *berat*. These interpreters could not be dismissed unless there were serious reasons concerning their honesty and good conduct. They were not paid by the state, but by the litigants themselves. Generally, they did not enjoy the prestige of dragomans, nor did they have similar wealth, privileges or political power within the mixed societies of the Cypriot cities, but unlike in the case of the dragomans, Greek Cypriots continued serving as court interpreters even after 1821 (see Dinç and Çelik 2012).

A very interesting aspect revealed by Çiçek is that members of the Christian community of Nicosia were very eager to bring their cases before the Muslim court of Nicosia even when they were not obliged to. The Ottoman judicial system allowed communities to have their own courts (usually for communal matters falling within the jurisdiction of the Orthodox Church), but criminal cases or any case between a Muslim and a non-Muslim had to be heard in the *kadı*'s court. Greek Cypriots very often resorted to the *kadı* even for communal matters and disputes within the Christian community. For Çiçek, this is an indication that the Greek Cypriots trusted the Muslim courts and that interpreters must have been appointed to a much larger extent than what is recorded in the sharia registers. The court interpreters were mostly Greek Cypriots who knew Ottoman Turkish. Building on Çiçek's work, Dinç and Çelik (2012) raise the question concerning the Armenians of Nicosia who had to appear before the Muslim court or also chose themselves to bring their cases to it. The absence of Armenian interpreters from the court records allows them to infer that Armenians must have been competent in Turkish to a much larger extent than Greek Cypriots. They support their opinion by referring to the results of the 1891 census (under British rule), where almost one quarter of the Armenian community indicated Turkish as their mother tongue.

Regarding the dragomans in foreign embassies and consulates, we return to the image of the dragoman of the Divan. They were highly esteemed officers appointed again by *berat*, enjoying the same privileges as the government dragomans. They were ranked very high within the embassy or consulate, right after the ambassador or consulate, and were responsible not only for the written translations but for all (oral) negotiations with officials speaking other languages. Diplomacy in Cyprus was conducted in Nicosia and in Larnaca, where most foreign consulates were situated, to be in close proximity to the main port of the island at the time, while the embassies were situated in Istanbul. As one can see from documents found in various archives, the dragomans of the consulates were not necessarily foreign nationals, but also locals, Greek Cypriots or Armenians, especially for consulates of countries with less internationalized languages, such as Danish or Dutch.

2.3 Types of translation and quality issues

It becomes obvious from the above that translation and interpreting in Ottoman Cyprus were focused on *pragmatic* genres. The main activities were interpreting for trade and legal matters, translation for legal, commercial and administrative documents and translation of correspondence. The correspondence was both between communities and among the communities, the government and the foreign representatives. It is also attested that locals in Cyprus were helping businessmen and traders ad hoc in their affairs, that is, for individual circumstances and without being officially appointed as interpreters (cf. Çiçek 2002: 7). On another note, quite demanding translation tasks such as the text of Ottoman laws for use in mainly Greek-speaking territories were not undertaken in Cyprus. They were probably conducted in Istanbul or elsewhere, as is evidenced by a letter sent on 31 January 1860 by the *mutasarrıf* (governor) of Cyprus to the Archbishop Makarios of the Cyprus Orthodox Church, informing him that the order of 100 volumes of the translation of the Ottoman Penal Code into Greek from the Porte had been settled (cf. Hidiroglou 1971: 102).

From a sociolinguistic point of view, it is interesting that official translation and interpreting for pragmatic purposes were needed and regulated through relevant policies when formal communication had to take place involving the high language varieties on the island. As concerns everyday communication in the respective vernacular varieties of the common people as well as in the other minority languages of the population in Cyprus, this was achieved either because the members of the various communities knew each other's language or because non-professionals practiced (mainly) oral translation ad hoc. This is not very surprising, given the social status of the population at the time, as well as the history of Cyprus. Nineteenth-century Cyprus was a mainly agricultural and trade society across population groups. All communities had their elite groups, but even the bulk of Muslim settlers from the sixteenth century onwards, that is, after the occupation of Cyprus by the Ottomans in 1571, were predominantly occupied in farming and trading, despite the fact that they belonged to the official ruling population group. Having common practical interests and purposes, living side by side, especially in dense populated areas such as Nicosia, having to deal with many foreign powers in trade and commerce and speaking at least four different languages, it was only to be expected that the people in Cyprus would find ways to communicate effectively in order to cohabit the same small space. In a sense, this period presents a more or less typical case of what Pennycook and Otsuji (2015) termed *metrolingualism*. This refers to the everyday multilingual practices relating to the spaces and rhythms of the city, practices that emerge and fluctuate bottom-up, coming from the diverse linguistic groups themselves instead of as a result of any policy (see also *metroethnicity* by Maher 2005).

After all, Cyprus has long been accustomed to diversity. Even a glimpse of its history since its Christianization immediately reveals that Cyprus has been in the hands of culturally quite different rulers, has used many different *linguae francae* across time (Greek, Arabic, French, Italian, Turkish) and the ethnic make-up of its population has often been modified. Moreover, the size of the island and, ultimately, its insularity has significantly contributed to the population experiencing these changes to a defining extent. That is to say, Cyprus may have been easily accessed because of its location at an important crossroads, but it was not a vast land where common people would stay culturally and linguistically unaffected from the ruling powers residing in a central, urban area. The cities of Cyprus were complementing each other in many respects and, despite the transportation difficulties of the time, urban and rural areas were still closely connected. Therefore, all imposed or naturally occurring societal and economic changes would reach across the island and would concern the everyday life of all people. This is why it can safely be assumed that diversity in Nicosia was a *lived* experience, expressed mainly through multilingualism and a more or less accepted sense of cohabitation.

The term *cohabitation* is deliberately chosen over *interaction*, here. To return to Simon (2012), the lived diversity of Nicosia and Cyprus had its limitations. The coexistence of many cultures and languages, though accepted and therefore peaceful for long periods, was controversial in that it was not deepened into real cultural interaction between the Muslim and non-Muslim communities through, for example, literary translation. In other words, there was no 'egalitarian conversation' of languages and cultures in Nicosia, since speaking or understanding the other's language in order to serve practical purposes is not tantamount to being genuinely interested in otherness. Interaction would imply the establishment of a much more complex network of relations than simply the satisfaction of commercial or administrative needs. Such a complex network did not seem to have been achieved in nineteenth-century Nicosia after centuries of manifold cohabitation. Literary as well as scientific translation between Turkish, Greek and various European languages, which would generate more substantial encounters among the communities, were happening outside Cyprus. For example, Kitromilides (2002) makes reference to very few Cypriot intellectuals from the whole history of Ottoman Cyprus who were involved with translation, such as Spyridon Valetas, Georgios Voustronios, Velissarion Donatos, Epiphanios, Sappho Leontias, Georgios Bellias, Markos Porfyropoulos, Ioanne Sozomeno, Philippos Protonotarios and Epameinondas Frangoudis. All of them were born in or had emigrated to various intellectual centres of the time such as Venice, Marseille, Bucharest, Jerusalem and Istanbul, translating predominantly religious texts, texts of religious interest or ancient Greek writers, but not Ottoman or Arabic literature that might be diffused to Cyprus as well. Another reason for the relative lack of interaction between the Muslim and non-Muslim communities of Nicosia is that the impressive translation policy of the late years of the Ottoman Empire in Istanbul, in the aftermath of European enlightenment, never reached the island of Cyprus or even damaged the traditional involvement of Greek-speaking population groups in translation affairs. After the Greek revolt at the beginning of the nineteenth century, Greeks seized to be appointed as dragomans and the Greek Cypriot community suffered repressive measures by the Porte. The central dragoman service in Istanbul was replaced by the *Tercüme Odası* (Translation Office) in 1821, and Muslims started being appointed as translators. A series of other translation or translating institutions were also established in Istanbul, such as the schools for military and medical training, where significant scientific translation of textbooks was undertaken, or the *Academy of Knowledge* and the *Translation Society* (in 1851 and 1865 respectively). Kamay (2012), Meral (2013) and Özmen (2016) offer comprehensive accounts on these institutions, their activities and their significance for the continuation and survival of the Ottoman Empire. It was the period of administrative reforms known as *Tanzimât* (reorganization, 1839–76). But the Tanzimat, as maintained by Michael (2013), led to unrest and to a climate of tension between the religious communities in Cyprus, plausibly leaving no room for constructive adoption of positive cultural developments through translation and other mediation policies.

There is practically no evidence about translation quality issues, either, mainly because archives do not record originals. In addition, there was not always an original in the form of a written text for all documents; neither was there any authority supervising translations, as was the case in central translation institutions in Istanbul. As a result, it is extremely difficult – if not impossible – to draw any conclusions about the choices made or the strategies followed by the dragomans and the court translators in Cyprus. The only assumption one can make should be based on analyses provided for translation in the Istanbul institutions, which might have had an impact on how non-trained translators and interpreters in the provinces were working. Particularly interesting is the differentiation between the terms *terceme* and *çeviri*. According to Paker ([2006] 2014: 344), the former is the traditional conception of translation and was twinned to imitation (*taklid*), while the latter is the contemporary Turkish term for translation and comes much closer to western conceptions.[2] The assumption, therefore, is that translation (in the wide sense) was not following any strict conceptions of faithfulness or fidelity, but was largely domesticating.

3 The first half of British rule in Cyprus (1878–1914)

The year 1878 marks a significant change for Cyprus. After the Russo-Turkish war, Cyprus became a protectorate of the British in exchange for their military help to the Ottomans against Russia. This was a rather peculiar situation, since British rule existed only de facto until 1925, when Cyprus officially became a Crown Colony, while Ottoman rule continued de jure and the population groups of the island were still Ottoman citizens. Practically, this meant that the British had to follow Ottoman law in the governing of the newly acquired territories (cf. Hill 1972). In charge of the administration and stationed in Larnaca – notably not in Nicosia – was the so-called *High Commissioner* of Britain, a denomination still in use for the British diplomatic representative in Cyprus today.

The British faced a multitude of challenges on the island. The first was a demographic one, with ethnic repercussions; the Greek-speaking population group had meanwhile become by far the largest one on the island (following the 1881 census, about 74 per cent of the population). In view of the obvious decline of the Ottoman Empire, and as a clear consequence of Greece's independence from the Ottomans in 1828, the Greek-speaking population group in Cyprus had already started contemplating the unification of the island with Greece, following the example of the Ionian Islands in western Greece, which had been annexed to the modern Greek state in 1864. While under Ottoman rule such ethnic aspirations were rather dormant, the arrival of the British sparked new hopes for the Greek-speaking population group (see Kyprianos 1878), whose elite – in addition – had started losing the privileges it enjoyed during Ottoman times (e.g. the institution of the dragoman). The other challenge the British faced was the heavy taxes they had to pay to the sultan, which, of course, led to the imposition of a heavy taxation system on the island. This, in turn, ignited ethnic unrest anew. On top of that, the new government needed to communicate both with the Turkish-speaking Ottoman Empire and with a multilingual local community.

In this significantly shorter part of the period under study, the Ottoman laissez-faire attitude (cf. Hadjioannou, Tsiplakou and Kappler 2011) towards language and educational policies on the island was not interrupted in the first three decades of British rule. The British, particularly the Anglican Church, maintained very good relations with the very powerful Greek Orthodox Church of Cyprus (see Hill 1972), and the main population groups continued being allowed to have their own schools and to take care of their own communal matters. Needless to say that the widespread *lingua franca* among the people on the island for everyday communication was meanwhile Greek. However, Turkish was maintained as the official language of Cyprus, despite repeated demands on the part to the church to introduce Greek as official language of the administration. Therefore, the British soon sought translators and interpreters ideally having command of all three languages involved in the administration and in the court hearings: English, Turkish and Greek. This is the reason why many of the new translators and interpreters no longer came from the Greek-speaking community, but from the Armenian-speaking one, since Armenians used Turkish to a larger extent than Greeks, as confirmed by Dinç and Çelik (2012). Although the 'administrative' nature of the British presence in the early years did not really favour translation between English and the local languages other than in pragmatic genres, the systematic translation of other genres gradually started in this period. Indeed, more than 900 texts by about 400 writers from European, Arabic and Persian literature were translated by 150 *literati* into Greek in the period 1880–1930 according to Papaleontiou (cf. 1997: 274). Moreover, an exceptional translation initiative by the British commissioner in Larnaca concerning literary genres is recorded within the first half of British rule in Cyprus: the *Excerpta Cypria* (Cobham 1908). According to Stephanides

(2011: 44) the Excerpta Cypria offers an anthology of the rich cultural history of Cyprus:

> One may find a kaleidoscopic perspective of this cultural history by navigating the Excerpta Cypriana – an anthology of translated writing on Cyprus compiled by the British commissioner of Larnaca and published in 1908. Including excerpts translated from various languages into English from ancient times up to the Ottoman period and evoking the gaze of travellers, settlers, Cypriots and conquerors, the anthology evokes the cross-cultural gaze on the island through the millennia: Strabo speaks of the temple of Aphrodite, unapproachable and invisible to women; the Spanish Jew, Benjamin of Tudela, speaks of the heretic Cyprian Jews, Epicureans who profane the sabbath and keep holy that of Sunday; Neophytus, the twelfth-century hermit speaks of England, a country beyond Romania out of which a cloud of English came with their sovereign; Capodilista, a 15th-century Paduan gentleman, marvels at banana trees with fruit like cucumbers, yellow when ripe and very sweet of savour; and a document of Ottoman law professes tolerance toward Christians.

Stephanides (2011) also stresses the cosmopolitan spirit that emerged as a result of the particular blend of colonial rule and Cypriot diasporic consciousness. For him, the first decade of British rule was defining for Cypriot literature, translation and criticism, as it brought to the island the first printing press and the first newspaper, published in Greek and English. This cosmopolitanism marked the island as a cross-cultural gateway between East and West.

Besides reinforcing the island of Cyprus as a cross-cultural gateway, the first half of British rule laid the foundations for an even more important development concerning cultural exchange and interaction within the communities of the island. It offered them a new *lingua franca*, English, which was soon established and embraced as the language of communication between the communities themselves, after the British took over. This happened not simply because English gradually became one of the official languages of the island, but probably because the various communities could maintain a convenient distance to it, as they did not necessarily identify it as part of their perceived ethnic identities. In other words, albeit the language of the rulers, it is logical to assume that the communities might have regarded it as a more 'neutral' means of communication dissociated from nationalist feelings, since no population group had English as their dominant language, as was the case, for example, with the Turkish-speaking minority during Ottoman times. Interestingly, English must have functioned as a common 'space' among communities despite its inevitable stigma as symbol of authority. Therefore, it should not be surprising that the communities resorted to it even after independence from British rule in 1960, notably not only for legal purposes (cf. Floros 2014) or negotiations (especially after the Turkish invasion of 1974) but also for cultural exchange between the communities and for reconnecting the Cypriot diaspora with the homeland, as asserted by Stephanides (2011: 51):

> A new generation has grown up since partition, and few Cypriot Greeks or Cypriot Turks speak each other's language so they rely on English as a lingua franca and as a language for mediation in translation. Many poets double as translators and translate each other's work mostly through the mediation of English, spawning an experimental literary dialogue and literary transculturation.

In sum, the 'duality' of the 'expanded' city found a new way of expression through English. English became a sort of pivot language, or a lingua franca as a solution to a difficult situation, a convenient reason for not learning each other's language. The translationality of Nicosia acquired another dimension: There was indifference and negation between Greek and Turkish, but engagement and creative interference just between Greek and English, or between Turkish and English, much less between Greek and Turkish.

4 The political implications of nineteenth-century practices for modern Nicosia

Without wishing to bypass or underestimate other important historical and political developments of the twentieth century in Cyprus, which led to the de facto division of the island and the continuing occupation of its northern part, it can safely been assumed that the language and translation policies of the nineteenth century – albeit seemingly liberal – have significantly contributed to the painful political and societal situation Cyprus and the city of Nicosia found themselves in since independence from British rule.

The laissez-faire attitude in religion, education and language, followed both by the Ottoman Empire and by the British in the early years of their presence on the island, could at first sight be seen as quite liberal, quite respective of the multiculturality of the conquered lands and – ultimately – quite innocent in terms of cultural imperialism. Both rulers of nineteenth-century Cyprus were more focused on matters of military power and economic growth, striving for their self-preservation and expansion mostly through armed supremacy and taxation; much less through cultural exchange and interaction. The provinces of the empires were seen more as exotic places (cf. Said's (1978) concept of *orientalism*) for exploitation rather than exploration. But the lack of measures that would foster cultural exchange through multilingual education for larger groups of the population instead of for the elite only, or through translation activities extending beyond pragmatic purposes, aiming to bring 'otherness' across both ways, ultimately laid the foundations for the formation of rather 'closed' (culturally), autonomous and self-sufficient groups within the Cypriot society, especially within cities. Contact in the wide sense was there, but it was only secured for the practicalities of everyday life, not in order to serve a deeper sense of belonging together. The lack of mild intervention policies thus fuelled the continuous attachment of the two main communities of Cyprus to their respective 'motherlands' (cf. Persianis 2003, quoted in Hadjioannou, Tsiplakou and Kappler 2011). Greek Cypriots adhered to the newly established Greek state and Turkish Cypriots adhered to the modern Turkey of Mustafa Kemal. Multiculturalism, multilingualism and the translation culture of the people of Cyprus in their everyday life, as described especially in Section 1, never managed to transcend the sense of each belonging to a different wider community. Therefore, developments that are more nationalist found a sound expression in the twentieth century and culminated in the de facto monolingual and non-translational spaces of today, as is evident in modern Nicosia.

The second half of British rule in Cyprus (1914–60) was characterized by the rise of an anti-colonial movement in Cyprus, which culminated in the armed campaign of 1955–9 by the EOKA (National Organization of Cypriot Fighters). Greek Cypriots and Turkish Cypriots seemed united against the common 'enemy', but this unity was rather superficial. Soon after independence, intercommunal clashes started and led to Nicosia being divided into two sectors, a 'Greek' and a 'Turkish' one, already in 1963. The commander of the British peace force drew a cease-fire line on a map of the city, using a green pencil; hence, this line is still known as the *green line*. Ironically, the green line follows *Hermes* street, the main commercial street of the walled city of Nicosia (after Hermes, the messenger of the ancient Greek gods and a symbol of translators and interpreters), and has remained a ghost street ever since. The armed clashes between the communities escalated after 1963, making Cyprus, but especially Nicosia and its surrounding areas, a site of conflict and hatred. A painful finale to these conflicts was given in July 1974, when the Turkish army invaded the northern part of the island and an exchange of populations was enforced soon thereafter. The resulting dividing line for the whole island (buffer zone) was an extension of the 1963 green line to the east and west. Within a very short period, Nicosia seized to be a multicultural and multilingual city, having been broken into two parts of ethnically almost uniform populations. The negotiations for the reunification of the island are still ongoing. The Republic of Cyprus maintains Greek and Turkish as its official languages to date, with Turkish practically not in use. The two parts of the island maintain diglossia, with the respective high varieties of Greek and Turkish being used for official purposes, while in everyday communication the dialectal varieties of Cypriot Greek and Cypriot Turkish are spoken. Multilingualism is also present; both parts of the island include minority communities of other languages. However, no official translation policy exists to cover possible communication needs, at least in the Republic of Cyprus. Nevertheless, there is little communication between the Muslim and Christian main population groups of the whole island. In fact, there was almost none until 2003, when some of the checkpoints reopened and north-south crossings were allowed again; since 2003, communication and cultural exchange between the two communities succeeds mostly through English, since all negotiation talks and the work of the bi-communal ad hoc committees are exclusively conducted in English.

5 Conclusion

This chapter examined the translation activity in the capital of Cyprus, Nicosia, which in the nineteenth century could be seen as an 'expanded' city, since the political, administrative, diplomatic and cultural life of the capital were complemented by activities in other cities of the island, mainly Larnaca. It could be shown that nineteenth-century Nicosia was a *dual* city in Simon's terms (2012), mainly through the fact that the inhabitants were multilingual and 'translational', with both official and unofficial translation activity taking place among the various population groups as well as between the population groups and the rulers. It could furthermore be argued that, unfortunately, the 'duality' of the city was not cultivated to a degree sufficient for bringing the communities together to such a degree for a sense of belonging to be created. As a result, other historical and political developments that ultimately caused ethic encapsulation and division found fertile ground and the lack of effective translation policies seems to have played a significant, albeit covert role in perpetuating the circumstances that made Nicosia to today's UN-monitored, divided space.

Notes

1 I would like to sincerely thank my colleagues Dr Theocharis Stavrides and Dr Michalis Michael from the Department of Turkish and Middle Eastern Studies at the University of Cyprus for guiding me through the variety of archives and for bibliographic suggestions, as well as Dr Ioannis Moutsis, historian, translator and visiting Lecturer at the University of Cyprus, for his invaluable help with sources in Turkish, as well as for archival research.
2 For translation conceptions and methods in Ottoman Turkey see also Tosun and Şimşek (2012).

References

Primary sources

Cyprus State Archives (2012–2018), Nicosia: Republic of Cyprus, Ministry of Justice and Public Order. Available online: http://www.mjpo.gov.cy/mjpo/statearchive.nsf

Holy Monastery of Kykkos Archives, Nicosia: Holy Monastery of Kykkos Research Center. Available online: http://kentromeleton.org.cy/?page_id=25

Stavrides, Th. (2016), *Ottoman Documents from the Archives of the Venetian Consulate of Cyprus, 1671–1765*, Nicosia: Cyprus Research Center

Secondary sources

Christodoulou, M. (1977), *Lefkosia. Name and Tradition*, Nicosia: Municipality of Nicosia.

Çiçek, K. (2002), 'Interpreters of the Court in the Ottoman Empire as Seen from the Sharia Court Records of Cyprus', *Islamic Law and Society*, 9 (1): 1–15.

Cobham, C. D. (1908), *Excerpta Cypria: Materials for a History of Cyprus*, Cambridge: Cambridge University Press.

Cronin, M. and S. Sherry (2014), 'Introduction: The City as Translation Zone', *Translation Studies*, 7 (2): 119–32.

Dinç, G. and C. Çelik (2012), 'Cyprus Court Interpreters during the Ottoman Period', *Mediterranean Journal of Humanities*, II (2): 45–55.

Dolgunsöz, E. (2014), 'Language Policies and Multilingual Education in Minority Schools in Ottoman Empire: Outcomes and Future Insights', *idil*, 3 (12): 97–108.

Ferguson, Ch. A. (1959), 'Diglossia', *WORD*, 15 (2): 325–40.

Floros, G. (2014), 'Legal Translation in a Postcolonial Setting: The Political Implications of Translating Cypriot Legislation into Greek', *The Translator*, 20 (2) *Special issue: Law in Translation*: 411–29.

Hadjikyriacou, A. (2016), 'The Province Goes to the Center: The Case of Hadjiyorgakis Kornesios, Dragoman of Cyprus', in Ch. Isom-Verhaaren and K. Schull (eds), *Living in the Ottoman Realm: Empire and Identity, 13th to 20th Centuries*, 239–53, Bloomington: Indiana University Press.

Hadjioannou, X. and S. Tsiplakou, with a contribution by M. Kappler (2011), 'Language Policy and Language Planning in Cyprus', *Current Issues in Language Planning*, 12 (4): 503–69.

Hidiroglou, P. (1971), *Επίσημα Οθωμανικά έγγραφα αναφερόμενα εις την ιστορίαν της Κύπρου* [*Official Ottoman Documents Referring to the History of Cyprus*], Nicosia: Cyprus Research Center.

Hill, Sir G. (1972), *A History of Cyprus: Volume IV; The Ottoman Province: The British Colony 1571–1948*, Cambridge: Cambridge University Press.

Johanson, L. (2011), 'Multilingual States and Empires in the History of Europe: The Ottoman Empire', in B. Kortmann and J. Auwera (eds), *The Languages and Linguistics of Europe*, Vol. 1, 729–44, Berlin: Mouton de Gruyter.

Kamay, B. (2012), 'Public Diplomacy and the Translation Office in the Ottoman Empire (1839–1876)', MA diss., Department of History, Bilkent University, Ankara.

Kitromilides, P. M. (2002), *Κυπριακή λογιοσύνη: 1571–1878* [*Cypriot Intellectual Life: 1571-1878*], Nicosia: Cyprus Research Center.

Kitromilides, P. M. (1992), *Κοινωνικές σχέσεις και νοοτροπίες στην Κύπρο του δεκάτου ογδόου αιώνα* [*Social Relations and Politics in 18th-Century Cyprus*]. Nicosia: Laiki Bank Educational & Cultural Center.

Kyprianos (Bishop of Kition) (1878), *The Times*, August 7.

Luke, Sir H. ([1921] 1989), *Cyprus Under the Turks –1571–1878*, London: C. Hurst & Co.

Maher, J. C. (2005), 'Metroethnicity, Language, and the Principle of Cool', *International Journal of the Sociology of Language*, 175/176: 83–102.

Meral, A. (2013), 'A Survey of Translation Activity in the Ottoman Empire', *The Journal of Ottoman Studies*, XLII: 105–55.

Michael, M. N. (2013), 'Trying to Impose the Reforms in the Periphery: Actions and Reactions to the Tanzimat in Cyprus: The Case of the Muhassıl Mehmet Talat', *OTAM*, 34/Güz: 163–84.

Michael, M. N. (2011), 'Local Authorities and Conflict in an Ottoman Island at the Beginning of the Nineteenth Century', *Turkish Historical Review*, 2: 57–77.

Myrianthopoulos, C. (1934), *Χατζηγεωργάκης Κορνέσιος, ο διερμηνεύς της Κύπρου, 1778–1809* [*Hadjigeorgakis Kornesios. The Dragoman of Cyprus, 1779-1809*], Nicosia: Mouson.

Özmen, C. (2016), 'Translating Science in the Ottoman Empire: Translator-educators as 'Agents of Change' in the Ottoman Scientific Repertoires', *Osmanlı Araştırmaları / The Journal of Ottoman Studies*, XLVIII: 143–70.

Paker, S. ([2006] 2014), 'Ottoman Conceptions of Translation and its Practice: The 1897 'Classics Debate' as a Focus for Examining Change', in Th. Hermans (ed.), *Translating Others*, Vol. II, 325–48, London and New York: Routledge.

Papadopoullos, Th. (1981), *Το άσμα των Διερμηνέων* [*The Song of the Interpreters*], Cypriot Studies ΜΕ, Nicosia: Society of Cypriot Studies.

Papaleontiou, L. (1997), *Τα πρώτα βήματα της κυπριακής λογοτεχνικής κριτικής (1880-1930)* [*The First Steps of Cypriot Literary Criticism (1880-1930)*], Nicosia: Cultural Services of the Ministry of Education and Culture.

Pennycook, A. and E. Otsuji (2015), *Metrolingualism: Language in the City*, New York: Routledge.

Persianis, P. (2003), 'British Colonial Higher Education Policy-making in the 1930s: The Case of a Plan to Establish a University in Cyprus', *Compare: A Journal of Comparative and International Education*, 33: 351–68.

Said, E. W. (1978), *Orientalism*, New York: Pantheon Books.

Salonen, A. (1952), 'Alte Substrat- und Kulturwörter im Arabischen', *Studia Orientalia*, xvii (2): n.p.

Simon, S. (2012), *Cities in Translation: Intersections of Language and Memory*, London: Routledge.

Stavrides, Th. (2012), *Studies on the History of Cyprus under Ottoman Rule*, Analecta Isisiana CXV, Istanbul: Isis Press.

Stephanides, S. (2011), 'An Island of Translation', *Kunapipi*, 33 (1): 42–53.

Theocharides, I. (1986), *Σύμμεικτα δραγομανικά της Κύπρου* [*About the Dragomans in Cyprus*], Ioannina: University of Ioannina, School of Philosophy, Department of History and Archaeology.

Tosun, M. and F. Şimşek (2012), 'Osmanlının son döneminden Türkiye Cumhuriyeti'nin ilk dönemine devlet eliyle yaptırılan çevirilerin toplumsal ve kültürel değişime etkisi' [The Effect of Translations, That Is Done Under the Control of State, on the Social and Cultural Change From the Last Period of Ottomans to the First Period of Republic of Turkey], *International Journal of Human Sciences*, 9 (2): 1719–35.

Name index

Abbott, A. 164–5
Adam, E. 69
Agstner, R. 148
Aguilar, E. 173
Ahačič, K. 186
Ahman y Nottbert, G. 172–3
Albani 27
Alexander III 128
Amon, S. 189
Anderson, B. 3
Ankersmit, F. 110
Arabia Solanas, R. 173
Arriaga, E. de 165–6, 177
Aškerc, A. 197

Bach, A. von 57
Bachleitner, N. 49–50, 55
Badeni, K. F. 47
Baggot, E. 154
Bähler, A. 72, 76–7
Baigorri, J. 166
Balibar, R. 3
Bárcena, V. C. 177
Baumbos, C. 151–2
Baycroft, T. 107
Beamish 151
Bech y Morera, F. 172, 175
Beecher Stowe, H. 194
Bellias, G. 220
Berger, A. von 51–2
Berthold V. 72
Bertillon 86
Beyen, M. 4
Billig, M. 4
Bittinger 101
Blåfield, O. 119–20, 123, 128, 131–2
Bogataj-Gradišnik, K. 192
Branchadell, A. 13
Breathnach, S. 151
Brenan, G. 152–3, 158
Briedis, L. 190
Broers, M. 27

Brunot, F. 33
Burke, J. 155
Bürki-Gyger, E. 69, 80
Butt, I. 149

Callanan, P. 154
Cañelles, C. 175
Canis 27
Cankar, I. 44
Cantillon, C. 149
Cardona y Robert, J. 172, 175
Carmichael, C. 186
Carreras 167, 176
Cartwright 151–2, 155
Castejón, R. M. 167
Castillo, D. 167
Çelik, C. 217
Certeau, M. de 92
Cervantes, M. de 194
Christodoulou, M. 210
Çiçek, K. 217–18
Clement, J. 93–5
Coakley, D. J. 145
Cobham, C. D. 222
Cola, M. G. 157
Colombi, M. 190
Comment, F. 69, 79
Condeminas y Torres, F. 172–6
Conrad, S. 4
Crivelli, J. 30
Cronin, M. 1, 43–4, 59, 115, 190, 211
Csáky, M. 44–5
Csendes, P. 43

Dambacher, E. 51
Daniëls, W. 93
Darquennes, J. 93
Declercq, E. 106, 110
De Groof, J. 96
Del Pozo, I. 162, 165–6
Del Vento, C. 24, 26
Demery, J. 150–1, 157

De Schutter, H.   7
D'hulst, L.   6, 11, 22, 36, 69, 78, 93, 95, 110, 202
Dinç, G.   217
Dizdar, D.   190
Dolgunsöz, E.   214–15
Donatos, V.   220
D'Ors, E.   174
Duchardt, H.   2
Ducommun, E.   85
Dullion, V.   11, 70, 80, 82
Duvosquel, J.-M.   106

Ebner-Eschenbach, M. von   51
Einsle, A.   49
Eixarch y Arberola, F.   172–4
Engman, M.   118, 123–4, 134
Epiphanios   220
Erjavec, K.   189
Eybl, F. M.   50

Felton, C. R.   156
Ferguson, C. A.   214
Figuerola, L.   167
Fischel, A.   61
Fischer, E.   50
Floros, G.   14, 224
Fogazzaro, A.   195
Foscolo, U.   23–6
Foucault, M.   116
Frangoudis, E.   220
Franklin, B.   194
Friedländer   44

Gabardini, M.   157
Gabrič   188
Garibaldi, G.   149
Gawrych, G. W.   3
Gerhartl, S.   49
Gipper, A.   190
Gobat, A.   85
Godechot, J.   26–7, 36
Goidanich, G.   153
Goidanich, P.   153
Goldsmith, O.   192, 197
González Núñez, G.   6, 69, 162
Gow, J.   186
Grant, S.   149
Grbić, N.   164

Gregorčič, S.   197
Grilli, A.   31–2
Grin, F.   115
Guillon de Montléon, A.   25

Habermas, J.   8, 48–9
Hadjikyriacou, A.   216
Hadjioannou, X.   212, 222
Hainisch, M.   44
Hammer-Purgstall, J. von   61
Hanley, J.   154
Hansen   157
Hartleben   55
Hartmann, S.   36
Hauser, O.   51
Heltai, J.   56
Hermans, T.   46
Herzfeld, M.   51
Hevesi, L.   56
Hidiroglou, P.   218
Hill, G.   211, 215, 221–2
Hlavac, J.   15, 178
Hobsbawm, E.   2
Hofmannsthal, H. von   51
House, J.   185
Howlin, N.   143
Hugelmann, K. G.   47
Humboldt, W. von   190
Humphreys, H.   142

Jalander, F. W.   120
Jenko, S.   197
Jernberg, F. E.   119–20, 123, 127, 131
Johanson, L.   214
John, M.   44
Jurčič, J.   195, 197, 201

Kalbeck, M.   52
Kamay, B.   220
Kang, J. H.   163, 178
Kappler, M.   212, 222
Kelly-Holmes, H.   93
Keman, H.   46
Kersnik, J.   197
Kitromilides, P. M.   214, 220
Ködel, S.   22
Konegen   55
Kopitar, T.   192
Kornesios, H.   215–16

Koskela, M.   15, 111
Koskinen, K.   12, 15, 68, 71, 82, 111, 116–17, 119, 121–5, 163–4, 178
Kraemer, M.   173
Kyprianos   222

Lah, Š.   189
Lambros   216
Lauer, R.   53
Lee Kun   142–3
Leerssen, J.   3
Leonard, C.   143
Leontias, S.   220
Leso, E.   36
Levstik, F.   197
Lewis, S.   145
Lichtblau, A.   44
Lönnroth, H.   129
Luke, H.   213, 215

Maher, J. C.   219
Makarios   214, 218
Mandado, L.   173
Marazzini, C.   31
Marcel, C.   147
Marcel, J.   147
Markiču   199
Marmion, A.   144–5
Martig, P.   73, 76
Mascaró y Gaurán, F.   172–4
McLaren, A.   150
Mendelssohn, P. de   51
Menou   33, 37
Meral, A.   212, 215–16, 220
Metternich   48
Meylaerts, R.   6, 8, 21, 45, 70, 74, 105, 108, 115, 162
Michael, M. N.   216
Michelli, F.   147–8
Miklošič, F.   188
Milčinski, F.   204, 207
Miloro, G.   147, 150
Miloro, G. V.   150
Minich, P. S.   147, 149–51, 157
Montero y Vidal, J.   165
Monzó, E.   164, 177–8
Mooney   143
Moormann-Kimáková, B.   178
Morabito, L.   27

Mörtengren   130
Muller, J.   156
Myrianthopoulos, C.   212, 215

Nikolaides, N.   216
Nouws, B.   105
Nuč, A.   62

O'Brien, P.   149
O'Donnell, H.   147
O'Donnell, S.   147
Ogris, W.   49
Ohnet, G.   200
Oliver y Riera, L. de   172–3, 176
Oller, J.   173
Opll, F.   43
Osterhammel, J.   4
O'Sullivan, A. E.   153
O'Sullivan, E.   156
Otsuji, E.   219
Özmen, C.   220

Pagliaruzzi, J.   197
Paker, S.   221
Paloposki, O.   84, 118
Papadopoullos, T.   215
Papaleontiou   222
Peñarroja, J.   166
Pennycook, A.   1, 219
Persianis, P.   213, 225
Phelan, M.   12
Pietikäinen, S.   93
Pillepich, A.   21, 23
Pini, V.   69–70, 75, 81–2
Pipp, L.   188
Pizzi, K.   190
Plessis, T. du   70
Pokorn, N.   13
Porfyropoulos, M.   220
Prešeren, F.   195–7, 201–2, 207
Protonotarios, P.   220
Puerta Reda, N. de la   167
Pym, A.   141–2, 157

Rafo, J.   167
Rahten, A.   189
Rasila, V.   119, 120, 122, 127–9, 132, 134
Rawley, J.   153
Reading   142

Reinke, K.   31
Reiter, C.   45
Ricart, J.   168, 175–6
Rilke, R. M.   51
Roberti, M.   22
Roselen, P.   173
Rumpler, H.   47
Ryckeboer, H.   105

Said, E.   225
Sakai, N.   190, 204–5
Salonen, A.   215
Santoyo, J. C.   141, 162, 165–6
Schjerve, R.   3
Schmid, C. von   194
Schreiber, M.   5–6, 9, 21, 31, 33, 35–6, 69, 93, 106, 190
Sela-Sheffy, R.   89
Selin, G.   125, 127
Seymour   157–8
Shakespeare, W.   194, 200, 205
Shaw G. B.   51
Shepherd   187
Silva Lima, A. da   147
Simon, S.   1, 43–4, 59–60, 190, 203, 210–11, 219, 226
Şimşek, F.   227
Slomšek, M.   188
Smith, R.   147
Snellman, J. V.   127
Soleil, S.   4, 36
Sozomeno, I.   220
Spiteri   156
Spolsky, B.   5–6, 12, 115, 162–3
Stavrides, T.   211
Stephanides, S.   222–4
Štih, P.   187
Stourzh, G.   47
Stritar, J.   192, 197, 202
Sumelius, F.   128
Swift, J.   200

Tacitus   25–6, 36
Taillefer, J.-B.-L.   110
Talavera y Barceló, S.   172, 175
Tallqvist   127
Tavčar, I.   197
Tedesco, E.   154
Theocharides, I.   215–16
Thiesse, A.-M.   3

Tomassini, A. P.   155
Tomassini, P.   155
Toran, R.   175
Toribio Sogorb, L.   172, 175
Torrents y Monner, A.   172–4
Tosun, M.   227
Trebitsch, S.   50–1
Tsiplakou, S.   212, 222
Turgenev, I.   201
Tusin, E. W. A.   146

Vähäpesola, J.   117, 119
Valdaliso, J. M.   167
Valenčič, V.   189, 205
Valeriani, L.   25–6, 36
Valetas, S.   220
Valsamachi, G. M.   157
Van Dam, H.   164, 178
Vandenbussche, W.   98
Van Gerwen, H.   6, 22, 36, 95, 108, 110
Van Ginderachter, M.   4, 109
Van Goethem, H.   92
Vanhecke, E.   96
Van Velthoven, H.   7, 93
Vetter, E.   3
Viljakainen, K   120
Voustronios, G.   220

Wagner, F.   58
Walter, F.   67, 72, 75–6, 79
Weber, E.   3
Weerts, S.   67, 71, 73–5, 83
Weilenmann, H.   67, 71, 73, 75
Werlen, I.   72–4
Widmer, J.   67, 71, 73–5, 83
Wiesmann, E.   22
Wilkinson, J. R.   148
Wilkinson, M.   148
Willemyns, R.   93
Wils, L.   93, 96
Witte, E.   7, 93
Wolf, M.   3, 8, 10, 43, 48–50, 59, 61–2, 77, 115, 163, 186, 188–90, 202, 203, 205

Yáñez   167
Yourdi, E. G.   148–9
Yourdi, N. G.   147–8, 151–2, 154–5

Zahra, T.   4

www.ingramcontent.com/pod-product-compliance
Lightning Source LLC
Chambersburg PA
CBHW052036300426
44117CB00012B/1843